The Cambridge Companion to Pushkin

Alexander Pushkin stands in a unique position as the founding father of modern Russian literature. In this *Companion*, leading scholars discuss Pushkin's work in its political, literary, social and intellectual contexts. In the first part of the book, individual chapters analyse his poetry, his theatrical works, his narrative poetry and historical writings. The second section explains and samples Pushkin's impact on broader Russian culture by looking at his enduring legacy in music and film from his own day to the present. Special attention is given to the reinvention of Pushkin as a cultural icon during the Soviet period. No other volume available brings together such a range of material and such comprehensive coverage of all Pushkin's major and minor writings. The contributions represent state-of-the-art scholarship that is innovative and accessible, and are complemented by a chronology and a guide to further reading.

ANDREW KAHN is University Lecturer in Russian at the University of Oxford and a Fellow of St Edmund Hall, Oxford.

THE CAMBRIDGE COMPANION TO PUSHKIN

EDITED BY

ANDREW KAHN

St Edmund Hall, Oxford

CAMBRIDGE UNIVERSITY PRESS
Cambridge, New York, Melbourne, Madrid, Cape Town, Singapore, São Paulo

Cambridge University Press
The Edinburgh Building, Cambridge CB2 2RU, UK

Published in the United States of America by Cambridge University Press, New York

www.cambridge.org
Information on this title: www.cambridge.org/9780521604710

First published 2006

Printed in the United Kingdom at the University Press, Cambridge

A catalogue record for this publication is available from the British Library

ISBN-13 978-0-521-84367-6 hardback
ISBN-10 0-521-84367-7 hardback
ISBN-13 978-0-521-60471-0 paperback
ISBN-10 0-521-60471-0 paperback

CONTENTS

ILLUSTRATIONS

CONTRIBUTORS

DAVID BETHEA, University of Wisconsin, Madison and University of Oxford

SERGEI DAVYDOV, Middlebury College

SIMON DIXON, University of Leeds

EVGENY DOBRENKO, University of Nottingham

CARYL EMERSON, Princeton University

BORIS GASPAROV, Columbia University

MIKHAIL GRONAS, Dartmouth College

ROBERT P. HUGHES, University of California, Berkeley

ANDREW KAHN, University of Oxford

MARCUS LEVITT, University of Southern California

OLEG PROSKURIN, Moscow

IRINA REYFMAN, Columbia University

STEPHANIE SANDLER, Harvard University

WILLIAM MILLS TODD III, Harvard University

MICHAEL WACHTEL, Princeton University

ACKNOWLEDGEMENTS

I wish to thank Rebecca Duplessis and Dominique Lussier for editorial assistance; Janet Godden for practical wisdom; and Dr Sarah Turner for translations of Chapters 7 and 14.

NOTE ON THE TEXT

Unless otherwise indicated, all citations of Pushkin's works are from A. S. Pushkin, *Polnoe sobranie sochinenii*, ed. M. A. Tsiavlovskii, B. Tomashevskii *et al.*, 17 vols., Leningrad, Akademiia nauk, 1937–54, henceforth, *PSS*.

Russian is transliterated according to the Library of Congress conventions except in the case of well-known surnames given in familiar form, e.g. Dostoevsky, rather than -skii. Russian first names are given in the original spelling, e.g. Petr rather than Peter and Ivan. For the sake of familiarity, however, the English spelling of names like Maria and Natalia is preferred, as it is with the name of a well-known figure like Pushkin, which appears as Alexander rather than Aleksandr. Following standard practice, rulers' names are given in their more familiar form (Nicholas I rather than Nikolai).

Until February 1918, Russia used the Julian (Old Style) calendar, which ran thirteen days behind the Gregorian (New Style) calendar used in Western Europe. To avoid complication, dates given in this volume are in the Old Style.

CHRONOLOGY

26 May 1799	Alexander Pushkin born in Moscow to Major Sergei L'vovich Pushkin 1771–1848 and Nadezhda Osipovna née Gannibal 1775–1836.
1811	Matriculates at the newly founded Imperial Lycée at Tsarskoe Selo as a member of its first class; makes lifelong friends with Baron Anton Del'vig.
20 June 1814	Makes his debut in print with the publication of two poems in the literary journal the *Herald of Europe*.
1815	Beginning of a lifelong friendship with the older poet and influential figure Vasilii Zhukovskii, who predicts his future greatness.
1816	Joins Arzamas, the most progressive and western of literary groups in St Petersburg.
June 1817	Graduates from the Lycée. Secures an appointment in the Ministry of Foreign Affairs.
April 1820	At the order of Alexander I, Pushkin is investigated for subversive behaviour linked to the inflammatory ode 'Liberty'.
1820	July publication of long poem *Ruslan and Liudmila* to popular and critical acclaim.
1820–24	Period of exile in southern Russia. From the autumn of 1820 based in Kishinev until June 1823, followed by time in Odessa from July 1823 until July 1824.
December 1824	*The Fountain of Bakhchisarai* is published. In August, Pushkin transfers from the south to confinement on the family estate at Mikhailovskoe until 1826.
1825	*Boris Godunov* completed, Pushkin has affair with the peasant girl Olga Kalashnikova.

11 January 1825	Pushkin visited by his Lycée classmate Ivan Pushchin, who hints at secret political activity.
18 February 1825	Publication of chapter 1 of *Evgenii Onegin*, with sales of 700 copies in February, decreasing steeply in the next months.
1 March 1825	Death of Alexander I.
14 December 1825	Coronation of Nicholas I disrupted by the Decembrists.
1826	*Poems of Alexander Pushkin,* Part I. In September, Nicholas I pardons him and becomes the poet's personal censor. Possibly advised by the critic and government agent Faddei Bulgarin, Nicholas blocks *Boris Godunov* for publication.
1827	Publication in July of the narrative poems *Brothers-Brigands* and *The Gypsies*, written in 1824. Publication in November of the burlesque poem *Count Null* to much indignation in prudish court circles.
1828	Chapters 4, 5 and 6 of *Evgenii Onegin* published to tepid reviews and modest sales. Second edition of *Ruslan and Liudmila* sells well. Investigated for the illicit circulation of stanzas from the poem 'André Chénier' under the title of '14 December'.
18–19 August 1828	Real threat of a second period of exile owing to the blasphemous *The Gabrieliad*. Made to sign a declaration stating that his verses will not henceforth be circulated in public without the censor's approval under a threat of severe punishment. Also placed under surveillance, which is to continue until his death.
1829	March publication of *Poltava*; *Poems of Alexander Pushkin*, Parts I and II.
May 1829	First proposal to Natalia Goncharova. Pushkin travels to Georgia and the Caucasus, recorded in *A Journey to Erzerum*.
January 1830	First number of the *Literary Gazette*, edited by Del'vig, to which Pushkin contributes.
Spring 1830	Del'vig publishes critical review of Faddei Bulgarin's play *Dmitrii the Pretender*, hinting at plagiarism of Pushkin and Bulgarin's status as a spy. Open hostilities prompt malicious epigrams from Pushkin;

	Bulgarin and his allies plague Pushkin henceforth. Engagement to Natalia Nikolaevna Goncharova, a beauty and favourite at court. Follows the July Revolution in France avidly.
September–December 1830	'First Boldino autumn'. Among other works, *Tales of Belkin*, The *Little House in Kolomna*, *Onegin's Journey* (original chapter 10 of the novel), the *Little Tragedies*, and over thirty lyric poems are composed.
January 1831	*Boris Godunov* published, 400 copies sell on the day of publication; receives 10,000 roubles from the publisher Smirdin, much of which goes to pay off debt.
18 February 1831	Marries Goncharova (having loaned her impoverished parents 11,000 roubles for the bride's dowry).
June 1831	The couple live in Tsarskoe Selo. The *Tales of Belkin* published.
August 1831	Russia retakes Warsaw, ending the Polish insurrection. Pushkin publishes the patriotic 'To the Slanderers of Russia', highly regarded at court but deemed craven by others.
November 1831	Nicholas I grants Pushkin permission to undertake historical research in the state archive, has him readmitted to a nominal position in the Foreign Office with an annual stipend of 5,000 roubles paid from July 1832.
Winter 1832	Chapter 8 of *Evgenii Onegin* published. Beginning of acute financial problems.
March 1832	*Poems of Alexander Pushkin*, Part III, published.
7 January 1833	Election to membership in the Russian Academy.
February–March 1833	Archival research on the Pugachev rebellion. First sketches of *The Captain's Daughter* penned. Travels to the Orenburg and Kazan districts to research the history of the Pugachev Rebellion.
March 1833	*Evgenii Onegin* published in book form.
6–31 October 1833	'Second Boldino autumn': 'The Queen of Spades', *Angelo*, several fairytales, the great lyric 'Autumn', and *The Bronze Horseman* composed. Financial woes mount and the family estate is almost forfeited to creditors.
1 January 1834	Appointment as Junior Gentleman of the Chamber.

March 1834	'The Queen of Spades' published. Researches the history of the reign of Peter the Great, works in Voltaire's Library in St Petersburg.
December 1834	*History of the Pugachev Rebellion* published with the tsar's approval. *The Tale of the Golden Cockerel* begun.
April 1835	*Poems of Alexander Pushkin*, Part IV, published.
1836	As editor publishes first volume of the journal *The Contemporary*. Three more volumes appear during the course of the year, including his only novel *The Captain's Daughter*, completed on 19 October, and published in December in volume iv.
29 March 1836	Death of Pushkin's mother.
26–29 January 1837	Wounded in duel and death.

Pushkin's Russia

ANDREW KAHN

Introduction

Alexander Pushkin changed the course of Russian literature. Ceaselessly experimental, he is the author of the greatest body of lyric poetry in the language; a remarkable novelist in verse, and a pioneer of Russian prose fiction; an innovator in psychological and historical drama; and an amateur historian of serious purpose. Pushkin's protean talent was legendary in his own lifetime. Both contemporary and later readers invoke the names of Shakespeare and Mozart to convey the impact of his artistic genius and the seeming effortlessness of his creative imagination. Russian writers of every generation, from Fedor Dostoevsky to Vladimir Nabokov and Joseph Brodsky, turn back to Pushkin, making him an interlocutor and acknowledging his presence as a continuous creative force. At the same time, he remains for Russians the indispensable writer, a genuinely popular classic, a cultural icon, a biographical obsession.

Underlying the protean diversity are unifying patterns of thought and theme. The interconnections between different types in Pushkin's creation bear witness to his impulse to refract historical, philosophical, psychological and autobiographical interests through multiple literary forms. This multiplicity of literary expression captures the essential mobility of Pushkin's thinking which preferred play and openness to definitive answers, and irony and ambiguity to didacticism, in the certain knowledge that these were the hallmarks of a free mind and in their own right anti-authoritarian. His preoccupations with numerous questions – the nature of the creative imagination, the meanings of love and the nature of betrayal, the connectedness of Russian and European cultures, the course of history in Russia and across Europe in the post-Napoleonic period – elicited masterpieces that often tend to incompleteness rather than dogmatic certainty, and to an openness of form that is radical from a writer also famed for the classical polish of his style.

Pushkin's sense of personal identity and his creative preoccupations grew out of a profound interest in the history of his nation. This is another unifying pattern across his diverse activities, reflected in the frequency with which historical topics and personal concerns are linked in his writings and in the chapters in this volume. His own coming of age occurred at a transitional moment in Russia's history that compelled him to wonder and write about the direction of the present in terms of the past. Russia's transformation during the epoch from Peter the Great to the end of Catherine the Great's reign in 1796 formed the backdrop for much of Pushkin's thinking about personal, historical and literary issues (discussed here in Chapters 1, 6, 7, 8 and 9). Bearing this in mind, it is helpful to understand certain aspects of Pushkin's life and artistic themes in the context of Russia's historical transformation during the eighteenth century.

The modern Russian state is often seen to originate in the reign of Peter I (1682–1725). The consequences of his reforms were still being felt in Pushkin's lifetime. When Peter the Great, as he was known, came to the throne in 1689, the social hierarchy and political structure of the medieval state were still largely intact. At the apex of the realm was the autocratic tsar; although he ruled unchecked by a constitution or parliamentary institutions, he ignored at his peril the advice of his aristocratic boyars, whose influence fluctuated from reign to reign. Their status, derived from their ancient lineage and military function, was defined by a complex precedence system known as *mestnichestvo* and was reflected in etiquette at the court of the tsar. As a way of guaranteeing conscription to the army and securing agricultural labour, the state had gradually imposed serfdom on the peasantry between the late-fifteenth century and 1649. In Peter's time, almost half the population of Russia was in bondage to a private lord; this remained the case in Pushkin's lifetime.

By the end of the seventeenth century, there was a growing sense that these structures were too primitive to meet the state's changing needs but it took the vision and energy of a determined moderniser like Peter the Great to achieve the necessary transformation. In order to establish Russia as a European power and to increase his country's status as a trading nation, Peter needed to defeat Sweden, Russia's strongest rival in the north. Such international ambition lay beyond the capabilities of the old Russia, requiring Peter to reform his army, create a navy and overhaul the major institutions of state. The tsar's governmental reforms were supplemented in 1722 by the institution of a Table of Ranks – an obligatory ladder for advancement in state service and an entry point into the nobility. Set against the old system of privileges that accrued to boyars by favour of the tsar and *mestnichestvo*, the new system encouraged the growth of a meritocratic elite to serve the renovated state. Ranked on three parallel tables – for civil, military and court personnel – entrants to the new system, whether of noble origin or drawn from the merchant class or free peasantry, were meant to ascend the ladder by dint of ability, knowledge and accomplishment.

Birth and marriage continued to confer privilege and status but by rewarding the service of commoners with noble rank, the Table fostered the view that nobility was a matter of performance and not simply pedigree. All those who reached the eighth of the fourteen ranks on the Table were granted hereditary nobility: the entitlement conferred status rather than land or wealth, but the effect was to dilute the perceived prestige of the ancient nobility and rapidly expand the gentry. Apart from a few aristocratic families that consolidated their wealth over the course of the next hundred years, the winners were largely 'new men', often regarded as social upstarts by more established nobles. Between Peter I's reforms and the mid-nineteenth century, the nobility increased rapidly in size (while remaining little more than 1 per cent of the overall population). Most of this metropolitan service gentry had few serf-holdings compared to the new magnates created in the reign of Catherine the Great (1762–96). Catherine's husband, Peter III, was assassinated as a consequence of the *coup* that brought her to the throne, but not before he had released the nobility from compulsory state service, encouraging them to continue to serve voluntarily on their provincial estates. By confirming and codifying noble privileges in her Charter to the Nobility (1785), Catherine maintained the tsars' traditional policy of granting nobles virtually unlimited social and economic control over their serfs in return for unquestioning political loyalty to the monarch. Any hopes of power-sharing entertained by the writers and intellectuals of her time were no more than fantasies.

Although the reality was that many ancient families were tenacious in their survival, it is no wonder that Pushkin, who admired Peter the Great, felt embittered about the declining status of the nobleman. Like other scions of ancient families, Pushkin was born into a family whose estates had been mortgaged or sold off and whose pedigree offered prestige without great preferment. Pushkin did not hanker for the days of the boyars, although he took pride in the Pushkin family pedigree. Despite ambivalence about Peter's documented inhumanity, Pushkin's respect for this ruler was constant and enhanced by the story of his great-grandfather Gannibal's rise under the tsar. His attitude towards Catherine the Great, however, was more personalised and complex, tinged with an animosity and blame for the way she had undermined the nobility, which, in Pushkin's view, deserved the sort of parliamentary influence it had gained in England.

Peter the Great also initiated a cultural revolution, discarding the old social conventions of the Muscovite state in favour of westernised manners and mores. He decreed against the wearing of beards and the old-fashioned caftan: his 'new Russians' were to dress in European costume and be clean-shaven. The push toward Westernisation led him to create a new capital, St Petersburg, founded in 1703 (an achievement that Pushkin described in *The Bronze Horseman*, his greatest narrative poem). Unlike ancient Moscow, famed for its gleaming cupolas, crooked streets and wooden houses, St Petersburg was designed to reflect the rational design of the new modern Russia. Its streets were laid out on a geometrical pattern, its buildings were topped with spires, feats of scientific engineering, and Colleges (precursors to the ministries created at the beginning of the nineteenth century) were housed in purpose-built Baroque accommodation. While Russia continued, under Peter's successors, to draw on a wide variety of European cultural influences, France became the main model for educated society, particularly in the reign of Catherine the Great. Though many provincial nobles remained illiterate, and were mocked as backward relics of a bygone world, French was the preferred language of the educated gentry, who aped French manners, dress and customs. Despite the satirists who lampooned their European ways, the cultivated Russian elite, like Pushkin's parents, took pride in their urbanity, polish and status.

By the time of Pushkin's youth, the accession of Alexander I (1801) had raised broader expectations of serf emancipation and constitutional reform. Doubts about the inhumane treatment meted out to their serfs were already troubling the more enlightened Russian nobles in the 1780s. The failure of the Decembrist Rebellion of 1825 (discussed in Chapter 7) reinforced Nicholas I's authoritarian streak. Demanding allegiance to the conservative values of 'Orthodoxy, Autocracy and Nationality', the new tsar outlawed dissent and inhibited open political debate. Pushkin's class was left marginalised without political influence, obliged to serve in the bureaucracy or consigned to slow decay in the countryside or Romantic escape in the Caucasus. Aristocratic disillusionment with Nicholas I's regime was largely captured by the next generation of writers, who came of age in the 1850s, but Pushkin's hero Evgenii Onegin was seen by that time as the prototypical 'superfluous man' doomed to boredom and inertia. Among the aristocrats of Pushkin's milieu, much pent-up energy was channelled into gambling to relieve boredom and the sense of stasis. A personal sense of honour became all the more important as an expression of self-worth in a society where thinking men and women were hardly free to act or take charge of their destiny. In this connection, the art of duelling, still alive in France, too, continued to be a means of settling scores. Pushkin's keen sense of honour, born both of his own accomplishments and of his self-identity as a nobleman, repeatedly involved him in duels. All of these historical issues, from state institutions like the Table of Ranks to the concept of individual status and honour, inform Pushkin's writings in ways that the individual chapters of this *Companion* elucidate.

It is also the case that Pushkin's creative life reached maturity at a time in the 1820s when Russia's literary culture, confined in the last third of the eighteenth century to a small urban elite, was slowly being transformed by growth in readership and commercial opportunities. Galvanised by the examples of Walter Scott and Byron – and aware that his own politically subversive persona attracted readers – Pushkin aspired to a similar level of popularity that would secure the status of the writer and also raise the taste of his readership. The success of the narrative poem *Ruslan and Liudmila* (1820), which appeared and sold out just as Pushkin departed to Southern exile, fuelled his ambition of establishing the professional status of the writer in a literary marketplace just as had occurred in Britain and in France. But the opportunities available to Pushkin as a writer, critic, and publisher were on a much smaller scale. While the first two cantos of Byron's *Childe Harold* were reprinted eight times in the six years following their original publication in 1812, and sold more than 20,000 copies, the print runs of chapters of *Evgenii Onegin* were relatively modest at a little more than 1,000 copies and never sold out. By the end of the 1820s, the growth of a readership in Russia made literary life almost viable commercially: publishers were paying authors several multiples of the sums offered to the previous generation. All the same, this was less than Pushkin needed and a fraction of the money that English and French writers normally – and some Russian writers exceptionally – earned (see Chapter 10). A wealthy magnate of the period might enjoy a quit-rent of 50,000 roubles from his landholdings, while Pushkin's salary as a courtier was closer to 5,000 roubles. The increasing popularity of low-quality fiction had made it difficult for poetry and high-quality fiction to compete. In 1831, when he published the *Tales of Belkin*, Pushkin hoped to sell 2,000 copies and walk away with a profit of 10,000 roubles after costs. In the event, only 1,200 copies were printed and he netted less than half his projected profit. By the end of his life, Pushkin's own works and his journal, *The Contemporary*, barely covered the cost of their publication. Awareness of the connection between economic pressures and creative choices informs our understanding of Pushkin at every level, whether he is projecting an image of genius in his poetry (Chapter 2) or managing a literary network in the ephemeral banter of correspondence (Chapter 9).

He was regarded as a classic by the time of his death, which occasioned widespread popular mourning. But his work was no longer fashionable and many of his greatest poems remained unpublished in his lifetime and proper editions did not appear till much later in the nineteenth century. The phenomenon of Pushkin appreciation only began to gain momentum from the

1870s: arguably, he became a truly popular writer only in the Soviet period. At the same time, although other Romantics like Byron or Hugo did battle with public opinion and censorship, Pushkin's career was also uniquely Russian in forcing him to negotiate with an autocratic government that saw a threat in the liberty of expression and artistic autonomy that Pushkin regarded as a right. His entire creative life amounts to an assertion of artistic freedom against the insuperable meddling and harassment of the government.

Readers have always been able to savour the beauty of Pushkin's language, famed for a surface clarity suffused with connotation and implication. But readers in the twenty-first century, approaching Pushkin for the first time, can now better see his creation, and his unique status in Russian culture, as historical phenomena in their own right. Over the past twenty years, major developments have occurred in the way Pushkin is understood. The chapters in this volume are shaped by the conclusions of specialist studies, and convey this contextualised portrait of the writer. We now read him with a greater awareness of his connection to the institutions of literature and the influence of market forces on literary production; with a fuller knowledge of his links to important trends in European Romanticism and aesthetics; and through the lens of modern critical theory, now including reader-response and Bakhtin as well as, from an earlier era, the influential Russian Formalists. This *Companion* affords an opportunity to consolidate and revise views of Pushkin's creative achievement in a post-Perestroika world where scholars from Russia and the West are newly collaborating in modernising their understanding of Pushkin's life and work. In areas such as politics and historiography, for example, where scholarship was contaminated by the Marxist ideology of the Soviet State, the present volume reconsiders Pushkin's connection to revolutionary groups of the 1820s, and his belief in the governing potential of his class of nobles.

The authors recognise that this book will most often be turned to by students of Pushkin and Russian literature, and the chapters in this volume reflect the great range of Pushkin's achievement as a writer and as a man of letters. But they are also aware of his impact in other media popular both in Russia and the West, whether in the drama of *Mozart and Salieri* or the operas of Tchaikovsky (Chapter 11); and of the perhaps unique experience of the Pushkin phenomenon as a case study in cultural politics (Chapters 12, 13 and 14). From the origins of the Soviet Union to its fall, there has scarcely been a moment when the spotlight has been off Pushkin as the symbolic centre of official ideology and unofficial dissent. Yet different visions of Pushkin, as much as an Iron Curtain, divided the literary cultures of the Russian diaspora and of the Soviet Union. Exploring the official and unofficial mechanisms behind Pushkin's role in the formation of twentieth-century Russian culture is an area that has been highly productive and one where even more exciting work is promised. In providing a detailed account of Pushkin's crucial role in the formation of Soviet and post-Soviet national identity and, in the case of émigré culture, alternative identity, the essays in the second section bear witness to a historical moment that is still being played out in Russia's perception of itself. The open-endedness of his legacy as a dynamic principle in a literature and culture seems particularly Pushkinian.

I

TEXTS AND CONTEXTS

I

DAVID BETHEA AND SERGEI DAVYDOV

Pushkin's life

Alexander Pushkin, like his near-contemporary Lord Byron, took great pride in his aristocratic ancestry. He was born into the family of Sergei L'vovich Pushkin and Nadezhda Osipovna Pushkina née Gannibal, whose ancestors on both sides included prominent figures in Russian history. Through his father, Pushkin belonged to an ancient line of nobility dating back to the twelfth century (not the thirteenth as Pushkin thought); their names are cited twenty-one times in Nikolai Karamzin's monumental *History of the Russian State* (1818), the authoritative historical work on Russia in Pushkin's lifetime. The Pushkin clan stayed close to power up to the end of the sixteenth century, falling from grace under the Romanovs, whose dynasty dates from the early seventeenth century. Several ancestors were conspirators and mutineers and suffered in particular under Peter the Great. By 1799, the year of the poet's birth, the Pushkin family had lost all their influence and most of their fortune, and, as he grew older, Pushkin came to identify with their lot: 'They were persecuted. And I am persecuted' (*PSS*, vol. xi, p. 388).

On the maternal side, Pushkin's great-grandfather, Abram (originally Ibrahim) Petrovich Gannibal was born in Africa in 1696; he may have been the son of an Abyssinian prince, as Pushkin believed. He was sent as a slave to the court of Peter the Great, where he became the tsar's informal secretary and constant attendant. Eventually he attained the status of hereditary nobleman and was awarded several estates for his loyal service.[1] While Gannibal achieved distinction as a military engineer, a notorious jealous streak marred his private life. This amazing figure with ties to Russia's greatest tsar and with a story of meteoric rise from slavery captured Pushkin's imagination and played a role in his self-projection (see Chapter 6). Pushkin was proud of his ancestors, accepting their heroic deeds and nobility along with the 'taint' of their passions and their penchant for self-destruction. Throughout his life he was sensitive about what he saw as his 'Negro ugliness' while fearing that his inherited temperament could – and given his poetic fatalism probably would – cast its shadow over his own life.

Childhood: 1799–1811

Alexander Pushkin was born on 26 May 1799 in Moscow. His parents endeavoured to maintain aristocratic appearances and constantly lived beyond their means. The podgy and clumsy Sasha (his affectionate Russian nickname) was their least favourite child; and while he felt this keenly he found refuge and warmth with his grandmother Maria Alekseevna and with his nanny Arina Rodionovna. From these two women the children learned Russian, as Pushkin recalls in the poem 'Sleep/Dream' ('Son', 1816), where 'granny' and 'nanny' merge into one appealing image. The children spent summers at their grandmother's estate in Zakharovo, near Moscow, where old-fashioned Russian life ruled. Pushkin addressed a number of moving poems to his nanny,[2] and as the ultimate token of his affection, he 'lent' her to his favourite heroine Tatiana in *Evgenii Onegin*.

Lycée: 1811–1817

The Lycée was an exclusive boarding school, directly attached to the Catherine Palace in Tsarskoe Selo, the royal summer residence. The emperor himself inaugurated it with pomp on 19 October 1811 in the presence of the court, the faculty and the first class of thirty students. It was the most progressive educational institution of its day in Russia.

Pushkin – nicknamed 'the Frenchman' for his brilliant command of French language and literature – was only a mediocre student. But he read avidly and began writing love elegies and verse epistles to friends. In the poem 'The Little Town' ('Gorodok', 1814) the teenage poet lists his favourite authors: classical and neoclassical writers like Homer, Virgil, Horace, Tasso, Molière, Racine, Voltaire, J.-B. Rousseau, Évariste de Parny, and Russian writers famed from the eighteenth century like the poet Gavrila Derzhavin, the playwright Denis Fonvizin, the historian and man of letters Karamzin, the poet Ivan Dmitriev and the fable-writer Ivan Krylov. To Voltaire and Parny he pays particular tribute. Pushkin started writing verse from an early age and published his first poem 'To a Poet-Friend' ('K drugu stikhotvortsu') in 1814. A more important debut was his public reading of 'Recollections in Tsarskoe Selo' ('Vospominaniia v Tsarskom Sele') during the qualifying examination at the end of the junior course on 8 January 1815. The greatest Russian poet of the eighteenth century, Derzhavin, was the guest of honour. He fell asleep during the examination, and only when Pushkin began reciting his poem – a gentle parody of Derzhavin's style – did the great man wake up: 'Here is the one who will take Derzhavin's place', he is alleged to have said.[3]

Pushkin's reputation grew by word of mouth, and he was encouraged by poets and men of letters close to the Karamzin circle, such as the poet

Konstantin Batiushkov, the writer and courtier Vasilii Zhukovskii and the satirist and critic Prince Petr Viazemskii who saw a bright future for the teenager. The final examination in May 1817, at which Alexander I was present, was allegedly a sham since the students probably knew their questions in advance. Even so, Pushkin managed to graduate at the bottom of his class, excelling only in Russian, French and fencing. Nevertheless, he had found at the Lycée the real home he did not know with his parents; he had made lifelong friends (Anton Del'vig and Ivan Pushchin to whom he wrote poems) and spent some of the happiest days of his life there.

Pushkin dreamt of a military career in the Guards, but because the uniform for the cavalry service was too costly, his father put him in for a government post instead. The eighteen-year-old Pushkin was assigned to the Ministry of Foreign Affairs in St Petersburg, with the rank of Collegiate Secretary and a modest annual salary of 600 roubles.

St Petersburg, Arzamas, Green Lamp, radicalism: 1817–1820

Pushkin's post at the ministry was purely nominal, enabling him to lead an idle and dissipated life akin to that of his hero in chapter 1 of *Evgenii Onegin*. While still at the Lycée, he had become a member of Arzamas, a literary-cum-dining society that took its name from the provincial town famous for its geese. In the first decades of the nineteenth century, Russian literary societies were divided on the basis of their attitude to the literary language. Members of Arzamas were followers of Nikolai Karamzin. In the early part of his career, before he turned to writing history in 1803, Karamzin had advocated that Russians cast aside an idiom based on the archaic Slavonic language of the Church, and use a more elegant version of the language spoken in polite society. Their views were opposed by the archaists, who were members of the group called The Colloquy of The Lovers of the Russian Word (*Beseda liubitelei russkogo slova*) and saw the Slavonic idiom as a matter of national pride. Many of Pushkin's literary friends felt an affinity for Arzamas and its programme. One exception was the poet Wilhelm Kiukhel'beker, who championed the archaic style (see Chapter 5) and became something of a figure of ridicule as well as a prototype for the character of Lenskii in *Evgenii Onegin*. Arzamas revelled in parody and subversive rituals. For instance, members staged mock burials of the members of the rival Beseda.

The other society to which Pushkin belonged was the Green Lamp (*Zelenaia lampa*), founded in 1819 as a champagne and theatre club with political overtones (see Chapter 9). Smart young military officers and men-about-town met 'under the green lamp' at the home of Nikita Vsevolozhskii to discuss contemporary theatre, issues of freedom, equality and the need for a constitution, and the beauty of ballerinas. They also used the meetings to drink and gamble. The latter activity became one of Pushkin's favourite and least successful pastimes: at one such gathering he forfeited a manuscript containing some of his earliest poems to satisfy a debt to Vsevolozhskii.

Pushkin had the reputation of a political liberal, sharing the expectations of his generation for the constitutional reforms that Alexander I had encouraged and then disappointed (for further discussion see Chapter 7). He also flirted with more radical politics. Once, for example, he publicly displayed in the theatre a portrait of Louis-Pierre Louvel, the assassin of the heir to the Bourbon throne, with the inscription 'A Lesson to Tsars'. Pushkin's friend Alexander Turgenev called his political bravado 'vulgar free-thinking' while the real revolutionaries, grown weary of Pushkin's fidgety nature and dissipated lifestyle, did not trust him and never offered him membership in their secret societies. Nonetheless, Pushkin's radical poems seemed to serve their cause and circulated privately, in manuscript. In 1819 they came to the attention of the government. The interior minister Count Arakcheev and Alexander I threatened to banish Pushkin to the remote Solovetskii Monastery on the White Sea or to Siberia, and in April 1820 he was summoned to the office of the Petersburg Governor-General Count M. A. Miloradovich who demanded to see the seditious poems. Pushkin, who had burned them, volunteered to write them down from memory, and the generous Miloradovich forgave him on the spot. It took the intercession of several influential people, among them Miloradovich, Karamzin and the emperor's mother, to prevail upon the tsar to commute Pushkin's exile to an administrative transfer to the south, where he would serve as translator to General Inzov, the senior military official of the colonies recently ceded to Russia by Turkey.

South, Caucasus, Kishinev: 1820–1823

In early May 1820, Pushkin left St Petersburg, unhappy but also relieved. In Ekaterinoslav (now Dnepropetrovsk), he met General Raevskii, hero of the Napoleonic campaign, who was travelling with his family to the newly conquered Caucasus. With the consent of his new chief, General Inzov, Pushkin spent a glorious three-month stay with the charming Raevskii family, admiring the mountains and the savage mountaineers, and reading Byron, in French translation. The group also visited the Crimea. On his way back, Pushkin fell ill with fever and during his convalescence made a trip to Bakhchisarai, the former capital of the Crimean Khanate. The khan's harem became the setting for Pushkin's Byronic tale, *The Fountain of Bakhchisarai* (*Bakhchisaraiskii fontan*, 1821–23). In September, Pushkin arrived at Inzov's new headquarters in Kishinev, Bessarabia. Here he befriended the division commander, General M. F. Orlov, a member of the Union of Welfare, a radical group that had a southern branch and a northern branch in St Petersburg, and was already preparing for an armed uprising to abolish the monarchy and all aristocratic privileges. Pushkin also spent two months at the Raevskii-Davydov estate in Kamenka, near Kiev, meeting other members of the secret society. In Kishinev, Pushkin finally met, and was impressed by, the leader of the movement, Colonel Pavel Pestel'.[4]

During his three years in Kishinev Pushkin fought several duels – all ending without bloodshed – for which he spent some weeks under house arrest. He also had an affair with Calypso Polichroni, the Greek girl reputed to have been loved by Byron. Here he saw into print *The Prisoner of the Caucasus* (*Kavkazskii plennik*, pub. 1822) and finished *The Fountain of Bakhchisarai*, the most popular work published in his lifetime. In addition, he wrote 'To Ovid' ('K Ovidiiu'), an elegy to the Roman poet who, like Pushkin, had in his own day been exiled to Bessarabia. One of his most notorious achievements, as circulated in manuscript copies, was the blatantly atheistic and obscene narrative poem *The Gabrieliad* (*Gavriiliada*, 1821). Inspired by Parny's *War of the Gods* (*Guerre des Dieux*, 1799) and Voltaire's burlesque of Joan of Arc in *The Maid of Orleans* (*La Pucelle*, 1755), Pushkin parodied the Immaculate Conception and made Satan the father of Christ. Another risqué work is the fairytale *Tsar Nikita and his Forty Daughters* (*Tsar Nikita i sorok ego docherei*, 1822). Most importantly, it was in Kishinev that Pushkin began *Evgenii Onegin*, his novel-in-verse loosely modelled after Byron's *Don Juan*, which took him eight years to complete (1823–31).

Odessa: 1823–1824

Pushkin was transferred in August 1823 to Odessa, a cosmopolitan European port on the Black Sea, and placed under the wing of Governor-General Count Vorontsov. This wealthy, English-educated aristocrat was a hero of the Napoleonic wars and a well-known liberal who had freed his serfs. The count opened his house and his library to Pushkin and offered him a post on his office staff. Pushkin's salary of 700 roubles a year was insufficient to support his lifestyle, with the result that he was forced to rely on income from publishers. This ungentlemanly need to haggle over money with publishers depressed and irritated Pushkin.

During his years in Odessa, Pushkin fell in love with three enchanting and experienced women: Amalia Riznich, a merchant's wife; Karolina Soban'skaia, a beautiful Pole to whom Mickiewicz's *Crimean Sonnets* are dedicated, and Countess Elizaveta Vorontsova, wife of the governor-general. The names Amalia and Eliza are found on the famous 'Don Juan list' that

Pushkin compiled in 1829. The intensity of what Pushkin felt for these 'Odessan muses' unites them despite their many differences.[5]

In Odessa, Pushkin was reunited with his friend, Alexander Raevskii, with whom he had travelled to the Caucasus. Raevskii also loved Elise Vorontsova and used Pushkin as a decoy in order to draw attention away from himself. On learning the truth, the trusting Pushkin was jealous and deeply hurt, portraying Raevskii as a Lucifer-like fallen angel in the poems 'Demon' ('Demon', 1823) and 'Treachery' ('Kovarnost'', 1824). The powerful count began to resent his subordinate's aristocratic tetchiness and the courting of his wife right under his nose. As tensions mounted, Vorontsov snubbed Pushkin by treating him as a petty civil servant, which Pushkin resented as an affront to his own 600-year-old lineage. Ultimately, Vorontsov requested Pushkin's transfer from Odessa, but Pushkin anticipated him by handing in a request for retirement and mocking the count in some brilliantly barbed epigrams.

To make matters worse, at around the same time the authorities in Moscow intercepted a letter from Pushkin to a friend in which he wrote that atheism is 'unfortunately the most plausible' belief. By now Pushkin's fate was sealed: an offence against religion was tantamount to an offence against the state. The tsar decided to dismiss Pushkin from service and to change his place of exile from the south to his mother's Mikhailovskoe estate in northern Russia about 300 miles south-west of St Petersburg.

There is evidence that during Pushkin's last week in Odessa, from 25 to 31 July 1824, he had a liaison with Elise Vorontsova that engendered a number of love poems written during his northern isolation.[6] On 1 August, dressed 'in yellow nankeen wide trousers and a Russian blouse', Pushkin left Odessa. In his luggage he was carrying the beginning of *The Gypsies* (*Tsygany*, 1824), the last and most complex of his three Southern poems, some thirty stanzas of chapter 3 of *Evgenii Onegin* and two gifts from Elise: a talisman-ring with a Hebrew inscription (which he wore to his last duel) and a golden medallion with her portrait.

Exile in Mikhailovskoe: 1824–1826

On 9 August 1824, Pushkin arrived in Mikhailovskoe where he was immediately placed under the surveillance of the police, the local abbot, and his own father. Relations between Pushkin and his father had always been tense, and Pushkin exploded in rage when he learned that Sergei L'vovich had consented to keep watch on him. Dishonour touched both father and son. In a letter to Zhukovskii he described his father's role in unsealing his correspondence, followed by a stormy confrontation that led to the father's departure.

Passionate longing for Elise Vorontsova tormented Pushkin. Arguably, what he felt for Elise he never felt again for anyone else. Whenever a letter arrived sealed with a talisman-ring (a match for the one Elise had given to Pushkin), he locked himself in his room for a protracted period and then burned the precious document.[7] From one of her letters Pushkin may have learned that Elise was pregnant with his child. In any event, approximately nine months after their last meeting Elise gave birth to a 'swarthy' daughter. The theme of an out-of-wedlock child appears in a number of works of this period.[8]

Pushkin often grew bored in the country. Despite the isolation, he was remarkably resilient and, tapping deep into private reserves, found a way to turn adversity to advantage and to grow remarkably as a thinker and artist during his confinement at Mikhailovskoe. The company of his old nurse, Arina Rodionovna, dispelled his melancholy. He wrote down songs and tales, the basis for later poetic gems of stylised folklore. Another refuge was found in the nearby Trigorskoe estate of Praskovia Osipova-Vulf, whose several daughters added a cheerful and much-needed feminine touch to his now severe male world. It was at this time that he had a sexual relationship with the serf girl Olga Kalashnikova.

The years 1824–25 found Pushkin at a crossroads. While the secret societies were preparing for an armed insurrection in the capital, Pushkin, holed up deep in the Russian heartland, was learning a different and thoroughly anti-romantic lesson. He finished *The Gypsies*, the last of his Southern narrative poems; the cycle 'Imitations of the Koran' ('Podrazhaniia Koranu', 1824), which paves the way for the 'negative capability' of the poet's later religious consciousness; the great Shakespearean historical drama *Boris Godunov* (1825, pub. 1830); the witty epic *Count Null* (*Graf Nulin*, 1825), modelled after Byron's *Beppo* and parodying Shakespeare's *Rape of Lucrece*; and chapters 4, 5 and 6 of *Evgenii Onegin*. The sustained reading of Shakespeare, Karamzin's *History of the Russian State* and the Bible convinced Pushkin that beyond individual will – noble or ignoble – ultimately stands a meaningful, if not always benign, historical destiny.

In November 1825, Alexander I died unexpectedly. His brother Grand Duke Constantine had in 1823 secretly renounced the throne in favour of a second brother Nicholas, but an interregnum of several weeks occurred while Constantine and Nicholas confirmed their plans. In St Petersburg, the members of the northern society of the Union of Salvation took advantage of the power vacuum and on 14 December mounted an armed insurgency. A group of officers commanding some 3,000 men refused to swear allegiance to Nicholas I and proclaimed their loyalty to 'Constantine and Constitution'. While the troops stood for hours in the cold on Senate Square, their leaders could not decide what to do next. Eventually, forces loyal to Nicholas opened fire, thereby ending the uprising.

Pushkin knew many of the rebels personally and was implicated because copies of his political verses were found among them. Yet he hoped that the interrogations of the insurgents would prove him innocent – after all, he was not a member of any secret society – and in May 1826 he appealed to the new tsar for a commutation of his exile. In July he learned about the execution of five of the rebel leaders, including the poet Konstantin Ryleev, the first such execution in Russia since the quartering of the Cossack rebel Emel'ian Pugachev in 1774. In the manuscript of chapter 5 of *Evgenii Onegin*, we find sketches of gallows with five dangling corpses, accompanied by an inscription, 'And like a fool, I too could have . . .' On 4 September 1826 a special courier arrived in Mikhailovskoe and whisked Pushkin away to Moscow.

After exile, Nicholas I, 1828, Erzerum: 1826–1829

Pushkin arrived in the Kremlin on 8 September. The first person he saw was the new tsar, who was still in Moscow after the coronation ceremonies. When the tsar asked whether Pushkin would have participated in the uprising had he been in St Petersburg, the poet is alleged to have confirmed that he would have done (see Chapter 7). The audience resulted in a truce of sorts. The tsar proclaimed Pushkin 'Russia's most intelligent man', ended his exile, and offered to be the poet's personal censor. For his part Pushkin presumably confirmed his pledge 'not to contradict the accepted order', something he had expressed already in his letter to Nicholas I the previous May.[9] In any event, he would pay dearly for this attempt to establish an understanding between poet and tsar.

Pushkin was slow to realise that he had fallen into a trap. Ostensibly free, he was actually the tsar's hostage under the supervision of General Benckendorff, the chief of the Third Department, the agency recently founded with responsibility for state security. Pushkin was not allowed to travel, publish or hold public readings without explicit permission. One of his first clashes with the authorities involved the poem 'André Chénier' (1825), presumed to contain a hidden reference to the Decembrist uprising, although it was written some time before and its subject was the fate of a poet in the French Revolution. Then, in 1828, the blasphemous *Gabrieliad* (written back in 1821) came to the attention of the Metropolitan of St Petersburg. Pushkin at first denied his authorship, but eventually confessed in a personal letter to Nicholas I, who forgave him and closed the matter. Even so, 1828 was an exceptionally bleak year for Pushkin. On his birthday (26 May) he wrote his most despairing Job-like lament, 'Futile gift, random gift' ('Dar naprasnyi, dar sluchainyi'). In the same year he repeatedly asked permission to undertake some activity that would alter the circumstances of his trapped existence: to join the army in the war against Turkey, to travel to France, to take part in a diplomatic mission to China. All requests were denied.

During these difficult years (1828–30) Pushkin was also searching for a wife. His gypsy-like existence had become a burden to him; he longed for some rootedness, for a home and family, yet he also realised that his reputation made him a less than attractive candidate for matrimony. He proposed to several women, but was rejected every time. Then in 1828 at a Moscow ball, he met the stunning sixteen-year-old Natalia Goncharova and proposed to her in May of the following year. After an indefinite answer from Natalia's mother, which Pushkin perceived as another rejection, he bolted on the same day for the Caucasus. There he visited his friends and his brother Lev at the front. Throughout his life Pushkin had wanted to experience the thrill of battle. Riding a Cossack horse in his frock coat and a top hat, lance in hand, he single-handedly 'attacked' the Turks; luckily he was rescued by Russian uhlans who took him for a mad German priest. In June, he rode along with the troops into the newly conquered Turkish town Erzerum – this was his first and last time abroad – where he remained until a plague epidemic chased him back across the Russian border. On his return he was reprimanded by Benckendorff for undertaking the journey without the tsar's express consent.

Boldino 1, marriage, historian, Pugachev, Boldino 2: 1830–1833

On Easter Sunday, 6 April 1830, Pushkin proposed again to Natalia Goncharova and was grudgingly accepted. Obliged by his future mother-in-law to provide a dowry for his bride, he set off for Boldino in the province of Nizhnii Novgorod (Gorky) to take possession of the tithes of two villages and 200 serfs – his father's wedding present to him. Confined to this backwater for almost three months due to an outbreak of cholera, Pushkin enjoyed an unprecedented spell of inspiration during this 'first Boldino autumn'. He wrote moving elegies in which he bids farewell to the female ghosts of prior love affairs; finished the last two chapters of *Evgenii Onegin* and burned chapter 10; inaugurated what he called his 'descent to prose' by penning the five experimental *Tales of Belkin* (*Povesti Belkina*); and rethought the concept of tragedy in four brilliant dramatic sketches known as the *Little Tragedies* (*Malen'kie tragedii*). He also produced a playful anecdote in the complex verse-form of *ottava rima*, *The Little House in Kolomna* (*Domik v Kolomne*), his first fairytale in verse, *The Tale of the Village Priest and His Workman Balda* (*Skazka o pope i rabotnike ego Balde*), and over a dozen dazzling poems, among them 'The Devils' ('Besy'), 'My Genealogy' ('Moia rodoslovnaia'), and 'The Hero' ('Geroi').

When Pushkin finally returned to Moscow he was confronted with the sad news that his closest friend from the Lycée days, Anton Del'vig, had died unexpectedly. On 18 February 1831, Pushkin and Natalia Nikolaevna Goncharova were married in Moscow. During the ceremony, the cross and Scriptures fell from the altar and the candle Pushkin was holding went out: 'Tous les mauvais augures', remarked the superstitious poet. Still, in the first blush of conjugal life he could remark to a friend that 'I am married, and happy'. His wife eclipsed all others with her exceptional beauty. Among her admirers was the tsar himself. If Pushkin believed in anything it was in the transfiguring power of beauty, whether the physical charm of Venus or the spiritual calm of the Virgin, and for him 'Natalie', perhaps unknown to her, was the embodiment of both.

During a meeting with Nicholas I in July 1831 the tsar mentioned that he wanted to obtain Peter the Great's house in Zaandam, Holland, from the Dutch monarch. Always ready with a quip, Pushkin replied that should this happen he would be interested in the post of janitor. Instead, the tsar promoted Pushkin to the rank of titular councillor and appointed him as court historiographer charged with researching in the imperial archives and writing a history of Peter the Great. Pushkin began work on *The History of Peter the Great* (*Istoriia Petra*), but he became curious about the Cossack rebellion of 1773–74, led by Emel'ian Pugachev; a daring Pretender to the throne, he spread the rumour that he was actually Tsar Peter III, the husband Catherine had had assassinated in 1762. In 1831 Pushkin responded to the Polish uprising against Russian domination with two 'patriotic' (that is anti-Polish, anti-European) verse invectives, 'To the Slanderers of Russia' ('Klevetnikam Rossii') and 'Borodino Anniversary' ('Borodinskaia godovshchina').

In the autumn of 1833, Pushkin travelled to the Urals to collect oral histories of the Pugachev rebellion from the few surviving eye-witnesses. On his way home he stopped again at Boldino. As it happened, he had written little since his last stay. Now, during his 'second Boldino autumn', the need to write again overwhelmed him. Within six weeks he had finished the *History of Pugachev* (*Istoriia Pugacheva*); two fairytales in verse, *The Tale of the Fisherman and the Fish* (*Skazka o rybake i rybke*), inspired by the Brothers Grimm, and *The Tale of the Dead Tsarevna* (*Skazka o mertvoi tsarevne*); the verse adaptation *Angelo* (*Andzhelo*), based on Shakespeare's *Measure for Measure*, a favourite work; and two of his greatest creations, the epic poem *The Bronze Horseman* (*Mednyi vsadnik*) and the prose tale 'The Queen of Spades' ('Pikovaia dama').

The year ended on a sour note: on 31 December 1833 Nicholas I awarded Pushkin the court title 'junior gentleman of the chamber' (*kammerjunker*), something usually conferred on younger scions of high aristocratic lineage. At the age of thirty-four, Pushkin felt humiliated, suspecting that Nicholas had made him a courtier as a pretext for inviting Natalia to royal balls at the Anichkov Palace.

Family man and courtier: 1834–1836

Pushkin did not hide the fact that life as a courtier was a burden. Indeed, he hated the frock coat that he was obliged to wear as a *kammerjunker*, regarding it as a symbol of his humiliation and called it 'a jester's motley'. He tried to avoid ceremonies at court where he was required to wear it. Moreover, the high style of living in the capital, the necessary appearances at court, the sartorial needs of his wife, the debts he settled for his spendthrift brother Lev – all these proved to be beyond the financial means of a professional writer and court historiographer. Pushkin was forced to ask for subsidies and credit from Nicholas, or turn to pawnbrokers for ready cash. By 1834 he was the father of two children (two more would be born later). Two of Natalia's unmarried sisters had come to live with the family indefinitely, which added a considerable burden. 'If I die, my wife will be on the streets and my children in misery', he wrote to his brother-in-law in 1833.[10] By the time of his death his debts had reached approximately 140,000 roubles, a ruinous sum.

Harassed by creditors, Pushkin made another request in 1835 for permission to retire for a time to his country estate in order to improve his finances. The request was denied. Instead, Pushkin was allowed to start a literary quarterly, *The Contemporary* (*Sovremennik*), a venture that only exacerbated his debts. In spite of his exhaustion and despondency, the poet still managed to finish several important works, including: *The Tale of the Golden Cockerel* (*Skazka o zolotom petushke*, 1834), based on a tale by Washington Irving; a complex cycle of poems, 'Songs of the Western Slavs' ('Pesni zapadnykh slavian', 1834); and *The Captain's Daughter* (*Kapitanskaia dochka*, 1836), the superb historical novel about the Pugachev rebellion that ingeniously reworked the plot line of Walter Scott's *Rob Roy*. He continued to solicit and edit contributions for *The Contemporary*.

Duel and death: 1836–1837

Throughout 1836, Georges d'Anthès, a handsome Frenchman serving in the Russian Royal Guards, relentlessly pursued Natalia Pushkina. In February, in the seventh month of her pregnancy, Natalia, who was clearly not indifferent, may have confessed to her suitor that she did love him but could offer him 'no more than [her] heart, because the rest does not belong to [her]'.[11] On 2 November 1836, d'Anthès contrived to arrange a secret rendezvous with her at the house of one of Pushkin's enemies. During the encounter, d'Anthès allegedly drew a pistol and threatened to kill himself in front of the distraught woman if she would not give herself to him. Somehow Natalia managed to escape.[12] Two days later, on 4 November, Pushkin received an anonymous 'diploma' stating that he had been unanimously elected to the post of Deputy Grand Master and Historiographer of the Most Noble Order of Cuckolds. In a gesture meant to humiliate him further, copies of the 'diploma' were sent to his friends for forwarding to him. Pushkin then confronted Natalia who confessed that d'Anthès had been pursuing her and that he had entrapped her just days before. She also showed her husband d'Anthès's letters to her and told him that the Dutch ambassador, Baron Louis van Heeckeren, d'Anthès's adoptive father, had pleaded with her to accept his son's advances. Convinced that his wife was innocent and enraged at her treatment, Pushkin resolved to defend both her and his own honour. That same evening he challenged d'Anthès to a duel. The conditions were calculated to produce a lethal outcome, with the barriers set a mere ten paces apart. 'The bloodier, the better', demanded Pushkin.[13]

Events did not follow the course that Pushkin had planned. The duel was postponed twice as d'Anthès suddenly claimed that he was in love with Natalia's sister Ekaterina and was preparing to propose to her. Pushkin tried to call d'Anthès's bluff, calculating that marriage to Ekaterina would be perceived in society, and more importantly in d'Anthès's regiment, as a cowardly ploy to sidestep the duel. Pushkin had also heard rumours that van Heeckeren had been having a homosexual liaison with his adopted son[14] and that in order to diffuse suspicion, which could compromise his army career, d'Anthès had sought a public affair with a brilliant society woman. After Natalia had rejected him, he began courting her sister. On 17 November, d'Anthès formally proposed to Ekaterina; and Pushkin, savouring victory, retracted his challenge. Nicholas I learned about the events and summoned Pushkin for an audience on 23 November. Pushkin assured Nicholas that he would not fight; he gave his word not to discuss the matter further and to inform the tsar in the event of any subsequent conflict.

The marriage between d'Anthès and Ekaterina Goncharova took place on 10 January 1837. Pushkin did not attend the ceremony and refused to receive the couple at his home. He believed that he had made the dashing French officer look like a coward in the eyes of society and had punished him sufficiently by forcing him to marry the unloved and unattractive Ekaterina, who was three years d'Anthès's senior and possibly pregnant with his child.[15]

D'Anthès resumed his pursuit of Natalia, insinuating that he had married Ekaterina in order to be closer to Natalia. High society viewed d'Anthès as a romantic hero who sacrificed his happiness to save the honour of his beloved. Juxtaposed with such 'chivalrous self-sacrifice', Pushkin's outbursts of jealousy and sullenness looked foolish even to well-wishers. Unable to forgive or forget the humiliating 'diploma', Pushkin grew increasingly agitated. Some friends saw his fits of rage, 'demonic laughter' and 'grinding of teeth', as signs of the fiery temperament inherited from his great-grandfather Gannibal.

During a ball on 23 January 1837, d'Anthès publicly quipped to Natalia that, according to the chiropodist shared by the Goncharov sisters, 'votre cor est plus beau que celui de ma femme' (your corn/body [*cor/corps*] is more beautiful than that of my wife's).[16] Pushkin was incensed when Natalia reported the remark to him. On the next day (24 January) Pushkin pawned his sister-in-law Alexandra's silverware for 2,200 roubles to purchase a pair of Lepage duelling pistols and a day later he wrote an insulting letter to Baron van Heeckeren. Pushkin accused the Dutch ambassador of acting like an 'obscene old woman' and of playing the 'pimp' for his 'bastard' and 'syphilitic' son who was also a 'coward' and 'scoundrel' (*PSS*, vol. xvi, pp. 221–22). A duel was now inevitable.

On 27 January 1837, the duel took place on the Black River, not far from where the Pushkins had summered in the past. Pushkin arrived at the barrier before his rival, but d'Anthès fired the first shot. Pushkin was hit in the abdomen and collapsed in the snow. He then raised himself on his elbow, took aim at his adversary and fired. When d'Anthès fell, Pushkin exclaimed 'Bravo!', and tossed away his pistol. D'Anthès was wounded lightly, Pushkin mortally. On his deathbed (in one account), Pushkin asked for Nicholas's forgiveness for breaking his word. 'Tell him that I'm sorry to die and that I would have been all his'.[17] He also asked that his second, Danzas, not be punished. It was decided to perform the last rites. Those present bore witness to the excruciating pain that Pushkin experienced in his remaining days, as doctors applied twenty-five leeches and gave him opium.[18] His final vision was one of ascent – he saw himself climbing out of his sickbed and 'crawling around his books and bookshelves high above'.[19] He died at 2.45 p.m. on 29 January 1837.

Thousands of people came to mourn Pushkin's passing. In order to prevent demonstrations the government moved the funeral in St Petersburg from St Isaac's Cathedral to the small church of the Saviour on Koniushennaia Street (near Pushkin's flat on the Moika Canal off the main thoroughfare, Nevsky Prospect). The area was cordoned off by police and admission tickets were issued to court members and diplomats. On 2 February the coffin with the poet's body was sent secretly, at midnight, to Mikhailovskoe. It was accompanied by an old friend, Alexander Turgenev, who had helped with Pushkin's admission to the Lycée, Pushkin's aged butler, Nikita Kozlov, and a gendarme. Pushkin was buried on 6 February 1837 next to his mother in their family plot in the grounds of Sviatye Gory Monastery. Nicholas I generously took on Pushkin's debts and provided for his family, granting pensions to his widow and daughters and allowances for his sons. He also promised to publish the poet's collected works at state expense for the benefit of Natalia and her children.

NOTES

1. See Hugh Barnes, *Gannibal: the Moor of Petersburg*, London, Gardner Books, 2005.
2. For example, 'Confidante of magical olden times' ('Napersnitsa volshebnoi stariny', 1822), 'Winter Evening' ('Zimnii vecher', 1825), 'To Nanny' ('Niane', 1826), 'Again I have visited' ('Vnov' ia posetil', 1835).
3. V. V. Veresaev, *Pushkin v zhizni*, 2 vols., 7th ed., Moscow, Sovetskii pisatel', 1936, vol. i, pp. 70–71 and 77.
4. 'Kishinev diary', 9 April 1821 (*PSS*, vol. xii, p. 303).
5. To Amalia: 'Under the blue sky of your native land' ('Pod nebom golubym strany svoei rodnoi', 1826) and 'For the shores of a distant fatherland' ('Dlia beregov otchizny dal'noi', 1830); to Karolina: 'I loved you . . .' ('Ia vas liubil . . .', 1829) and 'What is there in my name for you?' ('Chto v imeni tebe moem?', 1830); and to Elise a host of love poems, perhaps the most famous being 'Guard me, my talisman' ('Khrani menia, moi talisman', 1824) and 'The Burned Letter' ('Sozhzhennoe pis'mo', 1825).
6. See T. G. Tsiavlovskaia, 'Khrani menia, moi talisman' (1974), in R. V. Iezuitova and Ia. L. Levkovich (eds.), *Utaennaia liubov' Pushkina*, St Petersburg, Akademicheskii proekt, 1997, pp. 297–380.
7. See 'The Burned Letter'. Other poems related to Elise: 'All is finished, between us there is no tie' ('Vse koncheno, mezh nami sviazi net', 1824), 'The foul day has died down' ('Nenastnyi den' potukh', 1824), 'Let the one crowned with love of beauty' ('Puskai uvenchannyi liubov'iu krasoty', 1824), 'Guard me, my talisman' ('Khrani menia, moi talisman', 1824), 'All is sacrificed to your memory' ('Vse v zhertvu pamiati tvoei', 1825), 'Talisman' ('Talisman', 1827), 'Farewell' ('Proshchanie', 1830).
8. 'To an Infant' ('Mladentsu', 1824), *The Gypsies* (in an expunged passage written in January 1825), and the autobiographically motivated *The Blackamoor of Peter the Great*.
9. For a reconstruction of this audience see N. Eidel'man, *Pushkin. Iz biografii tvorchestva (1826–1837)*, Moscow, Khudozhestvennaia literatura, 1987, pp. 24–64.
10. *Vremennik Pushkinskoi Komissii za 1970 g.*, St Petersburg, Nauka, 1972, p. 7.
11. D'Anthès's letter to van Heeckeren of 14 February 1836 as published in S. Vitale and V. P. Stark, *Chernaia rechka*, St Petersburg, Zvezda, 2000, p. 112. This is a bilingual edition of the d'Anthès–van Heeckeren correspondence.

12. Reported by Vera Viazemskaia to Bartenev in P. I. Bartenev, *O Pushkine*, Moscow, Sovetskaia Rossiia, 1992 (orig. pub. 1888), p. 384. See also Stella Abramovich, *Pushkin: Poslednii god*, Moscow, Sovetskii pisatel', 1991, p. 396.
13. M. A. Tsiavlovskii and N. A. Tarkhova (eds.), *Letopis' zhizni i tvorchestva Aleksandra Pushkina*, 4 vols., Moscow, Slovo, 1999, vol. iv, p. 533.
14. See P. E. Shchegolev, *Duel' i smert' Pushkina*, Moscow, Zhurnal'no-Gazetnoe Ob"edinenie, 1936, p. 269.
15. Suggested by L. Grossman in 'Zhenit'ba Dantesa. Novye materialy o dueli Pushkina. Ocherk', *Krasnaia niva* 24 (1929), 10–12. See also Frans Suasso, *Dichter, dame, diplomaat: het laatste jaar van Alexander Poesjkin*, Leiden, De Slavische Stichting te Leiden, 1988, and the new evidence in Vitale and Stark, *Chernaia rechka*, pp. 175, 177, 189, 221–23.
16. *A. S. Pushkin v vospominaniiakh sovremennikov*, ed. V. E. Vatsuro *et al.*, 2 vols., Moscow, Khudozhestvennaia literatura, 1974, vol. ii, p. 305. See Abramovich, *Pushkin: Poslednii god*, p. 526.
17. Tsiavlovskii and Tarkhova (eds.), *Letopis'*, vol. iv, p. 598.
18. T. J. Binyon, *Pushkin*, London, HarperCollins, 2002, p. 629.
19. Tsiavlovskii and Tarkhova (eds.), *Letopis'*, vol. iv, p. 601.

2

ANDREW KAHN

Pushkin's lyric identities

Whatever else he was writing, Pushkin's energy for lyric poetry rarely seemed to dim. If he wrote for a coterie of friends and poets in early life, he looked forward in his late poems to a time when he would be a truly national poet, and many of his more than 700 lyrics have become canonical works of Russian literature. The corpus encompasses a wide range of genres, displaying Pushkin's mastery of the song, the poetic epistle, the elegy, epigram, the political ode, the landscape poem, the soliloquy, the poetic cycle, the fragment.

Poetry is often both a pragmatic and imaginary assertion of the self. The relationship between the first-person speaker and the author in Pushkin's lyric poems is no less complex than in *Evgenii Onegin* (see Chapter 3). Whatever the connection to the lived life, lyric poems project the sense that identity is continuous but also highly precarious. Lyric poetry also projects alternative senses of identity to different, sometimes overlapping readerships. By moving through Pushkin's career, this chapter discusses the shape of self-representation in his lyric works with a focus on the connection between poems that project the identity of a poet and poems where an inner and more private self speaks.

Poetic identity and literary traditions

In finding his own voice, the young Pushkin was happy to imitate other writers. He was always a literary poet, steeped in the lyric traditions of Russia and Europe, who also found poetic masters among contemporaries. During the affiliation with poets of the Arzamas group (1816–18), Pushkin expanded his poetic resources through the art of invention rather than through the faculty of imagination.[1] In these years, Pushkin repeatedly takes the nature of lyric talent as his subject. Identity is a function of how the poet defines his attitude to his art. The quest for self-definition is either projected through classical speakers, such as the bucolic poet who learns to play the flute in the exquisitely balanced 'Muse' ('Muza', 1820), where the development of the poet's technique matters more than the growth of his sensibility; or turned into sociable exchange with other writers open to dialogue with a younger poet keen to impress with enthusiasm, courtesy and frankness about his limitations and the uncertainties of his standing as a poet. Among early poetic influences the most prominent was Konstantin Batiushkov, a poet famed among the previous generation to Pushkin's as an elegist peerless in the portrayal of erotic anguish.[2] An accomplished translator, Batiushkov wove dense intertextual echoes into seemingly candid lyric confessions. His œuvre, ostensibly spontaneous yet highly crafted, established in Russian lyric a new standard of literary sophistication and emotional immediacy based on skills of imitation and smooth command of style. Through his voice sound echoes of Parny, Tibullus and Tasso, among others. In imitating Batiushkov, Pushkin learned to project a voice that was singularly fresh while also suffused with the tones of other poets.

The opening of 'To Batiushkov' ('Batiushkovu', 1815) describes the birth of poetic identity through affinity with the lyric style of the addressee and his models:

In the grottoes of Helikon
I was sometime born;
In the name of Apollo
I was anointed by Tibullus
And sated from childhood
By the clear water of Hippocrene
Under a roof of spring roses
I grew up to be a poet.

Written in a double quatrain stanza form of iambic trimeter, this song-like piece is a deceptively light vehicle for self-characterisation (see Appendix). Apart from its charming demonstration that poetic affinity is based on shared taste – both Pushkin and Batiushkov appreciate Tibullus and therefore must be drawn to one another – the poem makes a statement about self-definition achieved through self-limitation. At the beginning of stanza 3, the young poet refuses the challenge suggested by the older writer to abandon lyric and imitate Virgilian epic ('that I should / hurry after Maro'). In the final stanza, he proclaims the belief that as a lyric poet he must live within the limits of his talent, making perfect verse by practising the art that is given to him:

Phoebus has given me little:
Enthusiasm, a slender gift.
I sing under a foreign sky,
Far from my domestic Lares,
And, like bold Icarus,

Fearing to fly in vain,
I make my way:
Let each by his own lights.
(*PSS*, vol. i, p. 114)

Here Apollo is a figure of mere convention, whereas in the 1820s the god of poetry appears in Pushkin as the presence of a visionary inspiration associated with untutored (if not artless) genius. Pushkin would take up the challenge to enlarge his ambition as early as 1818 when he started composing *Ruslan and Liudmila* (see Chapter 5). The refusal to risk ending up like Icarus by putting ambition before ability leads to the final motto 'Let each [write] by his own lights'[3] (itself a quotation from Zhukovskii's own epistle 'To Batiushkov'). Pushkin, however, proves true to both Virgil and Batiushkov, since each perfected his technique in small forms before graduating to narrative. Fluency and elegance, and the ease of a highly imitative poet conscious of his forebears marks the attitude of the Pushkinian speaker. Yet there is also an element of displacement, for the speaker appears 'under a foreign sky' because he has yet to put a personal imprint on his craft and make his own home in the poetic world.

Even as he took his place among the highly polished older poets of Arzamas, Pushkin wondered about the meaning of genius as an inalienable and inimitable gift and the relation of originality and imitation. 'Rebirth' ('Vozrozhdenie') gives clues to Pushkin's early thinking about their complex interrelation and suggests anxiety about genius solely defined as imitation rather than in terms of original inspiration:

The painter-philistine, with lazy brushstroke,
Obscures the work of genius:
And his illegal sketch,
He paints over it thoughtlessly,
The alien colours, as years go by,
Peel away like old skin;
The work of genius before us
Emerges in all its former beauty.

Thus misconceptions disappear
From my tormented spirit,
And in it visions now appear
Of primordial, pure days.
(*PSS*, vol. ii, p. 111)

On the surface, the poem is about the distortions caused by imperfect artistic restoration or reproduction. The poem dates to the moment when Pushkin was about to start publishing works in separate editions, and we know from his correspondence that even from his Southern exile he paid obsessive attention to textual details and was tireless in correcting and revising. But the poem suggests a shift in Pushkin's thinking about the aesthetics of imitation. The copyist is a 'barbarian' because in a fundamental sense he fails to understand the meaning of the original and is alien to it as he imposes his corrective vision on it. The premise of the poem is that the original work of genius suffers through correction and improvement that also deprives the poet of ownership of his genius. The 'lawlessness' of the 'illegal sketch' lies in the licence that the improver takes without reference to the original intention. 'Rebirth' begins by making a statement about the psychology of art but finishes by using art to make a statement about psychology. Pushkin has begun to feel uncomfortable with the position of the imitative poet. Nonetheless, at the height of his maturity in 1836, Pushkin made one of his great declarations of poetic genius through an imitation of 'Exegi monumentum' ('I have built a monument'), the final poem of the Roman poet Horace's third book of Odes, in which Horace predicted that posterity would reward his poetic innovations with immortal fame. Even as he declared his artistic independence, by speaking through Horace Pushkin acknowledged his dependence both on a predecessor and on the recognition of posterity.[4]

Artistic identity and poetic authority

Poems of the 1820s show Pushkin learning how to confront and offset anxiety about readers and critics, in an increasingly commercialised literary marketplace. The new reading public, on whom the poet's commercial fortunes largely depended, offered none of the immediate support that friendly literary associations like Arzamas had provided. He did not try to negotiate and sidestep the dangers presented by his literary enemies or an uncomprehending public. Instead, he confronted them and tried to assert his authority. A number of poems balance a tension between assertions of individual identity and unwillingness to surrender identity to the fickleness of the public (or 'crowd') with its demand for genius and originality. Some works of the late 1820s ('The Poet and the Crowd' ['Poet i tolpa'], 1828) advocate a gap between the lofty poet and a readership condescended to as the 'rabble' (*chern'*). Assertions of the poet's genius and divine mission articulate an art-for-art's-sake refusal to satisfy any needs other than the author's own creative genius. But while Pushkin famously wrote that 'poetry by virtue of its highest, freest property ought to have no goal outside itself' (*PSS*, vol. xi, p. 235), he also believed that, once inspiration had produced a work, the goal of writing was to make money. To claim genius was also to advertise a rare commodity of higher value.

More than any other single work, 'The Prophet' ('Prorok', 1826) has shaped the view that poetry occupies a uniquely important place in Russian literature.[5] The exaltation of the poet as a visionary genius has become inseparable from Pushkin's own image, and has come to shape the Pushkin myth. It also needs to be seen within Pushkin's own economic and literary context, reflecting the poet's aspirations at a moment of uncertainty and promise in his career:

> Exhausted by spiritual thirst,
> I dragged myself in the gloomy desert, –
> And a Seraphim with six wings
> Appeared to me at the crossroads.
> With feathers as light as a dream
> He grazed my pupils.
> The prophetic orbs opened wide
> Like those of a startled eaglet.
> He touched my ears, –
> And filled them with noise and din:
> And I understood the motion of the sky,
> And the elevated flight of the angels,
> And the underwater motion of sea creatures,
> And the freezing of the grape in the valley.
> And he leaned over to my lips
> And ripped out my sinful tongue,
> Both idle and deceitful,
> And with his bloody hand
> He placed the stinger of the wise serpent
> In my lips as they went numb.
> And he cleaved my chest with a sword,
> And removed the trembling heart
> And in the open cavity he installed
> A piece of coal burning with flame.
> I lay like a corpse in the desert,
> And the voice of God called out to me:
> 'Arise, prophet, and see and understand,
> Become filled with my will,
> And as you traverse seas and lands,
> Scorch the hearts of people with your tongue.'
> (*PSS*, vol. iii. part I, p. 30)

When Pushkin gave programmatic importance to the poem by including it at the opening of his 1829 lyric collection, 'The Prophet' was intended to signal a radical departure in two ways. The exoticism and compressed plotting of his early Byronic imitations, like *The Fountain of Bakhchisarai*, had contributed greatly to Pushkin's success with his readership (see Chapter 5), and to the allure of his poetic personality. Only a few critics expressed the view that the poet 'ought to be in every work a creator and not an imitator', and acknowledged the right of the author to challenge readers with a new approach to themes and style.[6] The voice that emanates from poems such as 'The Prophet', 'Arion' (1827), and 'The Poet and the Crowd' does not belong to the conversational and stylish poetic persona admired by Pushkin's early readers. The theatricality and sacral distance manifested by the High Romantic mode make works like 'The Prophet' majestic but disconcertingly impersonal.[7] The facelessness and remoteness of the persona created a forceful contrast with the image of the poet Pushkin had cultivated in the early 1820s – feckless, stylish, Byronic, hedonistic.

Together with 'The Poet and the Crowd' and 'The Poet', 'The Prophet' marks a departure by depicting poetic genius as the inimitable and inalienable gift of a unique speaker. In 'The Prophet', inspiration happens before the reader's eyes. Other Romantic poets such as Victor Hugo also tapped into the legacy of such eighteenth-century thinkers as Herder and Vico, who accorded a position of eminence to poets in their theories of culture, attributing to them divine sight and prophetic power.[8] Few in Russia had ever coupled such extremes of ecstatic inspiration and violence as Pushkin does in 'The Prophet'. Using brutal and violent images to express the spiritual cost of the poet's epiphany, Pushkin's prophet is a poet of the revelatory and illuminating moment. Through violent divinatory utterance, Pushkin not only achieves a new artistic power, but he also markets his poetic charisma as exceptional and highly individual visionary power. The images of 'The Prophet' violate the rules of good taste and expression that had been the legacy of classicism to Pushkin's poetics. Genius in the prophet – and the genius of a poem such as 'The Prophet' – violently shatters the notion of poetry as a type of refined craft, precisely the hallmark of Pushkin's lyric artistry that his audience had been admiring since 1815. In 'The Prophet' the power to see afresh involves a process of physical annihilation and rebirth that is deliberately horrifying. No one would argue that the poem is Pushkin's manifesto for a kind of aesthetic, and this brand of bleakness and self-laceration only rarely occurs in his poetry. But in this work and the other texts of the so-called 'poet cycle' of the late 1820s, Pushkin employs dramatic discourse in order to force his readers to rethink their expectations of poetry and the nature of poetic genius.

Identity and friendship

In the 1820s, Pushkin found that one method for allaying his anxiety of reception, and the real anxiety caused by his political position, was to conjure in poems a spirit of friendship that transcended time and place while still rooted in his own experience. By writing about the shared affection of his classmates for Tsarskoe Selo and establishing its hallowed status in their own collective group mythology, Pushkin made their shared biography part of his own lyric identity and text.[9] In so doing, he both commemorated attachment to youthful literary and political ideals and also established the terms on which his friendships would evolve.

The six poems occasioned by the Lycée anniversaries picture a literary ideal of friendship, conversations and exchanges with friends about the bonds that hold them together. In these '19 October' poems, Pushkin drew on a rich source of his poetry, which is less a yearning for a specific landscape than the sense of emotional belonging invested in it through memory and friendship. Here his own feelings, his experience of attachment, loss, guilt and commemoration, invite exploration. The poems celebrate actual events and formulate an ideal of loyalty, affection and security that in Pushkin's later poems attain great significance as a counterweight to the unpredictable taste and commercial habits of an anonymous readership, and to the political vagaries of a hostile regime. In the great poem of friendship written during the second part of his exile in Mikhailovskoe ('19 October 1825'), Pushkin addresses his friends from a distance. Reunited with them through an act of poetic imagination, for the first time he begins to count the losses of friends who have died prematurely. More than a decade later, a cumulative sense of personal and collective tragedy suffuses the final poem of the cycle ('19 October 1836'), which Pushkin read at the jubilee celebration of his cohort. On this occasion, Pushkin offered a melancholy reckoning of his own fate and that of his generation. He reprised the same poetic form as the 1825 poem, including the use of caesura, which he otherwise had eschewed in his blank verse after 1830. The poem thus reverberates with the memory of earlier occasions, and its very sound becomes the one form of continuity that the poet can control despite the menace of random fate that has made the group, in his words, 'the plaything of a secret game'. Poetic identity merges with autobiographical identity, as the poem describes the details of the poet's life and those of his generation. Their span is measured against an epoch of historical change as the poet recalls their early enthusiasm for Napoleon and for Alexander I when he still enjoyed the reputation of a liberal reformer.

Personalising the anonymous reader

Two contradictory lyric stances dominate much Romantic poetry. On the one hand, the poetic persona appropriates the perceived world as part of the self in a kind of solipsistic self-diffusion. On the other hand, the poet searches for external recognition that will give this inner self form and definition. Whereas poems such as 'The Prophet' emphasise the distance between poet and ordinary readers, other works risk self-revelation to anonymous readers who are trusted to understand and share the poet's emotional vulnerability. In sharp contrast to the radical withdrawal of self that occurs at visionary moments, poems about love, jealousy, fear and self-disgust craft a special bond by allowing the reader into the poet's world of private feeling. Pushkin's love poems and elegies manifest a perfect ear for changeable emotional states of speakers caught in acts of self-discovery, self-recovery, ardent declaration or wistful aspiration.

Consider a brief masterpiece like 'What is there in my name for you?' ('Chto v imeni tebe moem?', 1830). While the poem grows out of a documented relationship, it is an excellent example of how Pushkin transmutes autobiographical circumstance into a work that puts the poet, and the poet's relationship to his addressee-reader, at the emotional centre of his text:

> What is there in my name for you?
> It will die, like the sad noise
> Of a wave, crashing on a distant shore,
> Like a nocturnal noise in the mute forest.
>
> On a memorial leaf
> It will leave a dead trace, like
> The pattern of a gravestone
> In an unintelligible language.
>
> What is in it? Long forgotten
> In new and violent tribulations,
> It will not give your soul
> Pure, tender memories.
>
> But on a day of sadness, in quiet,
> Pronounce it as you yearn;
> Say: there is a memory of me,
> There is a heart in the world, where I live . . .
>
> (*PSS*, vol. iii, p. 210)

Written as an inscription in the album of a young woman whose salon Pushkin frequented, the poem's life began as a communication of trust and affection between two real individuals. In fact the poet makes the capacity to understand his work a function of such personal affinity. The question for the professional writer is whether such a bond is possible with anonymous readers. Writing a poem, publishing it, gives the self up irrevocably to the eyes of the world and the possibility of distortion or misunderstanding occurs unless a reader of perfect sympathy, like the original addressee, understands his meanings and perpetuates his memory.

'What is there in my name for you?' itself occupies an eternal present tense, envisaging current and future readers who will be of comparable sensibility to the owner of the album in which the poet writes the poem. The manipulation of the timeframe is significant because it presents the act of reading as simultaneous to the act of writing, and the act of re-creation is tantamount to the act of creation. Even as Pushkin writes about dissolution the reader is made to engage in extending his life and identity. The second stanza likens the page of the album to a gravestone, and the comparison suggests a connection between this text and the genre of epitaph poetry that enjoyed widespread popularity in the pre-Romantic era. Readers of epitaphs momentarily revive the deceased, communing with them through the inscription on the tomb which speaks as the deceased subject might have spoken to the passer-by or reader. The purpose of the analogy is to place the reader of the album in exactly the same position and demand a similar insight in order to make the 'dead trace' come to life. Through emotional equivalences, the positions of the writer, original addressee and implied reader also converge. The precondition for writing poetry is a state of mind, marked by sadness and quiet, where recollection fills an emotional void and sense of emptiness. The same emotions will turn the despondent reader to poetry for renewal and give the poem its real value as the poet speaks to a reader once again. In the final stanza, the poet offers the poem as a formula of consolation that the dedicatee of the album and, in turn, any reader can repeat to themselves for all time. Playing on the verbal connection between the epitaph (the memorial leaf is a *pamiatnyi listok*) and memory (*pamiat'*), the consolatory formula turns the 'dead' poem into a living artefact that reproduces emotional memory. The original dedicatee of the album can open to the page and remember that it was Pushkin who through a poem gave a sign of their bond. The implication is that any reader will in future be able to enter into a dialogue through the printed words of the poet with any longed-for figure. The proof of that point, and the real beauty of the poem, lies in the reflexivity of the final two lines where the referents attaching to the pronouns are uncertain. As the dedicatee utters the lines, 'me' may refer to herself (that is to say, the poet remembers her). But as answer to the question 'What is there in my name for you?', the lines may refer back to the poet, whose name thus overcomes death and can inspire '[p]ure, tender memories'. A perfect reciprocity between author and reader is suggested.

In 'What is there in my name for you?' personal affection may thus be said to vouchsafe the immortality of the poet's creation; the poem is itself a token of emotional commitment and exchange, rather than a verbal artefact remembered by posterity for its literary accomplishment. The paradox of this particular poem – that the most enduring poetry is the most personal – is that it does not guarantee that the historical name of the poet as a real historical datum will survive. Pushkin's own name, which seems to echo through the consonant clusters of the first stanza, is nowhere mentioned. The poem turns every reader into a poet of a kind, thereby dissolving the original poet into the acts of the countless generations of readers who follow the emotional instruction given here and in reciting Pushkin's words first and foremost recall not Pushkin but the object of their attachment. The wish is that a certain idea of the self survive all these moments intact, and that this self withstand all change. Such transcendence of an irreligious kind also occurs powerfully in poems such as 'Again I have visited' ('Vnov' ia posetil', 1835), where the continuity of nature creates Pushkin's equivalent to a Wordsworthian 'spot of time' in which the poet who recalls his younger self also envisages later readers and visitors recalling him from these lines of verse. Such optimism about the power of the poetic word also emerges in Pushkin's last poems, most especially 'From Pindemonte' ('Iz Pindemonte', 1836), where a conviction about his creative faculty enables the poet, while being buffeted by personal turmoil and subjected to oppressive censorship, to declare his independence and proclaim the mundane world of politics no match for the power of art.

Psychological identity and Romantic anxieties

A reading of 'What is there in my name for you?' shows that Pushkin, like other Romantic poets, dwells on the search for right recognition, fearing both misprision in the eyes of the world and eventual neglect by posterity.[10] The quest for fame, search for authenticity and belief in inalienable genius carry a fear of isolation. This dialectic between the poet's sense of his artistic independence from popular demand and dependence on a readership leads to feelings of isolation and self-diffusion in Pushkin's lyric. In part, this tension is the natural result of a culture of publishing where copyright and royalties are marks of the authentic identity of the writer, material signs that should be inalienable from it.

In drama and narrative, Pushkin, like Shakespeare and Keats, is the epitome of the prehensile poet susceptible to 'filling some other Body' than his own. But powers of protean or Shakespearean empathy (possessed by poets such as Keats and Pushkin) lead to moments where the lyric speaker privately expresses a sense of not properly belonging to the world. This other side to Romantic lyric identity involves a subjectivity which threatens the integrity of the self. To keep from falling back into solipsism, the poet must make his own place and determine his own function in the world, in part by establishing some external means of validation that will recognise him as the poet he is. Poems in which objects of perception no longer necessarily exist outside the mind enact a withdrawal into a version of the visionary self (as in 'The Wanderer' ['Strannik', 1835]) and a state of subjectivity which characterises Romanticism generally, where identity is a matter of consciousness.[11] In several lyric poems, Pushkin confronts this as a problem by exploring identity outside the kinship group of friends and family. In these first-person meditations, the lyric persona is plunged in deeply private emotion such as longing, mourning, loving, anxiety and confusion. The world held suspended in the poet's mind can offer nothing apart from that mind to reflect his own real presence as something other than unanchored perception or series of perceptions of the world. In counterpoint to poems that assume the reality of the finite self in the eyes of the public are poems that speculate about identity in states of mind marked by uncertainty. Increasingly from 1828, Pushkin writes lyrics where the self becomes identified largely with the mind and dissociated from the body. The materialist-atheist in Pushkin continues to wonder about the nature of life. The speaker of the 1828 'Futile gift, random gift' ('Dar naprasnyi, dar sluchainyi') interrogates the universe with a sense of individual isolation and existential doubt that may have come to Pushkin through his reading of the *Pensées* of the seventeenth-century Christian moralist Blaise Pascal. Instead of making Pascal's leap of faith, Pushkin's speaker remains uncertain about the energy that turns brute matter into life:

> Who with inimical power
> Summoned me from nothingness [*nichtozhestva*]
> Filled my soul with passion,
> Disturbed my mind with doubt?
>
> (*PSS*, vol. iii, p. 104)

Although the mind rebels at its conclusions, the speaker is still able to give a name (*nichtozhestvo*) to death, and see it as a state of dissolution.

In works such as 'Elegy' ('Elegiia', 1830) this intense identification with consciousness is reinforced by encroaching night. Darkness suspends the poet's sense of embodiment, erasing the boundary between the mind and what it perceives. Such doubts about the substantiality of the self and its world became a central feature of late eighteenth-century poetry. Moments of doubt like this also recur frequently, and with greater intensity, in Romantic poetry, especially in high transports of imaginative revelation or visionary experience. The phenomenal world, perceived in darkness, isolation or at distance becomes dreamlike or gives way to a vision of the world as in Keats's 'Ode to a Nightingale' (1819) and Coleridge's 'Frost at Midnight'

(1798), both of which Pushkin read. The transformation of something outside the mind into something inside is facilitated by the poet's having momentarily lost, in the darkness surrounding him, the tenuous conviction of his embodied being that delimits outside and inside; as the world fades out, the body vanishes. The self merely as an object of consciousness is, like any other object, 'dead, fixed, incapable in itself of any action, and necessarily finite', as Coleridge, borrowing from the aesthetic theorist Friedrich Schelling, observed in his study of philosophy and criticism, *Biographia Literaria* (1817). Pushkin confronts a similar moment of disintegration in the 'Lines Written at Night during Insomnia' ('Mne ne spitsia, net ognia', 1830), where the monologue captures a state of consciousness suspended between sleep and apprehension. Through his reading of Shakespeare, Pushkin appreciated the richness of sleeplessness as a state that, while sometimes restorative of imaginative energy, can also destructively expose a state of powerlessness and loss of strength:

> I cannot sleep, there is no light;
> Everywhere gloom and tedious sleep.
> Only the monotonous running of the clock
> Sounds around me.
> The feminine babbling of the Parcae,
> The anxiety of the sleeping night,
> The mouse-like scampering of life . . .
> Why do you disquiet me?
> What do you, a boring whisper, mean?
> Are you a reproach, or the rumbling
> Of the day that has been squandered by me?
> Do you summon me or do you prophesy?
> I want to understand you,
> I seek sense in you . . .[12]
>
> (*PSS*, vol. iii, p. 250)

This is one of Pushkin's poems of existential questioning, cast as a dramatic interior monologue. The subject is the self, but the first-person pronoun occurs as an indirect pronoun ('me') and does not appear in the nominative case (as 'I') until the final two lines, where the speaker lays greater emphasis on the tone of personal trouble. The poem is a suppressed dialogue between the speaker and an unknown and unknowable force that can only be described as uncertain, like the mystifying noises that are outside the speaker. With line 10, however, they become interiorised as an effect of conscience. Night poems are often a setting for psychological doubling, and here the poet attempts to objectify himself by seeing his conscience as something that stands outside him. At the same time, the poet is incapable of complete self-distancing: reproach from outside and from within assail him, one being the voice of his conscience, the other being a deeper and less conscious sense linked to the buried memory of the day. This effect of being both within and outside the self corresponds to the liminal state of the speaker, suspended between sleep and wakefulness. The sounds that penetrate his mind and the hallucinatory image of the shuffling mouse – which may be the source of the whisper – indicate a mind on the brink of sleep. With line 10 the question of what external things signify becomes the question of what the self signifies. The function of the interior voice appears to be to summon or to prophesy, which suggests that the source of sleeplessness is an underlying expectation or anxiety, a waiting to be called or to learn the future.

Identity and posterity

Anxiety about posterity is a natural response for the atheist unconvinced of divine justice. Pushkin's intimations of mortality have a manifold complexion. There are works where the contemplation of death elicits an intellectual response shaped by philosophical language. There is an example of the last in a sonnet of 1823, 'While youthfully breathing sweet hope' ('Nadezhdoi sladostnoi mladencheski dysha'), one of the earliest Pushkin lyrics to enact a split between the observing consciousness and the emotional self. The text captures the state of resignation after a paradoxical assessment that follows from the atheist's first principles on mortality: the fact that there is no life beyond the grave feeds the poet's desire to live rather than impelling him toward suicide. Behind the pathos of the poem lies a serious reflection, complementing other lyrics (such as the early 'Grave of Anacreon', 1815) that make the connection between atheism and the desire to live. The argument for transcendence is made in the first part and is framed as a conditional statement. If it were possible to imagine that the soul were not subject to the same process of decomposition as the body, then the poet imagines a theoretical realm where death has been abolished and the soul will continue to flourish. The soul is seen explicitly as a type of intellectual capacity that will be enhanced by its freedom from the body, possessing in its disembodied state powers of extension such as endless memory. The intellectual sources of this position are complex. It brings together the materialist notion that the self is made up of matter or atoms that are destroyed at death and a Christian modification of this idea where the soul's atoms are given immortal properties and survive death. Pushkin presents this proposition in order to speculate about the eternal nature of intellectual and poetic matter. Memory, love, freedom and pleasure – the Epicurean imperatives of the materialist convinced of the complete corporeality of the self – are also the properties of poetry extended to the afterlife. The second section enacts an abrupt and highly compressed reversal by pitting the mind against its earlier optimism. In this part, reason is seen as distinct from the workings of hope:

> But in vain do I surrender to a seductive fancy;
> My mind resists, despises the hope . . .
> Nothingness awaits me beyond the grave . . .
> What, nothing! No thought, not a first love!
> I am terrified! . . . Once again I look at life sadly,
> And wish to live a long time so that a dear image
> Might long melt and flare up in my sad soul.
> (*PSS*, vol. ii. part II, p. 295)

Yet even now the speaker rebels against the nihilistic vision of an afterlife of nothingness. The motivation for the positive declaration about life and longevity is more fear of disintegration than love of life. At the very end social desire ('a dear image') dispels the potential for solipsism. Even here, while holding on to love as a consolation, the soul of the speaker remains forlorn (*unylaia*) because the suspicion of eventual nothingness cannot be eradicated. By contrast with the public identity of the speaker in 'The Prophet' and the dialogical self of 'What is there in my name for you?', the poet-speaker in 'While youthfully breathing sweet hope' is purely private and stripped of the confidence that the survival of his work will compensate for physical extinction. Other poems where the uncertainty of fate dominates share such foreboding. Still other poems such as 'Whether I wander along noisy streets' ('Brozhu li ia vdol' ulits shumnykh . . .', 1829) show a speaker who ponders the interrelation of natural growth and destruction, and manifest a special type of silence as a reaction to the poet's doubts. Contemplating death, this type of speaker, paradoxically, communicates by falling silent and attaining a Keatsian condition of 'negative capability' where the fascination of the unknown is a secret that cannot be revealed but also a dissolution of identity that must not be dreaded.

NOTES

1. For a documentary record of Arzamas's meetings and poetics, see Vadim Vatsuro and A. L. Ospovat (eds.), *Arzamas: sbornik*, Moscow, Khudozhestvennaia literatura, 1994; on Arzamas's idea of literary style, see B. M. Gasparov, *Poeticheskii iazyk Pushkina kak fakt istorii russkogo literaturnogo iazyka*, Vienna, Gesellschaft zur Förderung slawistischer Studien, 1992, part 1. All translations of poetry in this chapter are by Andrew Kahn.
2. See Oleg Proskurin, *Poeziia Pushkina, ili podvizhnyi palimpsest*, Moscow, NLO, 1999, chap. 1.
3. 'Bud' kazhdyi pri svoem / Rek tsar' zemli.'

4. See M. P. Alekseev *Stikhotvorenie 'Ia pamiatnik sebe vozdvignul': problemy ego izucheniia*, Leningrad, Nauka, 1967.
5. See Sergei Bocharov, 'Iz istorii ponimaniia Pushkina', in his *Siuzhety russkoi literatury*, Moscow, Iazyk russkoi kul'tury, 1999, pp. 230–45; Stephanie Sandler, *Commemorating Pushkin: Russia's Myth of a National Poet*, Stanford University Press, 2004, pp. 5–13.
6. See V. E. Vatsuro, 'Pushkin v soznanii sovremennikov', in Vatsuro *et al.* (eds.), *A. S. Pushkin v vospominaniiakh sovremennikov*, Moscow, Khudozhestvennaia literatura, 1974, vol. i, pp. 5–40.
7. See S. Shvartsband, 'O poeticheskikh "dinamicheskikh sistemakh"', *Pushkinskii sbornik*, Jerusalem, [no pub.], 1997, p. 97.
8. See the introduction by Michelet, read by Pushkin, in Giovanni-Battista Vico, *Principes de la philosophie de l'histoire*, Paris, 1827, pp. i–xxvi.
9. On poetic homes in Pushkin's lyric, see Vs. Grekhnev, *Mir Pushkinskoi liriki*, Novgorod, Volgo-Viatskoe knizhnoe izdatel'stvo, 1994. On the epistle and friendship, see William Mills Todd III, *The Familiar Letter as a Literary Genre in the Age of Pushkin*, Princeton University Press, 1976.
10. See Andrew Bennett, *Romantic Poets and the Culture of Posterity*, Cambridge University Press, 1999, chap. 1.
11. See Charles J. Rzepka, *The Self as Mind: Vision and Identity in Wordsworth, Coleridge, and Keats*, Cambridge, MA, Harvard University Press, 1986, pp. 6–7.
12. The impact of Shakespeare's historical plays on the writing of *Boris Godunov* is well known. Of particular relevance are *Henry IV* III.i.4, and *Macbeth* II.ii.33, as examples of self-confrontation caused by insomnia and guilt.

3

MARCUS LEVITT

Evgenii Onegin

Pushkin's masterpiece *Evgenii Onegin* (1823–30) is universally recognised as the starting-point of the classic nineteenth-century Russian novel, and has challenged generations of readers and critics. The period of writing *Evgenii Onegin* spanned an amazing epoch in the poet's creativity, and, as the leading nineteenth-century Russian critic Vissarion Belinsky aptly remarked, 'to evaluate this work is to evaluate the poet himself in the full range of his literary endeavours'.[1] The first impression *Evgenii Onegin* gives is of striking simplicity and disarming transparency – with its minimalist plot, formal elegance and economy and crystalline purity of language. Closer analysis reveals ever-new depths of philosophical, psychological and literary meaning, characteristic not only of great poetry but stemming from the work's radically innovative narrative structure. In its self-conscious play with narrative form and fictionality, *Evgenii Onegin* joins the novelistic tradition of Cervantes, Diderot and Sterne, while expanding the potential of mock-epic and burlesque poetry.

Outdoing Byron

A useful starting-point for approaching Pushkin's innovation is its acknowledged debt to, and differences from, Byron's 'novels in verse'. Like *Childe Harold's Pilgrimage* and *Don Juan*, *Evgenii Onegin* was written in numbered verse stanzas for which Pushkin devised a variant of the sonnet, in fourteen iambic tetrameter lines, that has become known as the 'Onegin stanza' (on which see the Appendix).[2] It was published in chapters that appeared irregularly over many years, with no ostensible end point envisaged, and featured a loose framework associated with the adventures of an eponymous hero that allowed the poet to incorporate disparate material (literary, historical, cultural and quasi-autobiographical). From chapter 1 to the 'Fragments of *Onegin's Journey*' appended to the final eight-chapter version, Pushkin's protagonist appears 'Childe-Harold-like' (I.38, VIII.24) – that is, as a type whose (in Byron's words) 'early perversion of mind and morals leads to satiety of past pleasures and disappointment in new ones'.[3] Pushkin's crucial move was to take what was a generally acknowledged weakness in Byron and turn it to his own productive advantage. In deciding to discontinue *Childe Harold*, Byron publicly admitted that he had failed to draw a clear distinction between himself and his fictional protagonist.[4] In *Evgenii Onegin*, Pushkin directly confronts this key problem of Romantic poetics, bringing these two aspects of authorial self into self-conscious dialogue. Pushkin's brilliance lies in playing them off one another, demonstrating the fundamental interdependence of art and life, 'literariness' and 'reality'. *Evgenii Onegin* thus marks a quantum leap in Russian literature, from the earlier century's mistrust of 'fiction' to a new conception of art. Pushkin offers a profound meditation on the ways in which cultural models (especially novels) shape modern identity.

The two realities

The interplay between art and life in *Evgenii Onegin* begins with the opening lines. Sub-textual reference veils caustic irony when Onegin refers to his uncle as a man 'of most honest principles', undercutting the ostensible praise by echoing Ivan Krylov's fable about an 'ass of most honest principles', who, despite good intentions, tramples his master's vegetable garden and gets a thrashing.[5] There are also more obvious meta-literary jokes, like the burlesque invocation of Zeus (suggesting Onegin as an epic hero) and the apology for skipping a formal epic introduction (postponed until the end of chapter 7). At the same time, two opposing ontological realities here come into play – that of the narrator, who in chapter 1 appears as a character, calling Onegin 'my good friend', and that of *Evgenii Onegin*'s creator, who stands outside the text and refers to 'the hero of my novel'.

The complexity of the narration also reflects the problem facing its narratees, *Onegin*'s readers, who appear as an explicit presence ('Onegin, my good friend / Was born on the banks of the Neva / Where perhaps you too were born / Or flourished, my reader', I.2).[6] From the outset, *Evgenii Onegin* sets extremely high expectations of its readers. It is assumed that they will get the joke when Evgenii makes his reference to Krylov's ass, that they are familiar with the problem of Byron's authorial persona, as well as a plethora of other literary, cultural and historical information. The great number of more or less hidden literary references and echoes continues to be uncovered and explored. The many blank stanzas where no text is given but the stanza number is retained serve as a purposeful 'minus device', also challenging the reader to 'fill in the blanks'. In some cases, these omitted stanzas were published separately, constituting a kind of 'penumbral text' beyond the published version; in some cases they were simply cut out; and in some probably never written; these marked excisions may serve various purposes, depending on context, but in general stress the open, unfinished, fragmented nature of the work.[7]

Evgenii Onegin does not merely imply the existence of an 'ideal reader' (that is, one able to fully appreciate authorial intention), but incorporates its own sliding scale of good and bad imagined readers. The scholar Sonia Hoisington describes this as its 'hierarchy of narratees' who are treated with differing degrees of irony, including parodic 'mock readers', that is, readers whose misreadings are anticipated. The main groups of readers addressed in *Evgenii Onegin* are the poet's 'friends' and the novel's 'readers'. This suggests the contrast between the work's 'two realities' but does not neatly accord with them. Gauging the distance between 'ideal' and 'mock' readers addressed in *Evgenii Onegin*, like triangulating the gaps in the narrator's multiple perspective, presents a fundamental challenge for us as readers. The judgement of 'readers' is generally treated with condescending irony, and while that of 'friends', who represent Pushkin's coterie of fellow-poets, is often privileged, they too are mocked at times. While some critics chart a movement toward 'stable irony',[8] others have stressed *Evgenii Onegin* as an 'essentially open dialogue . . . designed to exemplify a deep suspicion of all "statements" about the world – including its own'.[9]

From its opening stanzas, *Onegin* also calls upon the reader's familiarity with Pushkin's literary and public image. One is expected to understand the difference between Pushkin, mentioned as author of *Ruslan and Liudmila* who fictively befriended Onegin during the 1819–20 season in St Petersburg (the time described in chapter 1), and Pushkin the author who began *Evgenii Onegin* while in exile in the south of Russia. Furthermore, since Pushkin makes his created hero three to four years older than he is, it turns out that the Pushkin at the time of writing (1823) is at the same age as Onegin at the time recalled and depicted (1819–20), thus emphasising his own inner evolution and measuring it against that of his protagonist. While *Evgenii Onegin*'s 'two realities' may ultimately come together when we consider the characters as functions of the poet's self, it is incorrect to insist on the primacy of either aspect taken separately.

This chronological divergence in narrative perspective generates the novel's dialectical perspective on the problem of Byronic disillusionment.[10] I shall apply in my discussion the three stages of the author-narrator's development as established by J. Thomas Shaw. Stage one encompasses an initial period of youthful enchantment. Stage two is a phase of crisis. The final and third part is the synthetic stage of 'mature re-enchantment'. Chapter 1 establishes the pattern: the narrator's joyful optimism and subsequent Childe-Harold-esque alienation are revisited from a subsequent 'mature' vantage point. This defines the narrator's retrospective position as a poet and man of experience, and within the world of the characters marks the stages of their progress (or failure to progress) towards mature self-consciousness. The open, dialectical quality of the narrative consciousness thus spills over into the characters. It accounts for what Roman Jakobson has referred to as *Evgenii Onegin*'s 'elastically polysemantic' character, that has led historically to diametrically opposed interpretations of both author-image and protagonists.[11]

The fissure in the 'Byronic' narrator-protagonist had far-reaching consequences for all aspects of *Evgenii Onegin*, and is reflected in the fundamental open-endedness of its larger structure. The work was written over the course of seven years (1823–30), ten if we include the minor changes to the first full edition, and it was published in separate bound chapters over a similar span (1825–32). The action takes place over the course of five and a half years and is continuous except for the two-year gap between chapters 7 and 8 (the hiatus for Onegin's journey and Tatiana's move to Moscow and marriage).[12] The narrator-creator keeps evolving, responding to changes outside the text, and meditating on earlier aspects of his self and his creation. The serialisation of the novel at irregular intervals served to emphasise the openness of its structure, without foreseeable end, all the more so as the narrative incorporated the changing circumstances of its own production. If the first chapters recreate a relatively optimistic period of the poet's life before exile, the generally darker tone of the later chapters may be seen in the context of Pushkin's problematic attempts to come to terms with Nicholas's new and oppressive regime. The period of writing *Evgenii Onegin* also witnessed a major shift in the poet's critical standing, including a progressively more negative reception of the novel itself. Pushkin lamented the lack of decent literary criticism in Russia, and in *Evgenii Onegin* he compensated by offering a running commentary on the problem of its own reception – with critics and journalists being perhaps the bottom rung of the 'hierarchy of narratees'.

Genre and narrative

Evgenii Onegin's close attention to changing social, cultural and historical realities (from ballet and folklore to food and philosophy) have led critics ever since Belinsky to remark on its character as an 'encyclopedia of Russian life' and 'a historical novel'. Paradoxically, *Evgenii Onegin* is a historical novel by virtue of its vital connection to the open-ended present, whose 'historical' character is most clearly marked in the realm of changing fashions. This paradox of transforming chaotic, unfinalised reality into historical narrative was one which Tolstoy directly confronted in *War and Peace* (1865–68).[13] Yet however much Tolstoy might rework the Napoleonic narrative, the basic outcome was predetermined, and in this sense Pushkin's narrative experiment was far more open-ended and radical.

Evgenii Onegin foregrounds its ostensible lack of plan and the ad hoc process of its creation:

> I've thought about the form of my plan
> And what I'll name the hero;
> Meantime I have finished
> The first chapter of my novel;
> I've looked it over scrupulously:
> There are very many contradictions,
> But I don't want to fix them.
>
> (I.60.1–7)

The evolving 'form of [the] plan' is one of the clearest signs of *Evgenii Onegin*'s open-ended structure. The narrator-creator unapologetically challenges us here with what critics call *Evgenii Onegin*'s oxymoronic 'principle of contradictions'. The 'contradictions' do not highlight the artificiality of conventions in order to deny them in favour of 'reality', as some (most notably the influential Russian critic Iurii Lotman) have argued, but rather underscore the inevitability of mediation: 'reality' is always filtered through culture, convention, language, and it is the understanding of this necessary limitation that enables the poet's creative manipulations. In any case, *Evgenii Onegin*'s specific 'form of [the] plan' changed at least three times during the course of its writing and publication, from a projected two parts in twelve chapters, to nine chapters with a tripartite structure, and finally, to eight chapters, with the decision to destroy the (later very partially deciphered) politically sensitive – and unpublishable – 'chapter 10'.[14] The fact that the larger plan could change without destroying the integrity of the whole is another indication of *Evgenii Onegin*'s organic, dialectical structure.

Evgenii Onegin's hybrid status as a 'novel in verse' may also be seen as a consequence of its break from a Byronic type of lyrical narrative. According to the Russian literary theorist Mikhail Bakhtin, the novel is an 'anti-genre' in relationship to the classical Aristotelian hierarchy of fixed lyric genres, which it both recycles (or 'cannibalises') and subverts (or 'carnivalises'). True to this description, *Evgenii Onegin* absorbs and parodically reworks a panoply of literary discourses, both those of specific poetic genres (elegy, love lyric, epigram, friendly epistle, ode) and those of particular novelistic prose traditions. While the first hundred years of Pushkin criticism treated *Evgenii Onegin* primarily as a novel merely *written* in verse, since the Formalist critics in the 1920's, and especially in the last decade, commentators have insisted on the fact that it is a novel *in verse*, a work of poetry, and have redefined Pushkin's 'novel in verse' as a dialectical blending of the two. Pushkin himself famously commented apropos *Evgenii Onegin* that there is 'the devil of a difference' between a novel and a novel in verse,[15] but the precise bounds between novelistic (or prosaic) and lyric (poetic) principles remain slippery.

Stanzas 57–60 at the end of chapter 1 may be seen as a contrast between these two kinds of narrative. They follow a forceful rejection of the idea that Evgenii is a veiled self-portrait of the author – 'as in Byron' – and juxtapose the way 'all poets' operate to the narrator's own unique creative process. Love leads not to the spontaneous 'sacred frenzy' of creation but to silence ('I in love was deaf and dumb'); 'freedom' and the 'union of magical sounds, feelings and thoughts' – mature re-enchanted poetry – only appear afterward, after the storm of passion has passed. Narratives of the *Childe Harold* type, in which the authorial and fictional voice are one, may thus be equated to that of lyric poetry as a whole (especially love poetry), while the self-conscious writing of a novel in verse involves a fundamental break from the monological lyric persona where a single authoritative voice maintains control. This opens up space for a new, 'novelistic' discourse, which Bakhtin defined as dialogic and multi-voiced.[16]

Characters and traditions

Evgenii Onegin's characters are also 'novelised'. They fluctuate within *Evgenii Onegin*'s 'two realities', appearing to possess a fundamental verisimilitude while also serving as literary devices and reflections of dialectically evolving authorial consciousness. In sharp contrast to the canonical 'realist' novel that offers detailed context for a character's behaviour, thus circumscribing the reader's ability or need to make independent judgements, *Evgenii Onegin* is open, fragmented, leaving much for the reader to 'fill in'. The openness of the author-narrator's position and his evolving retrospective point of view determine the various shades of his irony that frame the fictional protagonists, who are situated at various stages in their own dialectic of self-consciousness. Character emerges through the interplay of lyric and novelistic perspectives that allow different degrees of self-revelation.[17]

Like the plot, the characters in *Evgenii Onegin* seem archetypal in their simplicity, but on more serious consideration challenge us with profound, perhaps irreducible, ambiguities and complexity. Broadly speaking, *Evgenii Onegin*'s three main protagonists represent the three main novelistic traditions of the day, English, German and French, that are presented consecutively in the first three chapters.[18] Evgenii, of course, assumes the mantle of the English Byronic protagonist, but also incorporates traits from the Gothic horror novel ('the British muse's eerie ravings', III.12, for example, J. W. Polidori's *The Vampire* and C. R. Maturin's *Melmoth the Wanderer*) and the (French) psychological novel, especially Benjamin Constant's *Adolphe.*[19] Vladimir Lenskii is 'impregnated to the core / With Göttingen and Kantian lore' (II.6),[20] in other words, with German pre-Romantic and Romantic idealism. As a novelistic hero, his main source is Goethe, while his poetry echoes Schiller's elegiac mode.[21] Tatiana Larina – 'in her hand a book from France' (VIII.5) – adopts sentimental epistolary novels as her own, those of Jean-Jacques Rousseau, Mme de Staël and Samuel Richardson.[22] As even this brief listing suggests, these three 'representative' traditions demand qualification. There are in fact numerous border-crossings among them, and a host of secondary cultural and literary cross-references. The challenge for Pushkin in creating a 'Russian novel' is mirrored for the characters of *Evgenii Onegin* in their need to pick and choose from among the styles, languages and roles that modern life offers and to negotiate a cultural identity that best 'translates' their individual needs. Conflicts emerge when the cultural and novelistic conventions that the characters adopt impinge on the fulfilment of their desires. This is a dynamic process, full of potential for self-discovery and realisation as well as the danger of miscarriage.

The duel is arguably the main action of *Evgenii Onegin*, and leads to a crisis for each of the main characters, paralleled by the author-narrator's own evolution. The narrator marks the decisive exchange between Lenskii and Onegin at Tatiana's name-day party (V.40) by forswearing digressions, associated with his happy-go-lucky, stage-one self. Similarly, in the next chapter he accompanies Lenskii's death with meditations on growing old and the denial of 'wild [*shal'naia*] rhyme' in favour of 'solemn prose' (VI.43). The duel highlights the basic conflict between Lenskii and Onegin as fundamentally opposite types, Lenskii in the naive enchantment of stage one, and Onegin mired in Byron's 'bleak egoism' of stage two (III.11). However, even 'ice and flame, verse and prose' turn out to be 'not so different among themselves' (II.13), and the duel suggests both characters' limitations as well as potential for change. Each plays out the problematic limitation of the monological Byronic narrative situation, Lenskii following the model of 'all poets', without critical distance from his own overly ecstatic self-expression, and Onegin his Childe-Harold-esque inverse – suffering from a lack of self-perspective due to hypertrophied cynicism. Onegin is trapped by the demon of irony, while Lenskii uncritically defines himself by the fixed clichés of his 'obscure and flaccid' 'Romantic' poetry, its inflexibility – as in Olga's case – marked by being 'always like this' (II.6, I.20). Lenskii's unhappy fate in *Evgenii Onegin* may then be ascribed to the immaturity of his self-consciousness as reflected in his poetry. A crucial moment comes the night before the duel when he visits Olga. He realises that his doubts about her that sparked the duel are groundless, and is ready to speak out, but he 'can't find the words' (VI.14). His anguished state is not communicated because 'he who is pampered by the muse / is always like that'. His poetic persona turns out to be a fatal obstacle to self-expression.

The duel is also a vivid example of the way in which the open structure allows for multiple possible outcomes. Many factors might have prevented the duel (VI.18): had Lenskii been a better poet; had he known about Onegin and Tatiana's affair; had Lenskii told Olga about his quarrel; had Onegin mentioned it to anyone; or had Tatiana found out – any of these might have prevented the disaster. Nanny alone had the opportunity to figure things out and take action (often the function of servant-confidantes in literature!), but chance had it that she was too old and farcically obtuse (compare III.19). Other circumstances also gravitate toward a bloody outcome. Lenskii's second, Zaretskii, is 'a duelling hawk' and, as critics have noted, he repeatedly violates or manipulates the rules: he fails to urge reconciliation when delivering the challenge and at the duel itself, and ignores Onegin's own breaches of etiquette (coming late, bringing his servant as second). Such factors suggest other potential results, what G. S. Morson has labelled as novelistic 'sideshadowing', that are also depicted in the several counterfactual scenarios offered had Lenskii not died (VI.36–40).[23] The alternatives are gauged both in terms of 'the world of the novel' and as corresponding to various readers' expectations. (Might the crisis of the duel have spurred Lenskii to true poetic greatness, or would he have abandoned the muse and sunk into domestic mediocrity?)

Onegin's crisis in *Evgenii Onegin* plays out as a conflict between the frigid egoism of his assumed 'Byronic' self and his potential for change. While Onegin is described from the start as *not a poet* (I.7, I.43), his advice to Lenskii that 'If I were a poet like you / I would have chosen the other one' (III.5) (that is, Tatiana) indicates a poetic intuition superior to that of Lenskii that suggests the potential to break out of his dead-end consciousness. This potential is also suggested by Onegin's relatively gentle spurning of Tatiana, when he felt 'long silenced feelings' newly awakened (IV.11–12). Nevertheless, Onegin gives Tatiana the logical arguments that refute the assertions he makes in their final meeting about his regained ability to love. Throughout, Onegin never completely accords with his Byron-esque (or any other) role – which may be appropriate insofar as stage two dictates scepticism towards *all* roles. He is only ever described as being 'like' (*kak*) a hero from Byron, a dandy, etc., and possible alternative definitions of him come with a question mark or a 'perhaps'.

Onegin's provocation of Lenskii marks his failure to achieve an alternative selfhood. When he takes misplaced revenge upon Lenskii at the ball for his embarrassment over spurning Tatiana, Onegin follows the pathological pattern of Byronic behaviour anatomised in the French psychological novel, most notably *Adolphe*. Similarly, Onegin's participation in the duel despite pangs of conscience (VI.9–11) marks his failure to throw off the Byronic mask. Still, it would be unfair to charge Onegin with cold-blooded murder unless we presume a moral objection to duels per se (as in Richardson's *Sir Charles Grandison*). As Tatiana learns, Onegin is 'no Grandison' (III.10), but neither does he violate the code of honour. Onegin's duelling, like his deliberate insult to Lenskii in the first place, represents an extension of his cold uncaring Byronic self, a 'correct' pose that becomes uncomfortably constraining. Both Lenskii and Onegin are coerced by the harsh code of 'false shame' imposed by duelling (VI.28), yet Onegin clearly shoulders the burden of responsibility. His very violations of etiquette, that might conceivably be taken as resistance to the duel, turn into fresh insult under Zaretskii's malevolent tutelage. Zaretskii here functions as Onegin's evil double, a personification of 'the tyranny of convention' whose yoke Onegin fails to shed.

Tatiana: 'love by the book'

Both Onegin and Tatiana undergo journeys of self-discovery, neither of which reaches full resolution. Onegin's killing of his friend sends him off on his 'aimless wanderings' in Europe (VIII.13). Tatiana is the most complex of the three major protagonists. Like Lenskii, she begins in naive enchantment (in effect, Shaw's stage one), and her interest in sentimental fiction likewise counterpoints Onegin's disillusion. If Onegin's behaviour in the duel reveals his failure to free himself from his social role, Tatiana's failure to win Onegin with her letter may be ascribed to unawareness about the conventional nature of her own behaviour.[24] Tatiana's love letter, one of four inserted verse texts not in the Onegin stanza,[25] is dictated by her reading of French epistolary novels ('love by the book', see also II.29, III.9–11), yet reveals her as a genuine stage-one lyric poet. Although she adopts the role of novelistic heroines like Rousseau's Julie de Wolmar, Richardson's Clarissa Harlowe or de Staël's Delphine, this is 'love without art' (*ona liubit bez iskusstva*) springing from her spontaneous inner need, and likened to a seed germinating in spring (III.9). Like Lenskii and 'all poets', she speaks directly from her heart, but unlike Lenskii's poetry, the author-narrator presents Tatiana's outpourings without irony, reverently offering his 'weak translation' of Tatiana's original French. Nevertheless, the irony here is multiple. There is the paradox of Tatiana's having unconsciously 'borrowed' her words – and the very idea of sending such a letter – from sentimental novels, and the author's apology for the fact that she wrote in French (since her written Russian was poor). These are set against the achievement of her 'artless art', and against the parallel feat of the author-creator, who describes what is generally acknowledged as the greatest example of love poetry in Russian as a weak paraphrase of Tatiana's French. Tatiana's authenticity of expression, despite its 'borrowed' foreign literary form, is thus identified with the narrator's genius in naturalising French amatory discourse into an expression of 'authentic' Russianness. This is consistent with other details that, alone among the major characters, closely associate Tatiana – 'Russian in her soul' (V.4.1) –with traditional folk traditions.[26]

Tatiana's path to understanding is hard-fought. Reacting to Onegin's rejection, Tatiana may be said to take several journeys: her dream in chapter 5, which reveals her own erotic desire and Onegin's violent capacity; the visit of this 'young pilgrim' (VII.20) to Onegin's library in chapter 7; and her trip to Moscow and married life. Her dream offers the most privileged view of any character, and may be read both as Tatiana's unconscious reprocessing of the letter and Onegin's refusal, as well as a prophetic warning of the duel to come. Onegin appears in the dream not as the virtuous hero of a sentimental novel as Tatiana had earlier imagined him, but as ringleader of a band of grotesque, monstrous creatures, as both a predator and object of desire. The dream enacts sexual confrontations in several forms (crossing the stream, being chased and carried by the bear, being laid down on the bench) and envisions Onegin's attraction and repulsion, power and violence. It has been mined for its Russian folkloric material and its psychoanalytical symbolism, both of which offer suggestive clues about Pushkin's – and his heroine's – sexual identity.[27]

Tatiana's search for answers to Onegin's rejection and Lenskii's death leads her to Onegin's library in chapter 7, where new knowledge appropriately comes in the form of reading novels (VII.21–25). Two statuettes preside over Onegin's library – Lord Byron and Napoleon – that serve as embodiments of those two or three 'Byronic' novels that reveal the true nature of Onegin's behaviour. Tatiana realises that she had 'misread' Onegin – he was 'not a Grandison' but in a class with these far less trustworthy protagonists who personify 'contemporary man . . . with his immoral soul' and 'malicious mind'. Onegin's association with Napoleon adds a further layer of cultural resonance to Tatiana's trip to Moscow, the place where destructive Napoleonic egoism (compare II.14) will seek sanction but again face harsh rebuff (VII.37).

Tatiana's road to self-consciousness thus entails becoming a critical reader. Nevertheless, her discovery remains relative (she understood *more clearly*, VII.24), and her revelations remain in an interrogatory mode:

> Sad and dangerous eccentric,
> Creation of heaven or hell,
> This angel, this arrogant demon,
> Which is it? Is he really an imitation,
> A paltry phantom, or also
> A Muscovite in Harold's cloak,
> Interpretation of foreign whims,
> A complete lexicon of fashionable words?
> Is he then but a parody? . . .
>
> Has she solved the riddle?
> Has *the word* been found?
>
> (VII.24–25.1–2)

The issue of his character is thus posed in terms of novels (how is one to 'read' him?) and the problem of his authenticity as a man is posed in terms of language: how to 'translate' words and cultural types into selfhood. In this case, translation means an 'imitation' of something ephemeral, a meaningless assemblage or parody of empty labels ('a complete lexicon of fashionable words'). Similar questions are posed by the public that greets Onegin after his return from his travels in chapter 8, questioning whether or not this is the same Onegin of old or in 'yet another faddish mask' (VIII.7–8). The passage ends, '"Do you know him?" "Yes and no"', and the answer to this question – key for *Evgenii Onegin*'s conclusion – is left to readers, who may ponder the frustratingly perfect Pushkinian ambiguity.

Conclusions and culminations

While the change in Onegin's character remains a question, Tatiana's dramatic transformation as revealed in chapter 8 is both a culminating moment of her trajectory and a key to the author-narrator's development. This is the point where *Evgenii Onegin*'s 'two realities' explicitly come together. The opening stanzas (VIII.1–6) give a short history of Pushkin's development as a poet described in terms of the metamorphoses of his Muse, from the one who 'revealed a feast of youthful pranks' in school years; to 'the young Bacchante' who inspired his 'Anacreontic' poetry, named after the lyric poet of classical Greece (this is the Muse of his boisterous life described in chapter 1); to the one who inspired the arch-Romantic heroines of his Southern poems. Then:

Suddenly everything was transformed
And she appeared here in my garden
A provincial maiden
With a sad look in her eyes
With a little French book in her hand.

And now for the first time
I am bringing my Muse to a society rout.
(VIII.5.11–14–6.1–2)

Tatiana is thus revealed as the personification of mature Pushkinian poetry. As William Todd has argued, Tatiana's new position as salon hostess and social 'legislatrix' (VIII.28) in chapter 8 represents 'the highest form of creativity open to a woman at this time':

> The author-narrator underscores the parallels between her creation and his by applying similar epithets to them – 'unforced' and 'free'. And just as Pushkin realises his freedom to play with literary conventions within one of the most intricate stanza forms in Russian poetry, Tatiana achieves her greatest level of creativity within the sphere of high society, with all of its norms, patterns, and potentially corrupting fashions.[28]

Tatiana's special status defies simple description, and is given primarily in negative terms, as the antithesis of everything 'vulgar':

Not cold, not garrulous,
Without insolent gaze at anyone,
Without straining for success,
Without any of those little contortions,
Without affected mannerisms,
Everything was calm, simple in her,
She seemed a true copy
Du comme il faut (Shishkov, excuse me:
I don't know how to translate this.)
(VIII.14.6–14)

As with her letter, Tatiana here is able to unite self and self-expression, without any suggestion of imitativeness. Earlier Tatiana embodies a spontaneous stage-one outpouring of emotion, paradoxically effecting a 'perfect translation' as ideal heroine of an epistolary novel. Here she personifies a dynamic synthesis, manifesting a mastery of many poses, discourses and conventions. In both cases she embodies an 'iconic', fully integrated self, paradoxically combining copy and authenticity (a 'true copy'), whose open-ended referent here is the universal yet indefinable 'comme il faut'. It has been observed that Tatiana can only be described by this kind of 'fundamentally untranslatable foreign concept', which alone can suggest her essential self – as opposed to Onegin, for whom foreign guises turn parodic.[29] Tatiana has mastered the distance between convention and self, sign and signifier, having both 'deeply assumed her role' (VIII.28) and realised its empty, contingent nature (as a 'masquerade', VIII.46).

Confronting this dramatically transformed Tatiana is what sets off the potential change in Onegin, although there remains a fatal ambiguity in his newly discovered love for her. On the one hand, Tatiana has every right to suspect Onegin's motives, supposing that he wants to make a scandalous social conquest now that she has become a princess. She has come to 'read' him as a Byronic villain (VIII.44); even the author comments on the attractiveness of 'forbidden fruit' (VIII.27). However, this does not necessarily mean that Onegin's feelings are false, only that he has no way to validate them. His past behaviour offers little or no basis for trust, and his words prove incapable of conveying authenticity, whether for an actual lack of integrity, expressive incapacity, or both. Still, the Tatiana of whom Onegin now dreams is not 'the unapproachable goddess / Of the luxurious, royal Neva' (VIII.27) but the young maiden sitting at the window of her rural home (VIII.37), and his renewed capacity to love is linked to meditations on Lenskii's death (in his letter, VIII.37). Perhaps the strongest – but still ambiguous – indication of Onegin's change is the fact that he is on the verge of *becoming a poet* (VIII.38). Tatiana's letter, previously in the author-narrator's possession (III.31), now belongs to Onegin (VIII.20), which might suggest the merging of poet and pupil, author and creation. But this change also remains only a potential, and Onegin's new poetic inclinations are rather pathetic.

The action of *Evgenii Onegin* ends much as it began, *in medias res*, emphasising the arbitrariness and conventionality of all endings and beginnings. While the open-ended form of *Evgenii Onegin* left room for a continuation (about which Pushkin joked), both thematic and formal elements suggest closure. In terms of their relationship, Tatiana and Onegin have nowhere further to go. With Tatiana's rejection, Onegin seems to have met a fundamental impasse in his attempt to free himself from the burden of his past (Pushkin suggested that Onegin would have ended up a Decembrist, though this may have been part of an earlier discarded plan). Tatiana has also reached a plateau, reflecting a new-found apprehension of what she has lost and gained. She cherishes her past self (the innocent maiden in the country garden), and understands the limitations of her new role, but she has also reached a level of freedom. Like a third-stage poet – or, more accurately, the Muse of such a poet – she is able to creatively manipulate the conventions of her culture. She has made peace with the strict limitations of her position and perhaps stands as Pushkin's analogy for himself as he confronted the limitations of his life under Nicholas I. From this perspective, Tatiana's situation suggests both Pushkin's wishful thinking for his own eventual married life and a reflection on his thorny position as a writer. He felt increasingly constrained (in a 'female' position of subordination) by the oppressive post-Decembrist political atmosphere, yet took fierce pride in his spiritual independence as a poet. If Evgenii is left as if thunderstruck, 'plunged in a storm of emotions' without release, Tatiana makes a self-conscious withdrawal. Indeed, nineteenth-century social critics (Vissarion Belinsky, Nikolai Chernyshevskii and Dmitrii Pisarev) found Tatiana's (Pushkin's) 'reconciliation with reality' unacceptable, and many subsequent novels – from Chernyshevskii's *What is to be Done?* (1863) to Tolstoy's *Anna Karenina* (1875–77) may be seen as offering alternatives or responses to her basic dilemma. Like the author-narrator in the final stanzas, her position suggests a mature elegiac sense of the world, one of loss and lost possibility, but also of clear-sighted vision.[30] This vision approaches the tragic: a new level of understanding, but one that entails knowledge of inevitable age, loss and death. Together with the shedding of this naive, Romantic self, *Evgenii Onegin* thus traces its own formal and spiritual movement away from the enchantment of poetry toward 'the severity of prose'.

NOTES

This chapter is indebted to the critical works listed in the Guide to Further Reading.

1. V. Belinsky, 'Eugene Onegin: an encyclopedia of Russian life', in Sonia Hoisington (ed. and trans.), *Russian Views of Pushkin's Eugene Onegin*, Bloomington, IN, Indiana University Press, 1988, p. 17.
2. For an introduction to the Onegin stanza, see A. Pushkin, *Eugene Onegin*, V. Nabokov (trans. and commentary), 4 vols., rev. edn., Princeton University Press, 1975, vol. i, pp. 9–15, and A. D. P. Briggs, *Alexander Pushkin: Eugene Onegin*, Cambridge University Press, 1992, pp. 8–27.
3. 'Preface to chapters I–II', in J. J. McGann (ed.), *Byron*, Oxford University Press, 1986, p. 21.
4. Ibid., p. 146.
5. Translations are my own, except where indicated. References in the text are to the standard edition by chapter, stanza, and line number.
6. S. Hoisington, 'The hierarchy of narratees in *Evgenii Onegin*', in Pushkin, *Evgenii Onegin*, translated by W. Arndt, pp. lxiii–lxxv; Iu. M. Lotman, *Roman v stikhakh Pushkina 'Evgenii Onegin'*, Tartu, Tartuskii gosudarstvennyi universitet 1975, chap. 2–4, *passim*.
7. Iu. Tynianov, 'On the composition of *Eugene Onegin*', in Hoisington (ed.), *Russian Views*, p. 77; on *Evgenii Onegin* as Romantic fragment, see M. Greenleaf,

Pushkin and Romantic Fashion: Fragment, Elegy, Orient, Irony, Stanford University Press, 1994, chap. 5.
8. The term – like the notion of 'implied reader' – is from Wayne Booth, *Rhetoric of Irony*, University of Chicago Press, 1974. For another view of irony in *Onegin*, see Greenleaf, *Pushkin and Romantic Fashion*, chap. 5.
9. G. S. Morson, *The Boundaries of Genre: Dostoevsky's Diary of a Writer and the Traditions of Literary Utopia*, Austin, TX, University of Texas Press, 1981, p. 143.
10. J. T. Shaw, 'The problem of unity of the author-narrator's stance in *Eugene Onegin*', *Russian Language Journal* 120 (1981): 25–42.
11. R. Jakobson, 'Marginal notes on *Evgenii Onegin*', in Pushkin, *Evgenii Onegin*, translated by Arndt, p. xliii.
12. See J. D. Clayton, 'Considerations sur la chronologie interne de "Evgenii Onegin"', *Canadian Slavonic Papers* 21:4 (1979), 479–88.
13. G. S. Morson, *Hidden in Plain View: Narrative and Creative Potentials in 'War and Peace'*, Stanford University Press, 1987.
14. In the final organisation, chapter 9 was transformed into the concluding chapter 8, and 'Onegin's Journey' (the former chapter 8) was included in fragmentary form as an appendix. See I. M. D'iakonov, 'O vos'moi, deviatoi i desiatoi glavakh "Evgeniia Onegina"', *Russkaia literatura* 3 (1963), 37–61.
15. Letters to P. A. Viazemskii of 4 November 1823 and 13 December 1825.
16. M. Bakhtin, 'Discourse in *Eugene Onegin*', in Hoisington (ed.), *Russian Views*, pp. 115–21. See also S. Bocharov, 'The stylistic world of the novel', in Hoisington (ed.), *Russian Views*, pp. 122–68.
17. Craig Cravens, 'Lyric and narrative consciousness in *Evgenii Onegin*', *Slavic and East European Journal* 46:4 (2002), 683–710.
18. L. Shtil'man [Stilman], 'Problema literaturnykh zhanrov i traditsii v "Evgenii Onegine" Pushkina', in *American Contributions to the Fourth International Congress of Slavists*, 's-Gravenhage, Mouton, 1958, pp. 321–67.
19. See Sonia Hoisington, '*Evgenii Onegin*: product of or challenge to *Adolphe?*', *Comparative Literature Studies* 14 (1977), 205–13.
20. Arndt's translation.
21. See Sonia Hoisington, 'Parody in *Evgenii Onegin*: Lenskii's lament', *Canadian Slavonic Papers* 29:2–3 (1987), 266–78.
22. S. Mitchell, 'Tatiana's reading', *Forum for Modern Language Studies* 4 (1968), 1–21.
23. G. S. Morson, *Narrative and Freedom: the Shadows of Time*, New Haven, Yale University Press, 1994.
24. M. Levitt, 'The dance of love in Pushkin's *Eugene Onegin* (the "Maiden's Song")', in J. T. Ryfa (ed.), *Collected Essays in Honor of the Bicentennial of Alexander S. Pushkin's Birth*, Lewiston, Edwin Mellen, 2000, pp. 75–91.
25. The others are: the dedication; the Maiden's Song; and Onegin's letter.
26. This is also suggested by her surname 'Larina', associated with domesticity (*lares*). Onegin and Lenskii's surnames may derive from bodies of water (Lake Onega, the Lena River), although Lenskii might also be associated with *len'* (laziness; compare his 'flaccid' verse) and Onegin with *nega* (languor), or, as Greenleaf suggests, negation (*o-ne* = 'oh no!').

27. Richard Gregg, 'Tat'yana's two dreams: the unwanted spouse and the demonic lover', *Slavonic and East European Review* 48 (1970), 492–505; D. Rancour-Laferriere, 'Puškin's still unravished bride: a psychoanalytic study of Tat'jana's dream', *Russian Literature* 25:2 (1989), 215–58; and J. D. Clayton, 'Towards a feminist reading of *Evgenii Onegin*', *Canadian Slavonic Papers* 29:2–3 (1987), 255–65.
28. William Mills Todd III, *Fiction and Society in the Age of Pushkin: Ideology, Institutions, and Narrative*, Cambridge, MA, Harvard University Press, 1986, p. 327.
29. Bocharov, 'Stylistic world', p. 153.
30. O. P. Hasty has also noted how women writers from Pavlova to Tsvetaeva could also 'enlist Tatiana to champion female creativity' (*Pushkin's Tatiana*, University of Wisconsin Press, 1999, p. 13).

4

CARYL EMERSON

Pushkin's drama

In the realm of theatre, Pushkin was a provocateur. Passionate about spectacle, he criticised most Russian performance practice of his time – neoclassical tragedy, melodrama, *vaudeville*, sentimentalist and patriotic-historical drama – for its pompous diction and predictable plotting. Only verse comedy and religious drama were exempt. He had strong opinions on theatre reform and hoped to enter Russia into pan-European debates over the proper purposes of drama.[1] As a playwright, however, Pushkin encountered constant obstacles. He abandoned all his teenage efforts at verse comedy; attempts to publish his play on Grishka Otrepiev and Tsar Boris were frustrated for years. Plans and dramatic fragments (about twenty-five) far outnumber the completed works.[2]

The masterpieces that did emerge, *Boris Godunov* (1825–30) and the four *Little Tragedies* (1830), have thrilled and mystified readers. But their stageability remains in dispute. Did Pushkin write 'closet drama'? In the plays themselves, events often occur with lightning speed, in improbable locales. Even with Shakespearean precedent, the on-stage battle scenes in *Boris* (where regiments gallop off and horses die on stage) are difficult to envisage; the penultimate scene of *Rusalka* takes place on the bottom of a river. Pushkin's words can be as difficult to realise as his spaces – especially the stage directions. How does one perform the powerful directive at the end of *Boris*, '*the people are speechless*', so that it can be heard? How should we experience those 'time-free' stage directions in the *Little Tragedies* – Laura's '(*she sings.*)' in *The Stone Guest* and Mozart's '(*he plays.*)' in *Mozart and Salieri* – which poetic metre simply leaps over, taking us directly and without missing a beat to the applause for Laura's completed song and to Salieri's tears upon hearing the *Requiem*? This is not the stuff of real staged time and space. Thus was born the idea that opera composers (Musorgsky, Dargomyzhskii, Rimskii-Korsakov) came to Pushkin's rescue, inserting the necessary songs, fleshing out the whole and saving these works for the stage.[3] Is Pushkin the playwright merely a stylised lyricist?

For Pushkin, drama always meant real theatre. His ambitious dramatic ideal was unrealisable then and perhaps even now. But as with so much in his protean output, Pushkin's dramatic works, including the fragments, cohere and satisfy on several levels. Even as we read what we could be viewing, certain constants – in choice of episode, collision of personalities, treatment of time and space, abrupt or startling ends – permit us to speculate on his constantly evolving theatrical vision. Each period of Pushkin's activity as dramatist reveals distinctive facets of this ideal.

Verse comedy: the stage as artifice and comic relief

Pushkin's appreciation of eighteenth-century French theatricals began in his childhood.[4] During and after the Lycée, entranced by Molière and Voltaire, he sketched several plans for a high-society verse comedy (one in iambic hexameter couplets) and in 1821 completed one scene of a melodrama on gambling. He also briefly tried his hand at verse tragedy: the Novgorodian tale *Vadim*. Until his Southern exile, Pushkin was an intimate of the major theatrical circles in the capital. The young poet was combative – but he was no genre purist. He encouraged Alexander Shakhovskoi (1777–1846, theatre director and author of popular verse comedies), to undertake stage adaptations of the Southern poems. The pleasure Pushkin received from light-hearted spectacle, together with his delight at ballet and his loyalty to Italian operetta, is a vital corrective to his later, more disillusioned critiques of theatre art. Although his own completed dramas were densely serious and morally freighted, Pushkin never lost his admiration for the pacing, wit, repartee and unexpected wisdom possible in formulaic stage comedy. He was sketching plans for a comedy as late as 1828. Comedic patterning would contribute vitally to Pushkin's later masterpieces in drama and prose (especially the *Tales of Belkin*).

This early period, before Pushkin's mid-decade encounter with Shakespeare, yielded no complete works or systematic statements on theatre. Judging by the conventional genres at which the aspiring playwright tried his hand, however, some general criteria might be posited. The stage must not bore us. Actors must speak, not recite, their lines – and their utterances must sound like living dialogue in a genuine present. Now that we are no longer obliged to see Pushkin's creative trajectory, in drama or elsewhere, as an inexorable progression toward realism[5] (a concept undreamt of in Pushkin's era), we can appreciate his tough-minded hopes for a hybrid drama combining the best of classical (and neoclassical) restraint with the flexibility of Shakespeare as revived by French and German Romanticism. Like the ancient Greek dramatists (and, of course, like Friedrich Schiller), Pushkin strove to unite in his person both the charismatic national poet and the national playwright, a prophetic seer of his own people's history as well as an improvisator on universal themes. For the mature Pushkin, the ideal spectacle would feature compact events, laconic expression, unexpectedness, and a ripening 'threshold moment' that people off stage could see while people on stage could not (because their world was limited to the time and space of that stage). Above all, it would presume an alert spectator willing to be brought to a moment of self-awareness that would bond him with the poet and the nation.

Dramatic patches (theatrical dialogue) inside the narrative poems

Four of Pushkin's *poemy* (narrative poems) contain substantial patches of theatrical dialogue: *The Gypsies*, *Tazit*, *Poltava* and *Angelo*. A 'dramatic patch' differs significantly from the direct speech of characters set off by quotation marks. It more resembles an inserted genre: suddenly the narrator dissolves, actors are 'labelled', the poem-text temporarily turns into a play-script, and the reader begins to realise (to hear and see) an embodied dramatic scene. What might have prompted Pushkin to 'bifurcate the matter' so that narrative declamation slides into stage speech – only to return, after a stretch, to a unified authorial voice?[6] No single answer suffices. The theatrical patches inside *Angelo* (1833) are largely technical: a selective, effective translation of key dialogues from Shakespeare's *Measure for Measure* that Pushkin's English was up to rendering.[7] The patches inside *The Gypsies* and *Poltava* are more revealing. Take, as an exemplar, *The Gypsies* (1824), penned one year before *Boris* and sharing much of that play's 'sense of a scene' without, of course, relinquishing the right to a generalising voice. All the major action of the poem is given in labelled dramatic patches: Aleko's arrival; the Old Man's stories; the double murder. The narrative frame is largely descriptive: one huge, thick stage direction on the sprawling gypsy camp, delivered in distanced epic tones. When Zemfira (with Aleko in tow) moves into the light of her father's campfire, the poem 'goes dramatic'. It drops back into authorial narrative whenever Aleko's psyche needs clarification – and especially during his terrible dreams. At the critical moment (Aleko's discovery of Zemfira's infidelity), a dramatic patch brings Aleko out of his dream and into a waking nightmare. The voices he hears, while creeping up on the illicit couple in the dark, have blind labels ('first voice', 'second voice'), for they are given not in the zone of the all-seeing playwright-narrator but in the zone of the hero's increasingly horrified consciousness. This blinkering of perspective prepares the reader for the two fatal stabbings, of Zemfira and her new lover, both of whom 'live out' (or 'die out') the violent prophecy of her song.

In this rounded scene from *The Gypsies*, we have the kernel of Pushkin's system for deploying actors in *Boris Godunov*. Characters are trapped in their own immediate circles of light. They are free agents in the present only; what they see of their own significance is fragmentary (and differs from what the audience knows of them). Each character's dreams, ambitions and fears infect the others on stage, but opportunistically, in keeping with their personal needs and horizons. Narrowly inscribed self-interest appears to govern every major event and personal decision. Nevertheless, in some uncanny way, symmetry is achieved in the play's action as a whole. The linear reveals itself as the cyclical; the seemingly innocent phrase hooks up and loops back to confirm or to condemn. 'The roundest writer in Russian literature, Pushkin everywhere exhibits a tendency to close the circle, whether it be the contour of events or the sharp outline of a stanza', Andrei Siniavsky wrote; 'there is something providential in Pushkin's consonances'.[8] Such providential roundedness, a striking feature in the Southern poems, would be all the more astonishing in historical drama, because Pushkin's hybrid genre – influenced (but less than is supposed) by Shakespeare, affected (more than is supposed) by archaic theatrical formulae – was factually accurate beyond what any historical playwright had previously attempted in the Russian tradition.

Boris Godunov and the tragicomedy of history

By the mid-1820s there were several reasons for Pushkin's turn to history, and to the catastrophic watershed of Russia's early modern period, the Time of Troubles. Between 1821 and 1824, Nikolai Karamzin, Russia's historian laureate and the poet's close friend, published volumes nine to eleven of his *History of the Russian State*, covering the reign of Ivan the Terrible's son Fedor (1584–98) to the accession of the False Dmitrii (1605). The story of Boris Godunov was their centrepiece: Russia's first elected tsar, the bridge between her two dynasties, and a surprisingly modern figure to emerge from the faceless piety (and faceless terror) of Muscovite rulers. The crime on Tsar Boris's conscience was his purported murder of the Tsarevich Dmitrii in 1591. That the ambitious, self-made Boris was responsible for this 'tsaricide' was doubted even in Pushkin's time. But the Russian Orthodox Church and the House of Romanov had long insisted on it, and the story of a political upstart punished for crimes against royal blood resonated well in the legitimist post-Napoleonic era. Pushkin blurred, but basically endorsed, the question of Boris's guilt. The resultant plot – with its hidden crime, preoccupation with kingship, aroused crowds and threat of civil war – was an ideal vehicle for Pushkin's growing interest in Shakespeare.

Although Karamzin was his primary source, the poet re-evaluated sensitive issues through independent research in medieval chronicles, his own family papers (several Pushkins took part in the Troubles), and impartial accounts by foreign mercenaries. Like Schiller before him, Pushkin saw no conflict between dramatic art and accurate documented history. Indeed, certain sentiments spoken in the play – on popular support for the Pretender, on Tsar Boris's tyranny and enserfment policies, on the psychology of the crafty Prince Shuiskii and the embittered, ambitious General Basmanov – were better and more bravely researched by Pushkin than by any Russian historian before or since. Upon finishing his play in November 1825, the poet knew he had authored a seditious text, politically and aesthetically.

Pushkin referred to his play by various names: a comedy (with a mock-chronicle title), a tragedy, a 'romantic tragedy', and on the title page in 1831 simply *Boris Godunov*, 'composition' (*sochinenie*). Its twenty-five short, unnumbered scenes ignore the unities of time, place, action and style. (As he expressed the matter in a jotting on tragedy in 1825: 'Interest [too] is a unity.'[9]) Formally, the play is bold. Its pattern of blank (unrhymed) iambic pentameter with caesura is broken by several rogue scenes: one in trochaic hexameter, another in free iambs and five scenes in prose (see the Appendix). Folk laments, commoners' speech and irreverent minstrel verse by vagrant monks add intonational and rhythmic variety. Action stretches over seven years (from the opening day to the closing day of the brief Godunov dynasty) and moves from Moscow to Poland, stopping at various borders and battlefields in between. We witness threshold moments for the heroes and for Russian history – but these moments are more often meditative or comic than authoritative and declamatory. The play contains only four showcase monologues. Recalling entries in a medieval chronicle, precise dates precede a scene at four points: 20 February 1598; the year 1603; 16 October 1604; 21 December 1604. Key events cluster around these dates: four scenes on Boris's election and coronation; two on the emergence of 'Dmitrii' out of Grishka Otrepiev, novice in the Kremlin Miracles Monastery; episodes from Tsar Boris's reign (first as seen from within the tsar's disillusioned mind, then through the eyes of Prince Shuiskii and Afanasii Pushkin); five Polish scenes of courtship and martial recruitment with the Pretender. The final nine scenes alternate at a dizzying pace between battles that the carefree, confident Pretender ought to have lost but inexplicably wins, and the Moscow scenes. There, to an undercurrent of rising terror, the Godunov claim on the throne becomes increasingly tenuous: Boris dies, Basmanov defects, Shuiskii ominously disappears from view, and the young Tsar Fedor is murdered, together with his hated mother, as Tsarevich Dmitrii prepares to enter the capital.

The famous final stage direction '*the People are speechless*' (*narod bezmolvstvuet*) is not to be found in any manuscript version of the play, which, under the title *Comedy about Tsar Boris and Grishka Otrepiev*, Pushkin tried to publish between 1826 and 1830. The censored version that appeared in 1831 was missing three scenes, dozens of lines of dialogue elsewhere, and no longer ended on the original cheer, 'Long live Tsar Dmitrii Ivanovich!', but on silence. Most of the omitted portions found their way into print by 1855. However, the People's final speechlessness became canonical in criticism about the play. Repercussions have been profound. With that ending in place, the People are enigmatic, fateful, pregnant with an unspoken word, which greatly appealed to populist (and later to Stalinist) mythologies. Pushkin could be aligned with official Russian State and Church doctrine, always hostile to Dmitrii (the poet, for his part, had assembled from non-Russian sources a very positive image of the Pretender). Pushkin also lost the 'roundedness' of his original Shakespearean structure, in which a new tsar is cheered by the populace in both the first and last scenes. But arguably, in the demoralising struggle between poet and imperial censorship, more was lost than the symmetry of this one play. A much larger symmetrical arc was never realised, whose conceptual shadow should complicate how we view Pushkin as historical dramatist.[10]

Beyond a ribald, mixed style, very little from Shakespeare's tragedies is reflected in *Boris Godunov*. Its compactness, emotional and rhetorical constraint, lack of titanic heroes, and reluctance to bring the supernatural on stage all set Pushkin's style apart. Another matter is the impact of Shakespeare's war-saturated chronicle plays. Pushkin endorsed August Schlegel's defence of the chronicle plays as vehicles for the inscrutable and organic workings of history, as well as François Guizot's distinction between tragedies and historical chronicles: tragic scenes must link up and explain, whereas chronicles need only fill out episodes with action.[11] In turning to chronicles in 1824 – both Shakespeare's dramas, and Russian medieval texts – Pushkin renounced the linear, elucidating power of tragedy as conventionally defined. A 'Muscovite' chronicle play could also draw satisfyingly on similarities between those two triumphantly rising empires, Elizabethan England and post-Napoleonic Russia.[12] But the obstacle to such parallels has always been the utterly bleak worldview at the end of *Boris*. Russia's national playwright had chronicled the nation's collapse, not its triumph.

There is good evidence, however, that the end of *Boris Godunov* was not intended to be the end.[13] The poet and critic Stepan Shevyrev, among others in the poet's circle, recalls Pushkin remarking that 'he still intended to write a *False Dimitrii* and a *Vasily Shuiskii* as a continuation of *Godunov*, and then to take something from the interregnum; it would resemble the Shakespearean chronicles'.[14] Sequels to the *Komediia* would bring the story to its logical culmination, the inauguration of the Romanov dynasty in 1613. Such a dynamic is itself comedic, in the spirit of Pushkin's early title. For comedy, while it can be black, is always forward-looking, focused on potentials in the present and future, as opposed to backward-looking tragedy, which it vanquishes. Boris was that backward-looking tragic figure; the triumphant Dmitrii in 1605 his vital and welcome (albeit transitory) replacement. When Pushkin wrote his initial 'comedy' under house arrest in 1825, he was an alienated man. When, after 1826, he spoke about further instalments – Shuiskii, the Pretender, and Marina Mniszech especially fascinated him – he hoped that his own life would take on noble Shakespearean contours: a playwright of genius serving a powerful monarch through an art so irresistible that injustice and suffering would cease to seem arbitrary and become glorious. To an extent this larger project would require a return to Karamzin's Statist, sceptical, somewhat fatalistic Enlightenment historiography. (In 1830, Pushkin sought and received the right to dedicate his play to the historian's memory.[15]) Unlike Karamzin's teleological narrative, however, the scenes in Pushkin's cycle would benefit from its specifically 'narrator-less' mode. Drama is perfect for pitting one explanatory strategy and one point of view against another. The workings of providence would compete alongside pure chance, political ambition, social injustice, popular revolt and personal vengeance. What principles might have governed this chronicle-play trilogy, had Pushkin written it?

Here we can only speculate. Most likely, comedy (in Pushkin's special sense of that word) would have remained central: a rejuvenating force, fertile, 'rounded', capricious, ultimately conciliatory. Providence, too, would be operative, not in the sense of predestination or punitive justice but more comedically – 'protecting' those figures (Dmitrii, Shuiskii, Gavrila Pushkin) who know how to benefit from accident or chance, and not protecting those (Basmanov, Boris Godunov) who calculate gains and losses, who complain and grieve.[16] In 1830, Pushkin took some notes on Mikhail Pogodin's historical play *Marfa Posadnitsa* that provide further clues to the trilogy's possible poetics.[17] European drama, he wrote, was born in the public squares and fairs. As a popular form, its primary task has always been to entertain and astonish. Thus the cruder emotions – laughter, pity, terror, surprise – are essential to its success. When 'poets moved to court', drama grew decorous, didactic and tedious. High tragedy in Russia still bore that official imprint; it had not yet shed its servile tone or rigidity of form. Characters had not yet learned to speak freely, without constraint, and the playwright was not yet as 'impartial as Fate'. Impartiality in historical drama meant 'expressing the people of the past, their minds, their prejudices' (that is, not removing them from their own circle of light). But Fate still displayed a pattern – and the playwright was obliged to see it.

The mixed reception of *Boris* in print soon confirmed Pushkin's fears. Its tone and genre pleased no one. It was not historical tragedy: the texture was too buoyant, the diction too conversational, and the secondary love plot so essential to kingship drama was parodied beyond repair. But the play also did not qualify as 'historical comedy' – that is, as a treatment of historical events from the perspective of a rogue, a Falstaff, or vagrant monks such as Misail and Varlaam. Its subject matter was too dark, the confessional monologues in it too lofty, and its concerns were unabashedly dynastic. In Shakespeare's hybrid spirit but with a neoclassical sense of proportion, Pushkin had produced something like a 'tragicomedy of history'. He had retold for the stage a piece of tragic, sacralised history so as to reduce the distance, mongrelise the language, focus on the present moment, allow intimate access to the heroes, enable chance events to make a difference, while prompting the audience to gasp and laugh. Russian precedents for this hybrid type of drama, such as the pious tragicomedy *Vladimir* (1705), were well known to Pushkin's generation. In *Boris*, of course, the blend of sacred with comic is thoroughly updated and passed through a Romantic-folkloric lens. Recent work on the play has disclosed close parallels between its topography and *vertep*, Russian folk puppet shows of the Nativity.[18]

Taken alone, *Boris Godunov* is that unclassifiable artefact that Pushkin called it: a 'composition'. It is not recognisable as a chronicle play in Shakespeare's sense. It leads nowhere. As a Russian history play, its historical accuracy and political wisdoms have been underappreciated – partly because opera cannot do them justice (and the operatised parts of Pushkin's play remain the most familiar); partly because Pushkin's skill as a historian in 1825 are assumed to be rudimentary and in competition with his ambitions as a dramatist; and partly because scholars have focused on the influences Pushkin himself named: Karamzin and 'our father Shakespeare'. Karamzin was indeed the starting-point, but not the end. Shakespeare (in French prose translation) was a crucial stimulus, but Pushkin would never have imitated a foreign nation's mode of historical dramatisation. His hybrid vision was cosmopolitan in its own way, drawing on monastic chronicles, Russified Jesuit school drama, the medieval mystery play and puppet show, accounts by foreign mercenaries in Russian pay. The stageworthiness of this hybrid composition was debated as early as 1826, but in fact its devices were well within the competence of popular theatre technology of the time (supernatural opera and *vaudeville*). More subtle realisations of Pushkin's mix of intimate, close-up lyric intonation with the *mise-en-scène* of a crowded square or battlefield had to await the advent of film. In 1830, Pushkin was quite certain that the play would fail.[19] That very year, he produced his next confounding masterpiece, the *Little Tragedies*.

The *Little Tragedies*: essences, epochs, personal exorcism

On 9 December 1830, Pushkin wrote to his friend Petr Pletnev: 'I shall tell you (as a secret) that in Boldino I wrote as I have not written in a long time.' The harvest included 'several dramatic scenes or little tragedies, to wit: *The Miserly Knight*, *Mozart and Salieri*, *Feast in Time of Plague*, and *Don Juan*'.[20] The idea of the dramatised miniature was not new for the poet. In an undated jotting *c.*1826, Pushkin listed ten topics that included, in addition to three actually written, 'Romulus and Remus', 'Jesus', 'Pavel I', 'the devil in love', 'Dmitrii and Marina' and 'Kurbskii'.[21] Why precisely four were realised during that 'first Boldino autumn' is uncertain. The completed tragedies have been seen as representing four epochs in European history – medieval, Renaissance, Enlightenment and Romantic – at points of crisis for their respective worldviews, which the topography of each tragedy symbolically reflects.[22] More frequent than historical readings, however, have been autobiographical explanations, many surprisingly non-reductive.[23]

Pushkin attended seriously to omens and thresholds. The autumn of 1830 was one: with his wedding negotiations stalled in Moscow, quarantined in a distant village because of a cholera epidemic, the poet found himself confronting death, the uncertainty (but necessity) of marriage, and his slipping fame, all of which conspired to raise his genius to fever pitch. The four tragedies can be seen as dramatisations of essential passions, or vices, that Pushkin felt obliged to discipline, perhaps even to exorcise, in order that the threshold be successfully crossed. The last play of the cycle, *Feast in the Time of Plague* (*Pir vo vremia chumy*), is the most immediately contextual. Unlike the companion tragedies, *Feast* concerns not a vice but an attitude: trapped in an ever-expanding circle of death, should one revel or repent? Its tableau-like, communal texture contrasts with the personal tone of the other three. Each little tragedy is a neoclassically sculpted confrontation between rivals – the peak moment or 'fifth act' of a crisis situation that 'moves swiftly and inexorably to its catastrophic climax'[24] – which bears within it a deeply private anxiety. But does the desired resolution or exorcism in fact occur? Upon closer inspection, the confrontation in each can be read as a bifurcation: two halves of one maximally stressed, but integrated, creative self.

Bidding farewell to bachelorhood, Pushkin worked through his prior, 'youthful' encounters with miserliness, envy, profligate lust and contempt for death. He stylised these liminal moments and attached them to a mainstream legend or personality in the European literary tradition. The plot of *The Miserly Knight* (*Skupoi rytsar'*) was closest – literally – to home: a contest between father and son over money. Its tensions so resembled those between Pushkin and his own frivolous, profligate, tight-fisted parent that the poet presented the piece as scenes from an eighteenth-century English 'tragicomedy', *The Covetous Knight* by William Shenstone, although no such play exists.[25] Albert, the neglected son, is honourable, impulsive, generous, and poor. His father the Baron is a miser of astonishing scope, who, in an ecstatic monologue, gloats over his coffers of gold, which in his fantasy provide him with power, creative genius, pleasure – and which he is determined to protect from the appetites of his heir. In the final scene, mediated by the Duke, the slandered Albert challenges his father to a duel, which is interrupted by the Baron's sudden heart attack and death.

This grim sequence of events is so melodramatic (and the Baron's monologue so famous) that it is easy to miss the oxymoron in the title. A true knight cannot be miserly (he can covet, but *skupost'* – miserliness – is not that). Pushkin understood coveting and to some degree respected it. He was, like his father, an extravagant spender. The difference was that the son, alone in his family, could also create wealth. For the problem with hoarding – and with the Baron's fantasy – is not the industry involved, but its dishonourableness and wrongness as an economy.

Those chests of gold do not make the Baron secure, serene, powerful or creative. Called before the Duke, he reveals himself to be a timid and lying courtier, so much so that at least one critic has suggested that *The Miserly Knight* is not a tragedy but a satire.[26] After all, greed on stage is conventionally resolved in a comic fashion. But Pushkin would come to admire Shakespeare's Shylock over Molière's Miser precisely because of the complexity of the Venetian moneylender's vice.[27] Although as a family man Pushkin felt acutely his duty to provide, 'asceticism as an extreme form of economy' and the equation of money with potency always remained suspect.[28] In 1830, the painful stand-off between a restless, creative son in need of means and an uncreative father who thinks he can withhold those means had a larger subtext: all value, to be valuable, was obliged to circulate.

The reduction of value to a good that is accounted and 'paid for' is the fraudulent move also governing the economy of art in *Mozart and Salieri*. The poet believed the legend that Antonio Salieri, Italian composer and pedagogue in Vienna, had poisoned his young protégé Mozart, or at least was capable of doing so ('competence to commit a crime' fired Pushkin's dramatic imagination as much as the crime itself; recall Boris Godunov's historically unproven guilt over Dmitrii of Uglich). In *Mozart and Salieri*, both the competence and the crime are presented in a complex manner. Since Salieri has a controlling monopoly on the words (the first act is given almost entirely in his zone, framed by two huge soliloquies), and since he is so gifted in self-criticism that is also self-justification, we do not doubt his sincerity. Conventionally, one does not lie in a soliloquy. But unlike the simpler, one-way passion of miserliness, envy is two-sided and dynamic. A highly unstable amalgam of opposites, 'hate–love' must constantly reconstitute itself with melodramatic stories, and it cannot be trusted. Mikhail Gershenzon noted that 'this drama is a drama solely about Salieri, Mozart is only the spark that ignites the flame'[29] – and this is largely true: a spark is unreflectively itself, a 'son of harmony' at home in its own element, whereas Salieri is an outsider, a 'servant of art' competent to appreciate greatness that he himself cannot create. In the first act, Salieri, pricked by the very existence of a Mozart, soliloquises at a slow burn. Mozart laughs.

But the second act, supposedly the zone of Mozart's buoyant genius and high humour, undoes this simple binary. It is true that Mozart would rather converse or make music than nurse past injuries, but in fact the content of his speech (on the Man in Black) and his music (a Requiem) is anything but radiant or comedic. The modesty of the true creative artist in the face of death is a major theme in all the *Little Tragedies*. But even here, Pushkin places hurdles. In Salieri's second monologue, we learn that the poison slipped into Mozart's glass is a potion that Salieri has been hoarding for eighteen years with the more likely intention of ending his *own* life with it. He is waiting for that moment when his own lack of genius becomes unbearable. Part of the tragedy, then, is Salieri's cry to Mozart: 'Wait, wait! . . . You drank it down! . . . without me?' (ii.50). Again, as in *The Miserly Knight*, we have multiple, mirrored victims. To Salieri's discredit, however, he recovers quickly and in cowardly fashion. It is not creativity that is primary for him, but an injured sense of justice.

With whom did Pushkin identify in this play? Of course great art requires both winged inspiration and sober revision. But Pushkin's 'Mozartian' buoyancy notwithstanding, great poets have tended to associate him with Salieri. In her essay 'Mozart and Salieri', Nadezhda Mandelstam notes how passionately her friend Anna Akhmatova insisted that 'Pushkin was juxtaposing himself to Mickiewicz' in this little tragedy: by his spontaneity, his responsiveness, his capacity to seize a cue and transform it into art on the spot, the great Polish poet could turn the fastidious craftsman Pushkin into a Salieri.[30] This argument – that inspired improvisation is the mark of both true poetry and true love – is pursued in the third and longest little tragedy, *The Stone Guest* (*Kamennyi gost'*).

Autobiographical resonances abound here as well. Pushkin himself kept a Don Juan list, womanised indefatigably, and in 1830 must have been intensely curious about the effect of his impending marriage on this defining aspect of his life. Remarkable in Pushkin's version of the Don Juan legend, however, and what perhaps prompted him to add his word to the masterpieces of Molière and Mozart, is his emphasis on two themes not immediately related to libido: the all-conquering nature of poetry, and the claims of the present against memory and a burdened past.[31] *The Stone Guest* is the most dialogic and 'performative' of the tragedies. Its four scenes are packed with movement. Oddly, however, the scenes 'forget' one another. In the first, Don Juan, escaped from exile, plans seduction strategies with Leporello. In the second, Laura, who 'cannot love two men at the same time' (ii.51), is revealed as a double for Don Juan, whose verses she sings in inspired improvisation (when Juan appears and kills Don Carlos, the two reunited lovers behave as if Carlos had never been). By scene three, Laura is forgotten. Doña Anna has now become all – and Don Juan, stripping off disguise after disguise, brings her to the brink of a kiss. The Statue finally intervenes and the successful seducer dies uttering Doña Anna's name. At any moment, arousal in the present is the only reality.

Part of the drama of a poetic temperament – such as we see in the Baron, Mozart, Salieri, Don Juan, Dmitrii the Pretender – is its need to posit an ideal and pursue it fearlessly, so that it fills the whole of the poet's space. Single-minded pursuit becomes tragic for the artist when he attempts to attain this absolute through the imposition of finalised form.[32] If the Baron's gold represents this form in its crudest incarnation, then Doña Anna, at the other extreme, is the muse at her most refined and veiled. But to the experienced poet, she is malleable material too. Able to create a whole out of the tiniest glimpse of her heel, Don Juan comes to the end of his outward-seeking desires; compelled to break down her resistance and finding none, his only path is his own 'death and transfiguration'.[33] Pursuing this theme in *Rusalka*, his final finished drama, Pushkin will create an entirely new cast of characters in a new sort of space, at once superstitious and non-sentimental, where death is not an end. It is scarcely even a boundary.

Medieval 'prose drama' and folklore tragedy

Pushkin was to undertake two more dramatic experiments. One, composed in 1835, remained a fragment in four brief scenes, known as *Scenes from Times of Chivalry* (*Stseny iz rytsarskikh vremen*). Uniquely for Pushkin the dramatist, the text is in prose. In plot and dialogue, it closely resembles

La Jacquerie, a drama of feudal-age peasant insurrection written in 1828 by Pushkin's contemporary (and admirer) Prosper Mérimée. Mérimée was influenced by Shakespeare as well as by Walter Scott, and in the plot of Pushkin's 'Scenes' – in which a disenchanted, disinherited son becomes a bandit – we detect traces of both those writers and of the poet's own (unfinished) prose work *Dubrovskii*. As in the *Little Tragedies*, autobiographical motifs abound. The hero, Franz, a poet, under threat of expulsion by his miserly merchant father, dreams of becoming a knight. He takes up as an equerry in a castle only to discover that serving these capricious, violent men is no better than serving his father; he is expelled for impertinence. Penniless and homeless, he organises a revolt of vassals, during which he is wounded and captured by the very knights he had insulted. Only after performing for them as a Minnesinger, a bard of courtly love, is his sentence of hanging commuted to life imprisonment.

'Scenes' has almost no stage history. But one interpretation of its poetics is suggestive for this final phase in Pushkin's dramaturgy: its fairytale (*skazka*) structure, which explains the disjointed action, non-developmental characters, sparse repetition-laden dialogue and abstract, ethnically mixed names and locales.[34] Pushkin was not repeating here, on medieval western soil, a history play such as *Boris*, with its precise dates and documented events. Nor did he intend another little tragedy, where a single passion plays out at crisis pitch. 'Scenes' is a social panorama of 'Europe in general' at a threshold moment, suspended between magic and science, pared down to its symbols, with each social class allotted one type only: merchant, knight, scholar-alchemist, poet. According to Pushkin's plan, a major role was to be played by the alchemist Berthold Schwarz, inventor of gunpowder, and the drama would end with Faust's arrival on the devil's tail. If this reading is valid, then Pushkin's condensation and cross-section of European class history in a new type of hybrid drama can be seen as an extension of his mature fascination with folk-and-fairytale denouements (as in *The Captain's Daughter* and *Angelo*) during dark times. Real-life injustice cannot ultimately appeal to the law, but only to magic and grace.

Pushkin's other dramatic experiment, *Rusalka* (*The Water-Nymph*), also requires a supernatural, fairytale poetics. But it is aesthetically far more complex. The story of a maiden seduced, abandoned, with child, who drowns herself in despair and is transformed into a mermaid, was popular on various national opera stages, usually in a comic or sentimental vein. *Rusalka* joins the *Little Tragedies* as a Russian 'translation' of a familiar pan-European theme. But in this case, death puts an end to nothing. Indeed, the disgraced Daughter's 'life' is her prehistory. The six compact scenes cover seven years (like *Boris*) and observe the same tripartite geography: home (the mill on the

Dnieper, where the Miller reproaches his daughter and where she is deserted by her Prince) – away (the Prince's castle, where he is married and where his Princess spends seven childless years) – home (again the Dnieper, both underwater and on shore, where the Prince, urged on by a strange yearning, encounters the mad Miller and glimpses Rusalochka, his daughter). So very distant from the comic-operetta mode is Pushkin's treatment that one critic has elevated its *skazka* element to high tragedy, albeit of a lyric sort, and connected *Rusalka* with Pushkin's renewed hopes for radical reform of the stage.[35]

Arguably, more Shakespearean tragedy resonates in this 'fairytale' drama than in *Boris Godunov*. In addition to the drowned Ophelia, driven mad by the behaviour of her Prince, there are ominously chanting *rusalki*, who recall the witches in *Macbeth* (in an early draft, not only the voice but the full-bodied ghost of the Daughter appears at the Prince's wedding feast, dripping wet and green-haired). And framing the whole is *King Lear*: a wilful father who, having lost his beloved (and wilful) daughter, goes mad – and in his madness, finally acknowledges his responsibility for years of bad parenting and greed. In condensing these episodes, Pushkin increases their moral weight. Consider the motif of madness. The Prince's horrified response to the mad Miller's ravings recalls Pushkin's own lyric on losing one's sanity. Crucial, however, are the differing contexts for such anxieties in lyric and drama. King Lear, for all the magnificence of the tragedy that surrounds him, speaks his truth 'lyrically', to the audience, alone to the wild elements on the heath, ignoring even his Fool. The Raven-Miller rants crazily to the clear-minded Prince, who is brought to even more certain sanity in the presence of this madness. The ethical scenario in *Rusalka* is not open, as in lyric, at the mercy of its outside addressee for closure; drama traps and completes from within itself.

Or consider the Miller's Daughter. She is no Ophelia, no Cordelia; for that matter, she is no Tatiana, Doña Anna or Masha Mironova. She is that rare female figure on Pushkin's literary horizon, one far more common in Dostoevsky: the infernal woman. Pushkin generally prefers the introspective, decorous, vulnerable or reconciled woman to the vengeful one. The Miller's Daughter, however, is single-minded in her fury at abandonment, on both sides of her death. 'Tell him,' Rusalka instructs her daughter, 'that I still remember him and love him and await him here [*zhdu k sebe*]' (v.29–30). This vengeance is fertile. Her steadiness in refusing to forgive brings the men to their senses, forcing them to remember: the Miller, that he looked the other way and hoped to profit thereby, and the Prince, that he was relieved to be married according to his rank. As always in Pushkin, when a bond of love, family or pledged loyalty is broken by calculation – Boris Godunov,

Basmanov, Salieri, the Baron – the punishment is barrenness or the loss of one's line.

Given the sexual mores of Pushkin's social class, it is unlikely that *Rusalka* reflects any guilt on the poet's part over his affair with a serf girl and the birth of his illegitimate son in 1826. A more likely autobiographical subtext in the *Rusalka* project, which bracketed Pushkin's marriage, was the poet's utopian hope that a woman of such fierce fidelity could exist at all – a woman who, unlike Doña Anna, could not be re-seduced. Family, children, a cult of the hearth were essential parts of this hope. It has long been assumed that Pushkin left his *Rusalka* unfinished (a single scene remained to be written), but the contrary case is more persuasive. The play ends abruptly, but with perfect 'roundedness': the innocent child who trembles under the Daughter's heart in the first scene appears incarnated, to bewitch the responsible party at the end. Rusalochka running to her father on the Dnieper shore echoes Dmitrii of Uglich appearing to Boris, and also the young Tsar Fedor Borisovich whom his father could not save. But in this fairytale setting, the dynamic is de-historicised and death is not forever.

Theatrical consciousness and dramatic wisdom

How might one sum up Pushkin's dramatic genius? First, staged art, to be profound, did not have to be busy, over-full or long. A poetics of *Rusalka* and the *Little Tragedies* invokes the ideal of 'chamber drama' by analogy with eighteenth-century 'chamber music'.[36] Even *Boris Godunov*, with its mob scenes, military battles and cast of many dozens, could be staged almost neoclassically, for each scene revolves around key conversations or confessions with a handful of participants.

Second, drama for Pushkin was essentially a retelling. Stories came from Karamzin, Mérimée, Shenstone, Wilson, or more broadly from European legend. Because he retells, the playwright is free to dramatise only thresholds, interweaving his personal experience with universal plots. But Pushkin's use of the threshold is extraordinarily complex. In his dramas there is no protagonist, only antagonists. We cannot tell whose fate to follow. Boris and the Pretender never meet, and each fades out before the end of the play (in the original *Komediia*, both names had equal billing). Even the Baron and Don Juan are storyless without their antagonists. The main plot line of *Rusalka* is equally compelling told from the perspective of the Prince, the Miller or the Daughter. This impulse to decentralise lyrical perspective, to dare to dispense with a narrator and thereby to even the playing field for all consciousnesses, may have prompted Pushkin to include dramatic inserts or 'patches' in the long poems.

Finally: if all the world's a stage, then the mark of a competent playwright is to exercise constraint on that stage, to remain within the mind of each antagonist and speak only from that delimited place. Pushkin's friends noticed this aspect of the poet's remarkable readings of *Boris* in the fall of 1826. 'Pushkin was born for drama', Ivan Kireevskii wrote in 1828, remembering those readings; even in his long poems each part strives to break loose and speak its own truth, which means 'he is too multisided and objective to be a lyricist'.[37] About that judgement, readers of Pushkin will never agree.

NOTES

1. For the French 'war of dramatic manifestos' in the 1820s, see Douglas Clayton, *Dimitry's Shade: a Reading of Alexander Pushkin's Boris Godunov*, Evanston, IL, Northwestern University Press, 2004, pp. 30–53.
2. S. Fomichev, 'Dramaturgiia A. S. Pushkina', in *Istoriia russkoi dramaturgii (XVII – pervaia polovina XIX veka)*, Leningrad, Nauka, 1982, pp. 261–95, here p. 261.
3. Modest Musorgsky's *Boris Godunov* (1869–74); Alexander Dargomyzhskii's *The Stone Guest* (premiered 1872); Nikolai Rimskii-Korsakov's *Mozart and Salieri* (1898); César Cui, *Pir vo vremia chumy* (1900).
4. Simon Karlinsky, *Russian Drama from its Beginnings to the Age of Pushkin*, Berkeley, CA, University of California Press, 1985, pp. 312–38. Karlinsky dismisses *Boris Godunov* as an inferior play. See also M. Virolainen, 'Dramaturgiia Pushkina', in David M. Bethea (ed.), *The Pushkin Handbook*, Madison, WI, University of Wisconsin Press, 2006, pp. 190–209.
5. For this Soviet-era line, see Sergei Bondi, *O Pushkine: stat'i i issledovaniia*, Moscow, Khudozhestvennaia literatura, 1978.
6. S. A. Nebol'sin, 'Drama Pushkina, evropeiskaia drama i sovremennyi teatr', in his *Pushkin i evropeiskaia traditsiia*, Moscow, Nasledie, 1999, pp. 13–29, here p. 17.
7. See Alexander Dolinin, 'Pushkin and English literature', in Bethea (ed.), *The Pushkin Handbook*, pp. 424–57.
8. Abram Tertz (Andrei Sinyavskii), *Strolls with Pushkin*, New Haven, CT, Yale University Press, 1993, p. 66.
9. 'Interes – edinstvo', 'O tragedii', *Pushkin: Polnoe sobranie sochinenii*, vol. xi, Moscow, Akademiia nauk SSSR, 1949, p. 39. Henceforth *PSS*.
10. See Chester Dunning, *The Uncensored Boris Godunov*, Madison, WI, University of Wisconsin Press, 2006, chap. 2 and 3.
11. See G. O. Vinokur, *Kommentarii k 'Borisu Godunovu' A. S. Pushkina*, Moscow, Labirint, 1999, pp. 323–35; and S. Bondi, 'Dramaturgiia Pushkina i russkaia dramaturgiia XIX veka', in *Pushkin: Rodonachal'nik novoi russkoi literatury*, Moscow, Leningrad, Akademiia nauk, 1941, pp. 365–436, here p. 381.
12. John Bayley, *Pushkin: a Comparative Commentary*, Cambridge University Press, 1971, p. 109.

13. See especially Pushkin's draft of a letter to N. N. Raevskii *fils*, 30 January or 30 June 1829, in J. Thomas Shaw (ed.), *Letters of Alexander Pushkin*, Madison, WI, University of Wisconsin Press, 1967, pp. 365–66.
14. S. P. Shevyrev, 'Rasskazy o Pushkine', in V. E. Vatsuro *et al.* (eds.), *A. S. Pushkin v vospominaniiakh sovremennikov*, 2 vols., Moscow, Khudozhestvennaia literatura, 1974, vol. ii, p. 40.
15. See Pushkin's request to Pletnev, 29 October 1830, in Shaw (ed.), *Letters*, p. 434.
16. Compare Tertz (Sinyavskii), *Strolls with Pushkin*, pp. 60–69.
17. *PSS*, vol. xi, pp. 177–83 ('O narodnoi drame i drame *Marfa Posadnitsa*', 1830).
18. I. L. Popova, '*Boris Godunov*: misteriinye korni narodnoi dramy', *Moskovskii Pushkinist*, vol. vii, Moscow, Nasledie, 2000, pp. 65–73.
19. See Tatiana Wolff (ed. and trans.), *Pushkin on Literature*, rev. edn., Stanford University Press, 1986, pp. 245–50, here p. 247.
20. Letter of Pushkin to Pletnev, 9 December 1830, in Shaw (ed.), *Letters*, p. 446. 'Covetous' in the title has been changed to 'miserly'. See n. 25 below.
21. See M. A. Tsiavlovskii in *PSS*, vol. xvii, 'Rukoiu Pushkina', Moscow, Voskresenie, 1997, pp. 213–15.
22. N. V. Beliak and M. N. Virolainen, '*Malenkie tragedii* kak kul'turnyi epos novoevropeiskoi istorii', in *Pushkin: Issledovaniia i materialy*, vol. xiv, Leningrad, Nauka, 1991, pp. 73–96.
23. Two English translations provide useful interpretive essays: Nancy K. Anderson, *Alexander Pushkin: the Little Tragedies*, New Haven, CT, Yale University Press, 2000; and Svetlana Evdokimova (ed.), *Alexander Pushkin's Little Tragedies: the Poetics of Brevity*, translated by James E. Falen, Madison, WI, University of Wisconsin Press, 2003.
24. Anderson, *Alexander Pushkin: the Little Tragedies*, p. 6.
25. The Russian title has conventionally (and inaccurately) been translated into English as *The Covetous Knight*; see Anderson, *Alexander Pushkin: the Little Tragedies*, pp. 199–200.
26. Richard Gregg, 'The Eudaemonic theme in Pushkin's *Little Tragedies*', in Andrej Kodjak and Kiril Taranovsky (eds.), *Alexander Pushkin: a Symposium on the 175th Anniversary of his Birth*, New York University Press, 1976, pp. 178–95.
27. In *Table-Talk* (1836): 'Molière's Miser is miserly – and that is all; Shakespeare's Shylock is miserly, resourceful, vindictive, a fond father, witty.' Quoted in Wolff, *Pushkin on Literature*, p. 464.
28. Svetlana Evdokimova, 'The anatomy of the modern self in *The Little Tragedies*', in Evdokimova (ed.), *Alexander Pushkin's Little Tragedies*, p. 119.
29. M. Gershenzon, 'Motsart i Salieri' (1919), in *'Motsart i Salieri', tragediia Pushkina. Dvizhenie vo vremeni 1840-e–1990-e gg.*, ed. V. S. Nepomniashchii, Seriia 'Pushkin v XX veke', vol. iii, Moscow, Nasledie, 1997, pp. 115–22.
30. Nadezhda Mandelstam, *Mozart and Salieri: an Essay on Osip Mandelstam and the Poetic Process* (1972), translated by Robert A. McLean, Ann Arbor, MI, Ardis Publishing, 1973, pp. 14–15.
31. See Anderson, *Alexander Pushkin: the Little Tragedies*, pp. 156–81; and David Herman, 'Don Juan and Don Alejandro: the seductions of art in Pushkin's *Stone Guest*', *Comparative Literature* 51:1 (Winter 1999), 3–23.

32. Marina Kostalevskaia, 'Duet – diada – duel' (Mozart i Salieri)' (1996), in Nepomniashchii (ed.), *'Motsart i Salieri'*, pp. 807–21.
33. The phrase is from Robert Louis Jackson, 'Moral-philosophical subtext in *The Stone Guest*', in Evdokimova (ed.), *Alexander Pushkin's Little Tragedies*, pp. 191–208, here p. 206.
34. Stanislav Rassadin, 'Posledniaia skazka', chap. 7 in his *Dramaturg Pushkin*, Moscow, Iskusstvo, 1977, pp. 297–358.
35. V. E. Retsepter, '"Vysokaia tragediia" ("Rusalka" i dramaticheskaia reforma Pushkina)', *Moskovskii Pushkinist*, vol. iv, Moscow, Nasledie, 1997, pp. 233–77.
36. See Evdokimova, 'Introduction', *Alexander Pushkin's Little Tragedies*, pp. 3–28.
37. [Ivan Kireevskii], 'Nechto o kharaktere poezii Pushkina', anonymous (signed '9.11') in *Moskovskii vestnik* 8 (1828), 195–96. Cited in Vinokur, *Kommentarii*, p. 204.

5

MICHAEL WACHTEL

Pushkin's long poems and the epic impulse

In Russian, the long poem (*poema*) is generally defined as an extended verse narrative in contrast to the shorter and less plot-oriented lyric (*stikhotvorenie*). Like all genre classifications, the term has its limitations. The long poem need not be antithetical to the lyric (indeed, lyric insertions are frequent), and some forms of the lyric can be dependent on plot.[1] Such ambiguities notwithstanding, Pushkin himself used the term, and it has become traditional in editions of his work.[2] Pushkin turned to the long poem throughout his career, completing ten and leaving substantial fragments of others. The present chapter focuses on *Ruslan and Liudmila* (*Ruslan i Liudmila*, 1818–20), *The Gypsies* (*Tsygany*, 1824) and *The Bronze Horseman* (*Mednyi vsadnik*, 1833).

Epic and mock-epic (*Ruslan and Liudmila*)

To the end of his life, Pushkin was as much a product of the Russian eighteenth century as he was of contemporary European Romanticism. Russia's eighteenth-century poets had established a hierarchy of genres, each of which demanded a specific style and vocabulary. At the pinnacle was the epic (*poema*), for the creation of a national epic was deemed the ideal means of 'legitimising' both the country and its nascent literary tradition. In practice, however, the eighteenth-century poets had far less success with the epic than with the solemn ode (*torzhestvennaia oda*), a relatively lengthy and formally strict poem commemorating events of national significance (battles and court festivities). To this genre they redirected the topoi, rhetoric and elevated lexicon prescribed for the epic. Pushkin studied this poetry at the Lycée, and his own 'Recollections in Tsarskoe Selo' ('Vospominaniia v Tsarskom Sele'), written for a school celebration, demonstrates a complete mastery of the odic style.[3] That he did not consider himself beholden to that tradition is evident in *Ruslan and Liudmila*.

Pushkin's work on an extended verse narrative attracted considerable attention, and when it finally appeared in print (1820), critics weighed in immediately. Few doubted the young author's talent, but many were puzzled by the work itself. Iurii Tynianov has called *Ruslan and Liudmila* a 'revolution in genre',[4] and indeed, it was the genre more than anything else that puzzled contemporaries. Even the poem's metrics caused confusion. It was written in freely rhymed iambic tetrameter, which would soon (thanks to Pushkin) become the standard for the long poem. But at this point it was a novelty. Iambic tetrameter had been widely used throughout the eighteenth century (even in the ode), but not in epics.[5] More striking still, Pushkin's lexicon violated the canons of the eighteenth-century ode writers (who felt that epic themes demanded epic style, that is, church slavonicisms) and of Pushkin's friends, who sought a 'middle style'.

The opening of *Ruslan and Liudmila* situates the action at the court of Vladimir in ancient Kiev. However, such temporally precise allusions quickly recede, supplanted by improbable heroes who left no trace in the historical record. At times, Pushkin appears to direct us to Russian folklore, but the motifs, such as the damsel in distress, the sleeping beauty and the heroic quest, are hardly unique to Russia.[6] Much more influential was the tradition of light verse and mock-epic, which Pushkin knew from French and Italian poetry. Even the authorial digressions, constantly interrupting the 'heroic' narration, were borrowed from western models.[7]

The plot of *Ruslan and Liudmila* concerns Ruslan's attempts to recover his beloved Liudmila, who is whisked away on their wedding day in the moment before they consummate the marriage. This abduction could set the stage for a Russian *Iliad*, yet rather than exploit its epic potential, Pushkin chooses to titillate his readers and manipulate their expectations:

> The precious hopes have been realised,
> The gifts of love are readied;
> The jealous garments fall
> On the Turkish carpets . . .
> Do you hear the enamoured whisper
> And the sweet sound of kisses
> And the interrupted murmur
> Of final timidity? . . . The husband
> Already senses raptures;
> And now they have arrived . . . Suddenly
> Thunder crashed, light shone in the haze,
> The lamp goes out, smoke rises,
> All around it has become dark, everything trembles,
> And Ruslan's soul freezes . . .[8]
>
> (*PSS*, vol. iv, p. 9: canto I, lines 108–21)

Using the familiarity of direct address, Pushkin offers us seemingly unmediated access to the bridal suite. His description is both visual (Ruslan's desires are projected in the line 'the jealous garments fall') and aural (Liudmila's 'murmur of final timidity'). Our voyeuristic pleasure is then cruelly interrupted, with the surprise accentuated syntactically (enjambment), rhythmically (the spondaic 'Gróm gríanul'), and through rhyme ('Suprug'/'vdrug' [husband/suddenly]). When eventually – and it takes another ten lines for this to become explicit – the reader learns that the heroine has mysteriously disappeared, he is almost as disappointed as the protagonist.

Pushkin devotes the rest of his poem to the quests of four heroes (Ruslan and three antagonists), who set off in different directions in search of the princess. The tone is often comic and at times overtly parodic. The humour is both situational and stylistic. Curiously enough, the most obvious parodied text was written not by any of the fusty eighteenth-century Russian poets (the most likely targets), but by Pushkin's friend and mentor Zhukovskii. In the fourth canto, Pushkin explicitly reminds the reader of the plot of Zhukovskii's recently completed ballad 'Twelve sleeping maidens', but turns these chaste maidens into seductresses. Upon hearing their tantalising song of invitation, Ratmir, one of Ruslan's antagonists, enters a mysterious castle. He is greeted by a 'swarm of charming hermitesses' ('otshel'nits milykh roi', IV.105 – the lexical clash of the religious and erotic produces a comic effect), who lead him to a 'magnificent Russian bath' ('k velikolepnoi russkoi bane', IV.112) and then to a sumptuous feast. At this point, the poet interrupts his narration:

> I am not Homer: in lofty verses
> He alone can sing
> The banquets of Greek warriors
> And the sound and foam of deep goblets.
> For me it is more pleasant,
> Following the footsteps of Parny,
> To praise with my careless lyre
> Nudity in the shade of night
> And the kiss of tender love![9]
> (*PSS*, vol. iv, p. 54: canto IV, lines 142–49)

This passage appears to demonstrate Pushkin's rejection of Homeric epic in favour of Parny, an affiliation both generic (erotic elegies) and stylistic ('careless').[10] Pushkin's love for Parny was genuine, and abundant evidence can be found throughout his early poetry. However, the dismissal of Homer demands closer attention. The humility topos ('I cannot sing of banquets') is itself a marker of high style, not of light verse. As so often in epic, in the guise of diminishing the poet, it serves to glorify him. Given that the first canto of Pushkin's work had featured a memorable description of a Russian feast at the court of Vladimir (I.38–60), the present statement cannot be taken at face value. Pushkin belittles his connection to Homer, yet simultaneously affirms it through his very denial (litotes).[11] Such a claim is admittedly expressed humorously, coming amid a parodic scene in what is essentially a brothel. Yet it found support among an audience eagerly yearning for a national epic. One of Pushkin's defenders even went so far as to name the *Odyssey* as a precursor text.[12]

Ruslan and Liudmila takes advantage of the trappings of epic, but the wealth of extraneous material and tongue-in-cheek humour undoes the potentially heroic plot.[13] Nonetheless, it contains individual episodes heavily indebted to the themes and language of eighteenth-century odes (for example, the battle of the Russians against the Pechenegs [VI.244–319], which delighted the arch-archaist Kiukhel'beker).[14] If nothing else, such passages raised hopes in many literary 'camps' for the appearance of a genuine national epic from this precocious author.

Ruslan and Liudmila was by far the longest *poema* that Pushkin was to write. The relative figures are striking: *Ruslan and Liudmila* (approximately 3,000 lines), *The Gypsies* (569 lines) and *The Bronze Horseman* (481 lines). Despite its popular success, there is little question that its sheer length precluded the lexical focus that Pushkin would bring to all subsequent works in the genre. In later long poems, the individual word is marked, and the reader is expected to think of the initial usage when it recurs. In *Ruslan and Liudmila*, such repetitions are virtually insignificant, and even stylistic variants of the same word are used interchangeably.[15] In the later long poems, carefully structured repetitions and internal echoes become an essential part of Pushkin's poetics.[16]

Epic as tragedy (*The Gypsies*)

It is difficult to recognise the author of *Ruslan and Liudmila* in *The Gypsies*. Though only a few years separate these works, Pushkin's life and poetic orientation had changed radically. In the Southern exile that followed the completion of *Ruslan and Liudmila*, he first encountered Byron's verse. Though the meeting was mediated by French prose translations, Pushkin still found much to admire in the impetuous Byronic hero, the exoticism of the plots and their fragmented presentation. According to Viktor Zhirmunskii, Byron's poetry represented 'freedom from conventions, from classical poetics, from the poor and decrepit rules and schemes of French classicism'.[17]

For all the talk of Byronic influence, Pushkin's Southern poems differ markedly from his English 'models'. Pushkin incorporated Byronic elements that he found congenial, but combined them with a host of other sources to create a unique form of Romanticism. The plot of *The Gypsies* concerns Aleko, who flees 'civilisation' to join a band of gypsies. He is initially attracted by the beautiful young Zemfira, whose father invites Aleko to stay 'until the morning . . . or longer' (lines 51–53). Aleko, about whom we – and Zemfira – know only that 'he is pursued by the law' (line 47), chooses to stay longer. He sires a child with Zemfira and participates in all aspects of gypsy life. After two years have passed, he discovers that Zemfira is unfaithful and, in a fit of rage, brutally murders her and her new lover. His revenge, a blatant violation of gypsy custom (as presented by Pushkin), leads Zemfira's father to rebuke Aleko, who remains behind as the gypsies continue their wanderings.

Like all the Southern poems, *The Gypsies* surprised contemporaries with its unusual narrative construction. Time passes either at lightning speed ('two years passed', line 225) or not at all (the constant plot repetitions, which suggest that gypsy time is circular rather than linear). Essential plot details occur 'off-stage'. For example, the sole reference to Zemfira and Aleko's child occurs in the sentence 'At the cradle [the old man's] daughter [Zemfira] sings of love' ('U liul'ki doch' poet liubov'', line 257).[18] In terms of genre, the confusion is vastly greater than in *Ruslan and Liudmila*. The narrative frequently veers off into drama, replete with stichomythia (verse dialogue in alternate lines), soliloquies and even stage directions. At two essential moments, the freely rhymed iambic tetrameter is interrupted by interpolated poems in other metres.

Beneath this chaotic exterior is a meticulously constructed work in which lexical, motivic and formal echoes compensate for uneven narrative development. A *kurgan* (pagan funeral mound) is where Zemfira first meets Aleko; it is also the place where he eventually murders her. The provocative song with which Zemfira declares her disdain for Aleko dates from the time when Zemfira's mother betrayed her father; in different ways, it reflects the fate of both generations. The domesticated bear, compulsively gnawing at its chains, offers an ironic (yet never explicit) commentary on Aleko; both are slaves within a world of freedom.[19]

The Gypsies is framed by two bird metaphors, and a comparison of these passages shows the subtlety of the work's architectonics. When Aleko first joins the gypsies, he becomes a 'free inhabitant of the world' (line 99), and

Pushkin – despite a few dark hints about his protagonist's past – inserts a joyful song in trochaic tetrameter:

> God's little bird knows
> Neither care nor toil;
> He does not carefully weave
> A permanent nest;
> In the long night he dozes on a branch;
> The fair sun rises;
> The little bird hears God's voice,
> It awakens and sings.
> After the spring, the beauty of nature,
> The hot summer passes –
> And fog and bad weather
> Are brought in by the late autumn:
> People are bored, people are sad;
> The little bird [leaves for] distant countries,
> To a warm land beyond the blue sea
> It flies away until spring.[20]
> (*PSS*, vol. iv, p. 183: lines 104–19)

In the Russian tradition, trochees are often linked to folklore. When inserted into an iambic poem – and amplified by diminutives, insistent negations (the first three lines of the song), and oral formulae (for example, 'solntse krasnoe', 'za sine more') – the association becomes unmistakable. This 'artless' song underscores the simplicity of gypsy existence. Taking his thematic material from the natural world, Pushkin shows that the gypsies (and their new convert Aleko) live in the present without fear (or care) about the future. In the subsequent lines, he explicitly compares Aleko to the happy bird, stating (albeit with a certain semantic tension between adjective and noun): 'he also [is] a migratory exile' ('I on, izgnannik pereletnyi', line 121).

At the end of the work, Aleko commits the murder, and Zemfira's father in effect banishes him from the tribe. After this speech, Pushkin reprises the poem's opening line ('Gypsies in a noisy crowd' – 'Tsygany shumnoiu tolpoi') to accentuate the notion of circularity. But this is repetition with a marked difference:

> [He] spoke – and in a noisy crowd
> The roaming gypsy encampment rose up
> From the vale of its terrible night dwelling.
> And soon everything in the distant steppe
> Disappeared; only one cart,
> Covered with a poor carpet,
> Remained in the fateful field.

Thus sometimes before winter,
In a time of hazy morning,
When from the fields there rises up
A flock of late cranes
And with a shriek rushes south into the distance,
One, struck by a fatal bullet,
Remains sadly behind,
Its wounded wing drooping.[21]
(*PSS*, vol. iv, p. 202: lines 521–35)

In contrast to the earlier folkloric passage, Pushkin here uses an epic simile, a highly oratorical trope with roots in Antiquity, but also common in Russian eighteenth-century odes. The key to an epic simile is not a one-to-one correspondence between the 'tenor' (the subject) and the 'vehicle' (the thing to which it is compared), but rather the rhetorical force that the simile attains as it spins seemingly out of control. This is the only epic simile in the entire work, and its presence is striking, even incongruous.[22] Rather than the generalised bird of the earlier passage, we encounter a crane, here not for folkloric associations but because of its Homeric provenance (e.g. the opening of book 3 of the *Iliad*). The emphasis is no longer on the natural world, but on the intrusion of human violence in that world. If the folkloric insert featured Aleko as a migratory bird, a 'voluntary exile' (the oxymoronic 'dobrovol'noe izgnan'e', line 176), the epic simile portrays him as an abandoned, involuntary exile.

Zhirmunskii has identified the source of this passage as the final lines of Byron's *Parisina*.[23] However, that poem ends with an extended comparison, not an epic simile. Pushkin did not simply borrow a Byronic technique; by casting his comparison as a stylisation of Antiquity, he profoundly altered it. Once the Homeric allusion is recognised, other perplexing elements fall into place. Pushkin's contemporary Viazemskii noted that the final line of the epilogue ('And there is no defence against fate' – 'I ot sudeb zashchity net') sounded like it came from the chorus of an ancient tragedy.[24] In fact, several elements of the poem recall Greek tragedy. Zemfira's father, the only significant character who lacks a proper name, is called 'old man' ('starik'). His speeches are lexically and stylistically inappropriate for an uneducated gypsy. For example, the final lines of his lengthy speech about Ovid (yet another reference to Antiquity) are syntactically so convoluted that even educated Russians parse them with difficulty.[25] His final speech, in which he chastises Aleko, is introduced by the verb 'rek' ('spake'), highly incongruous when applied to a gypsy. However, Pushkin is not aiming for 'realism' here; he is reaching back to eighteenth-century aesthetics, according to which a profound statement demands an elevated lexicon. In the larger context of the work, the old man plays the role of a Greek chorus. He is an elder whose views of life reflect the wisdom of his years rather than the ignorance that the educated but uncomprehending Aleko repeatedly attributes to him. Like the chorus in Antiquity, he observes and comments, but does not act (hence his essential passivity as a character). The old man recognises and accepts fate (an 'epic' perspective), while Aleko impulsively but ineffectively rejects it.[26]

In *The Gypsies*, Pushkin gives epic breadth to a Romantic escape-and-adventure narrative. This is not an epic in any strict sense, but rather Homer as reflected in Russian eighteenth-century poetics, where tragedy, ode and epic form a unified whole. Ultimately, the grim, fatalistic acceptance of life as a tragedy and of individual experience as endless repetition brings the work closer to Antiquity than to Byron. In the epilogue, the epic sweep becomes especially pronounced when the poet recalls how he himself travelled with the gypsies and repeated 'the tender name of dear Mariula' (lines 560–61), the woman whose betrayal set the entire plot inexorably in motion. This reference not only shows the chronology of the poem to be a continuum (reaching from the *Vorgeschichte* to the poet's own time and place), but also suggests that the poet is at the mercy of the same passions and punishments as his characters.

National epic (*The Bronze Horseman*)

Subtitled 'A Petersburg Tale', *The Bronze Horseman* draws its material from myth, history and recent events. Like *The Gypsies*, it reflects the poet's obsession with the role of the individual in society, but it also shows his increasing fascination with Russian history and, in particular, the person of Peter the Great. The Introduction begins by depicting Peter on an empty shore, dreaming of his future city. A hundred years pass in a single poetic line ('Proshlo sto let', line 21 – one recalls a similar device in *The Gypsies*), the glorious city is already built, and the poet celebrates its beauty. Part One introduces Evgenii, a lowly clerk, who aspires to marry Parasha and raise a family. His modest dreams are interrupted by the cataclysmic flood of 1824. At the end of Part One, Evgenii is precariously perched on a statue of a lion, water lapping at his heels, while the Bronze Horseman looms up before him. In Part Two, the flood recedes and Evgenii sets off in search of Parasha. Upon discovering that she – and her house – have disappeared, he goes mad. Wandering aimlessly, he finds himself before the Bronze Horseman and, in a moment of spontaneous rebellion, utters a threat to it. The statue seems to come alive and pursue him for an entire night, ultimately humbling him. In the final lines Pushkin portrays a desolate island landscape, adorned only by a house (presumably Parasha's) that had been dragged there by the flood's fury; Evgenii's corpse is found on the threshold and unceremoniously buried.

By Pushkin's time, it had become commonplace to compare St Petersburg to ancient Rome, a connection that Peter and his successors had cultivated. The famous equestrian monument that serves as the poem's title and symbolic centre exemplifies this tendency; it was created in response to the ancient Roman statue of Marcus Aurelius.[27] Even the lion statue that Evgenii sits upon has Italian origins; it is the traditional symbol of the Medici family.

Given St Petersburg's historical status as a 'new' Rome and Pushkin's focus on Peter as its heroic founder, *The Bronze Horseman* invites comparisons to Virgil's *Aeneid*. However, as in the case of Byron and the Southern poems, the differences are more illuminating than the similarities. Virgil's epic was essentially commissioned to glorify the present, but it ends long in the past. The many trials Aeneas undergoes are all of divine provenance, and they ultimately lead to a commensurate reward. In contrast, Pushkin completely avoids mentioning the difficulties that accompanied the founding of St Petersburg. The city turns from a swamp to a magnificent metropolis as if by magic. Pushkin's emphasis is on the suffering not of the past, but of the present.

What connects Pushkin to Virgil is the epic treatment of the subject matter. Once again, epic must be understood broadly, in the spirit of the Russian eighteenth century. In a brief foreword, Pushkin insists that his tale is based on 'truth' (*istina*) and even names the journalistic accounts he consulted. However, his depiction of the flood borrows more from Genesis than from the contemporary press. Pushkin uses the biblical word for 'flood' ('potop', II.147) and explicitly introduces the notion of divine retribution when 'the populace sees God's wrath and awaits execution ('Narod / Zrit [B]ozhii gnev i kazni zhdet', I.104). In this line the thematic allusion to Genesis is poetically amplified through lexicon (archaisms [*zrit*] and Biblicisms [*gnev*]) and diction (the monosyllabic words and consonantal clusters are typical of the eighteenth-century ode). Elsewhere, Pushkin uses the most obvious formal marker of epic style: an epic simile, which likens the flood to marauders who enter a village, wreak havoc and drop booty as they depart (II.1–14). In these ways, a recent event in the history of St Petersburg is given elevated, even mythical status. Indeed, the biblical substrate is amplified through references to Greek Antiquity (for example, Triton and Charon).

At the poem's centre is the contrast between the epic figure of Peter and the anti-hero Evgenii, the 'little man' who struggles to find his way in 'Peter's creation' ('Petra tvoren'e', line 43). Pushkin carefully parallels his antagonists thematically while differentiating them stylistically.[28] When writing about Peter and his achievements, the tone is elevated and the language odic. The passages about Evgenii rely on a distinctly prosaic type of language (befitting a *povest'* [tale], the genre designation in the work's subtitle). This technique is evident in the characters' very first appearances:

> And he [Peter] thought:
> From here we shall threaten the Swede,
> Here a city will be founded
> To spite [our] haughty neighbour.
> Here we are fated by nature
> To hack through a window to Europe,
> To stand with firm foot by the sea.
> Hither along waves new to them
> All flags will come to visit us
> And we shall celebrate on the expanse.[29]
>
> (*PSS*, vol. v, p. 135: lines 12–20)

> What then did he [Evgenii] think about? About the fact
> That he was poor, that through work
> He had to attain for himself
> Both independence and honour;
> That God might have given him more
> Brains and money. That after all there are
> Such lazy happy people,
> Idlers not terribly swift,
> For whom life is so very simple![30]
>
> (*PSS*, vol. v, p. 139: part I, lines 31–39)

In both passages, the characters think, but the distinctions are numerous and essential. 'And he thought' ('I dumal on'), though not a complete line of verse, is placed on its own line to give it prominence. In Russian, the lapidary phrase 'I dumal on' has the same intonational pattern as 'Let there be light' ('Da budet svet'), and in the context of the emptiness, land and water (compare 'On the shore of an empty wave' ['Na beregu pustynnykh voln'] of line 1 with Genesis i.2), the parallel is striking. A powerful rhetorical display follows, replete with archaisms ('otsel''), bookish syntax (the double dative 'po *novym im* volnam' [on waves new to them]), metaphor ('to hack through a window to Europe' – the 'window to Europe' originates in a French source Pushkin explicitly names in a note, but the brutality of the verb is his expressive addition), metonymy ('all flags' meaning 'all ships'), and synecdoche ('the Swede' instead of 'the Swedes'). Peter thinks in the first-person plural, reflecting a concern less with himself than with the fate of his people.

A godlike figure, Peter cannot be paraphrased: his thoughts – 'translated' into words – are cited directly. Evgenii's thought process, in contrast, is mediated. The narrator leaves biblical style behind, opting for an interrogative and almost chatty 'What then did he think about?' In fact, Evgenii thinks only about himself (singular). His pedestrian thoughts are expressed through uncomplicated parallel syntactic constructions peppered with colloquialisms ('uma nedal'nego lenivtsy', 'kuda legka'). While Peter ponders the future, Evgenii is mired in the present. When, in the subsequent passage (I.56–62), Pushkin finally gives an unmediated presentation of his thoughts, there is a shift to plural as he considers the future, but the 'we' is simply 'Parasha and I', and the future consists solely of domestic concerns.

It would appear, then, that *The Bronze Horseman* glorifies Peter at the expense of Evgenii. However, the plot development runs counter to this seemingly obvious reading. Peter's expectations for his city are fulfilled, but certainly not as he anticipated. It was he who insisted that 'Here we are fated *by nature* . . . To stand with firm foot by the sea.' In an odic reprise of this statement, the narrator had addressed the city (as 'grad Petrov', a standard eighteenth-century collocation): 'Let even the conquered element [nature] / Make peace with you' ('Da umiritsia zhe s toboi / I pobezhdennaia stikhiia', lines 86–87). Yet the events of the poem contradict both Peter's confidence and the hopes of the admiring narrator. The divine Peter is transformed into the demonic Peter, whose attempts to subdue nature lead to a world turned upside down. And the unassuming Evgenii manages to summon unforeseen powers to challenge Peter's hegemony.

Were the poem to end with the epic confrontation (rich in odic echoes) in which Peter subdues his challenger, it would be easy to conclude that Peter's work, for all of its brutality and tragedy, was a historical necessity. But Pushkin ends his poem quite differently, with an anti-idyll of sorts.[31] The locus is an uninhabited island without a blade of grass growing on it. The lexicon insistently draws on the nature description of the poem's opening. 'Empty island' ('pustynnyi ostrov', II.212) recalls the empty waves ('pustynnykh voln') of the poem's first line, the poor fisherman ('rybak', II.208) who stops there obviously reprises the lone fisherman who plied his trade on the river in pre-Petrine days ('rybolov', line 25). Even the decrepit house (which stands 'like a black bush above the water', II.215–16) recalls the poor settlements of the Finns, which 'showed black' in the first stanza of the Introduction (line 7). Both are scenes of sparseness and poverty, and they suggest the closing of a circle. Ultimately, the sound and fury of Peter and his superhuman quest ends where it began, with the inhospitable and indomitable emptiness of nature. In the form of the flood and its aftermath, the apparently 'conquered element' has triumphed over both Evgenii and Peter.

In his first Southern poem, *The Prisoner of the Caucasus* (*Kavkazskii plennik*, 1820–21), Pushkin had related an ill-fated love story between a Russian prisoner and a Circassian girl. To this elegiac tale, he appended an epilogue that glorified Russian imperialism, causing confusion in generations of readers. Was this a tale of individual emotions or a grand historical narrative of inevitable conquest? In *The Bronze Horseman*, Pushkin uses a similar technique, but turns it on its head. To the epic story of the construction and destruction of St Petersburg, he adds an elegiac conclusion.[32] The reader is torn between recognising Peter's divine mission and rejecting his brutal and ultimately futile attempt to usurp God's role. In unforgettable verses, Peter's legacy is both revered and reviled.

In his long poems, Pushkin displayed a remarkable ability to synthesise vastly diverse materials, styles and genres. Of these, the seemingly archaic epic – with its highly marked lexicon, tropes and syntax – assumed a position of special prominence. Pushkin never wrote exclusively in epic style, but by allowing it to coexist with more 'contemporary' idioms, he gave his narrative poems extraordinary breadth. In a brief sketch of 1825 'On the national element in literature', he approvingly cited Viazemskii's evaluation of the two most famous eighteenth-century epics: 'What is national about [Lomonosov's] *Petriad* or [Kheraskov's] *Rossiad* besides the proper names?'[33] The same criticism, of course, could be directed at *Ruslan and Liudmila*. However, in *The Bronze Horseman*, Pushkin did indeed create a genuine if highly idiosyncratic national epic. He showed Peter in a battle with destiny, but refused to judge the outcome: 'Where are you galloping, proud steed?' (II.159).

NOTES

1. For conflicting views of the long poem in Pushkin's day, see V. E. Vatsuro and S. A. Fomichev (eds.), *Pushkin v prizhiznennoi kritike 1820–1827*, St Petersburg, Gosudarstvennyi Pushkinskii teatral'nyi tsentr, 1996, pp. 69, 74, 207, 258, 263, 281, 315.
2. At times, Pushkin subdivided his long poems still further, into *poema* and *povest'* ('tale'). E. I. Khudoshina, 'K voprosu o stikhovom epose Pushkina kak tselostnoi sisteme', *Boldinskie chteniia*, Gorky, Volgo-Viatskoe knizhnoe izdatel'stvo, 1983, pp. 180–88.
3. Anna Lisa Crone, 'What Derzhavin heard when Pushkin read *Vospominaniia v Tsarskom Sele* in 1815', *Pushkin Review* 2 (1999), 1–23.
4. Iurii Tynianov, *Pushkin i ego sovremenniki*, Moscow, Nauka, 1968, p. 135.
5. Tynianov (*Pushkin i ego sovremenniki*, p. 136) overstates his case, but only slightly. See V. Zhirmunskii, *Bairon i Pushkin*, Leningrad, Academia, 1924, p. 328, n. 10, and A. N. Sokolov, *Ocherki po istorii russkoi poemy XVIII i*

pervoi poloviny XIX veka, Moscow, Izdatel'stvo Moskovskogo universiteta, 1955, pp. 326–55.

6. Russians often associate *Ruslan and Liudmila* with folklore because of the opening passage: 'There is a green oak by the seashore' ('U lukomor'ia dub zelenyi'). These lines, a veritable compendium of folkloric images, were written later (1824–25) and have only minimal relevance to the original poem. Even Pushkin's 'fairytales' (*skazki*) draw far more from western models than from native oral tradition. M. Azadovskii, *Literatura i fol'klor*, Leningrad, Khudozhestvennaia literatura, 1938, pp. 65–105.
7. G. L. Gumennaia, 'Pushkin i shutlivye poemy XVIII veka', *Boldinskie chteniia*, Gorky, Volgo-Viatskoe knizhnoe izdatel'stvo, 1982, p. 145. These digressions set Pushkin's work apart from the few examples of Russian eighteenth-century mock-epic. Contemporary critics rightly recognised, for example, Pushkin's debts to Bogdanovich's 'Dushen'ka', (1783), a Russianised rewriting of the myth of Cupid and Psyche. However, Bogdanovich's narrator does not digress.
8. Translations are my own. 'Svershilis' milye nadezhdy, / Liubvi gotoviatsia dary; / Padut revnivye odezhdy / Na tsaregradskie kovry . . . / Vy slyshite l' vliublennyi shepot, / I potseluev sladkii zvuk, / I preryvaiushchiisia ropot / Poslednei robosti? . . Suprug / Vostorgi chuvstvuet zarane; / I vot oni nastali . . . Vdrug / Grom grianul, svet blesnul v tumane, / Lampada gasnet, dym bezhit, / Krugom vse smerklos', vse drozhit, / I zamerla dusha v Ruslane . . .'
9. 'Ia ne Omer: v stikhakh vysokikh / On mozhet vospevat' odin / Obedy grecheskikh druzhin, / I zvon, i penu chash glubokikh. / Milee, po sledam Parni, / Mne slavit' liroiu nebrezhnoi / I nagotu v nochnoi teni, / I potselui liubovi nezhnoi!'
10. On the sources of this 'carelessness', see Svetlana Evdokimova and Vladimir Golstein, 'Pushkin's aesthetics: *Sprezzatura* in *Eugene Onegin*', in Lazar Fleishman, Gabriella Safran *et al.* (eds.), *Word, Music, History: a Festschrift for Caryl Emerson*, Stanford, CA, Berkeley Slavic Specialties, 2005, pp. 121–46.
11. The identical technique can be found in Pushkin's other mock-epic *The Gabrieliad*. In this case (lines 474–77), the similarity to Homer – which is, on the surface, mocked – is still more obviously relevant, because the premise of the entire work is to retell the story of the Annunciation (and the Fall) in the spirit of ancient Greece, where the immortals have the same earthy (sexual) appetites and character flaws as mortals.
12. Vatsuro and Fomichev (eds.), *Pushkin v prizhiznennoi kritike 1820–1827*, p. 29.
13. Mark Altshuller, 'Pushkin's *Ruslan and Liudmila* and the traditions of the mock-epic poem', in Derek Offord (ed.), *The Golden Age of Russian Literature and Thought*, New York, Macmillan, 1992, pp. 7–23. Proskurin (*Poeziia Pushkina, ili podvizhnyi palimpsest*) aptly entitles his chapter on *Ruslan and Liudmila* 'The sham *poema*' ('Mnimaia poema').
14. V. K. Kiukhel'beker, *Puteshestvie, dnevnik, stat'i*, Leningrad, Nauka, 1979, p. 414.
15. G. Vinokur, 'Nasledstvo XVIII v. v stikhotvornom iazyke Pushkina', in D. D. Blagoi and V. Ia. Kirpotin (eds.), *Pushkin: Rodonachal'nik novoi russkoi literatury*, Moscow, Akademiia nauk, 1941, pp. 524–5.

16. See L. S. Fleishman, 'K opisaniiu semantiki "Tsygan"', in Nils Ake Nilsson (ed.), *Russian Romanticism: Studies in the Poetic Codes*, Stockholm, Almquist & Wiksell, 1979, pp. 94–109.
17. Zhirmunskii, *Bairon i Pushkin*, p. 30. French classicism, of course, had been the primary source of Russian eighteenth-century poetics.
18. With his fanatic concern for concision, Pushkin removed a lengthy passage he had originally written about the birth of their child (vol. iv, pp. 444–50), leaving only the metonym 'cradle'.
19. Once again, Pushkin relies on metonymy, having Aleko lead the bear when the gypsies perform before villagers. Contemporaries criticised the fact that Aleko would take on such a lowly task, arguing that it was ignoble and not poetic. Ryleev thought it would be more appropriate were Aleko to become a blacksmith (vol. xi, p. 153), while Viazemskii thought he should be a horse-thief (Vatsuro and Fomichev, *Pushkin v prizhiznennoi kritike 1820–1827*, p. 321). But the connection of Aleko to the bear was symbolically essential to Pushkin, and it clearly trumped all other considerations. Pushkin was even willing to sacrifice metaphorical precision to this higher goal. The description of the bear as a 'fugitive from its den' ('Beglets rodnoi berlogi', line 239) is transparently inappropriate, since a captive animal can hardly be deemed a 'fugitive' – yet it has obvious relevance to Aleko.
20. 'Ptichka [B]ozhiia ne znaet / Ni zaboty, ni truda; / Khlopotlivo ne svivaet / Dolgovechnogo gnezda; / V dolgu noch' na vetke dremlet; / Solntse krasnoe vzoidet: / Ptichka glasu [B]oga vnemlet, / Vstrepenetsia i poet. / Za vesnoi, krasoi prirody, / Leto znoinoe proidet – / I tuman i nepogody / Osen' pozdniaia neset: / Liudiam skuchno, liudiam gore; / Ptichka v dal'nye strany, / V teplyi krai, za sine more / Uletaet do vesny.'
21. 'Skazal – i shumnoiu tolpoiu / Podnialsia tabor kochevoi / S doliny strashnogo nochlega. / I skoro vse v dali stepnoi / Sokrylos'; lish' odna telega, / Ubogim krytaia kovrom, / Stoiala v pole rokovom. / Tak inogda pered zimoiu, / Tumannoi, utrennei poroiu, / Kogda pod''emletsia s polei / Stanitsa pozdnikh zhuravlei / I s krikom vdal' na iug nesetsia, / Pronzennyi gibel'nym svintsom / Odin pechal'no ostaetsia, / Povisnuv ranenym krylom.'
22. Pushkin employs similar epic similes (with birds as the 'vehicle') in *Ruslan and Liudmila* (II.184–203) and in *Count Null* (*Graf Nulin*, 1825), lines 250–57, but for comic effect.
23. Zhirmunskii, *Bairon i Pushkin*, p. 71.
24. Vatsuro and Fomichev, *Pushkin v prizhiznennoi kritike 1820–1827*, p. 322. Viazemskii disapproved, writing in the margin of his own copy of the text, 'the conclusion is too Greek' ('slishkom grecheskoe okonchanie', Vatsuro and Fomichev, *Pushkin v prizhiznennoi kritike 1820–1827*, p. 458). However, he had not recognised the extent of Pushkin's allusions to Antiquity in this work, nor had he considered the motivation behind them. For a corrective, see Viacheslav Ivanov, 'O "Tsyganakh" Pushkina', *Sobranie sochinenii*, Brussels, Foyer chrétien oriental, 1987, vol. iv, pp. 299–323.
25. Viacheslav Ivanov cited this passage to prove that Pushkin's 'simple' style was not so very accessible after all. M. S. Al'tman, *Razgovory s Viacheslavom Ivanovym*, St Petersburg, Inapress, 1995, p. 40.

26. Tynianov (*Pushkin i ego sovremenniki*, pp. 144–45) sees Pushkin's experiment as placing Aleko, a 'lyrical' and 'elegiac' hero (the poetics of the early nineteenth century) in an epic context (the eighteenth century). See also Proskurin, *Poeziia Pushkina, ili podvizhnyi palimpsest*, pp. 108–39.
27. Alexander M. Schenker, *The Bronze Horseman: Falconet's Monument to Peter the Great*, New Haven, CT, Yale University Press, 2003, pp. 188–98, 287–89.
28. L. V. Pumpianskii, *Klassicheskaia traditsiia: sobranie trudov po istorii russkoi literatury*, Moscow, Iazyki russkoi kul'tury, 2000, pp. 158–96.
29. 'I dumal on: / Otsel' grozit' my budem shvedu, / Zdes' budet gorod zalozhen / Na zlo nadmennomu sosedu. / Prirodoi zdes' nam suzhdeno / V Evropu prorubit' okno, / Nogoiu tverdoi stat' pri more. / Siuda po novym im volnam / Vse flagi v gosti budut k nam / I zapiruem na prostore.'
30. 'O chem zhe dumal on? o tom, / Chto byl on beden, chto trudom / On dolzhen byl sebe dostavit' / I nezavisimost' i chest'; / Chto mog by [B]og emu pribavit' / Uma i deneg. Chto ved' est' / Takie prazdnye schastlivtsy, / Uma nedal'nego lenivtsy, / Kotorym zhizn' kuda legka!'
31. The unambiguous conclusion of the long poem *Poltava* (1828–29) provides an instructive contrast. In this case, Peter's decisive victory is followed by the ignominious disgrace of his rival. A hundred years later (the familiar 'proshlo sto let', *PSS*, vol. v, p. 63 [*Poltava* canto III, line 425]) Peter has created an 'enormous monument to himself' (canto III, line 434) while his enemy is forgotten (canto III, line 450). See Svetlana Evdokimova, *Pushkin's Historical Imagination*, New Haven, CT, and London, Yale University Press, 1999, pp. 202–04.
32. B. M. Gasparov, *Poeticheskii iazyk Pushkina kak fakt istorii russkogo literaturnogo iazyka*, Vienna, Gesellschaft zur Förderung slawistischer Studien, 1992, pp. 291–96.
33. *PSS*, vol. xi, p. 40.

6

IRINA REYFMAN

Prose fiction

Narrative experiments

Alexander Pushkin turned to prose fiction in 1827, when he began working on *The Blackamoor of Peter the Great*. The body of his prose fiction is not large: finished and unfinished works as well as outlines, sketches and variants fit into a single volume of any standard popular edition of his writings. Of about thirty contemplated works, Pushkin completed only four: The *Tales of Belkin* (1831), 'The Queen of Spades' (1834), 'Kirdzhali' (1834) and *The Captain's Daughter* (1836). Of these 'Kirdzhali', a biography of a brigand subtitled 'a tale', can hardly be called a work of fiction. It is a tale (*povest'*), only in the idiosyncratic sense Pushkin sometimes gives the word to emphasise the narrative's supposedly factual nature.

Prompted partly by the growing commercial success that other less talented writers were having with popular prose works, Pushkin turned his creative energies to writing fiction. Here, as in poetry, Pushkin remained committed to the principles he associated with high-quality literature, and while he may have aimed to make money in practice, he approached prose writing with the same spirit of refined experimentation, artistic innovation and irony familiar to readers of his poetry. The most productive analyses so far have identified either unsure experimentation or Pushkin's attraction to Romantic fragmentation as the causes of his halting results in prose fiction. Paul Debreczeny sees inexperience in Pushkin's search for effective narrative voices.[1] For Pushkin the central formal challenge of storytelling was how to develop a narrative voice appropriate to his plot. In *The Blackamoor of Peter the Great*, the fragment of historical prose that developed out of non-fictional sources, he cultivated a detached mode of storytelling with the narrator functioning as a chronicler of events. The challenge of sustaining the omniscient mode of narration, which had little precedent in Russian fiction, may have led him to abandon this work.

In his first major work, the now classic *Tales of Belkin* (1831), he stepped away from his omniscient narrator, appropriating instead conventions like the frame tale of the found manuscript and the fictitious narrator. These devices had been successfully used by popular writers like Washington Irving, E. T. A. Hoffman and, above all, Sir Walter Scott. The *Tales of Belkin* are introduced in a preface by the publisher (known only as A. P.) who relates how the works were discovered in manuscript after Belkin's death and sent to him for posthumous publication. Each tale is the work of a different internal narrator who tells his or her story to Belkin. It is never clear whether Belkin is an able transcriber of the stories of these characters; or a purveyor of hackneyed plots with no awareness of his unoriginality; or whether he is a parodist of genius. As a cycle, the five stories show a mastery of the main fictional codes of the period and reveal Pushkin's gift for telling a story (or, in Debreczeny's phrase, playacting). Yet even as Belkin's distressed heroes and heroines convincingly relate their tales of military adventure ('The Shot'), successful and unhappy courtship ('The Blizzard'), prodigal morals ('The Stationmaster') and sentimental love ('The Squire's Daughter'), the reader attuned to the wide range of literary subtexts gains an ironic perspective on these stories as parodies of their kind.

Experimentation remained the watchword as Pushkin attempted to work in longer forms. The few surviving chapters of a historical novel provisionally titled *Roslavlev* are largely told in the first person of the heroine Polina, but her personality is so passive that the narrative verges on the third person. Once again, Pushkin's ease in creating pastiche of first-person narratives clashed with his aspirations to produce an omniscient narrator. In the unfinished *Dubrovsky*, which is indebted to popular robber novels of the period (especially Scott's *Rob Roy*, 1818) as well as Stendhal's *The Red and Black* (1830), Pushkin managed omniscient narration on a much larger scale. The work is a significant step forward because it confirmed his growing ease with the formal variety and structural complexity of the novel, containing more types of description and dialogue than Pushkin had previously incorporated in any earlier fiction. *Dubrovsky* appears to have petered out only because the extant chapters exhausted the main plot. In his only completed novel, *The Captain's Daughter* (begun in 1833), Pushkin reconciled his ease in creating authentic-sounding first-person speakers with an omniscient narrator. The novel, which follows the adventures of a young provincial nobleman caught up in the peasant revolt of 1774, is told many years after the events by the older hero. Although the use of an older self creates a double perspective, Pushkin limits the younger narrator's knowledge of events: the narrator knows the truth about odd coincidences and unlikely outcomes, yet events are recounted with seeming objectivity and much of the historical narrative is in the omniscient third person. Pushkin's work as a historian led him to understand the Pugachev rebellion through eyewitness accounts, government documents and private writings. His work in producing a strict historical narrative facilitated his success in creating a third-person omniscient voice that could be spliced into Grinev's memoiristic account.

An alternative is offered to Debreczeny's approach by Monika Greenleaf, who argues that Pushkin tended to abandon his prose projects not because he was dissatisfied with the results of his experimentation with narrative modes, but rather because he was attracted to the genre of the Romantic fragment. Developing the Formalist critic Iurii Tynianov's approach, she suggests that the boundaries between Pushkin's sketched programmes and his finished prose effectively dissolved. In this view, the result was that sometimes his rough drafts became in themselves finished products.[2]

Modest as it is in scope, Pushkin's fiction, both completed and abandoned, proved crucial for the subsequent development of Russian prose. Nineteenth-century Russian prose writers, from Nikolai Gogol to Anton Chekhov, had Pushkin to thank for a rich variety of narrative techniques and generic forms, as well as for specific plot ideas. Gogol and Dostoevsky inherited Pushkin's use of a naive and unreliable narrator and borrowed some of his themes. In writing *Anna Karenina* (1877), Tolstoy was inspired by Pushkin's fragmentary attempts at a society tale or novel.[3] For his novel *A Hero of our Time* (1840), Mikhail Lermontov adopted (and adapted) the format of the *Tales of Belkin* as well as Pushkin's use of multiple narrators. Ivan Turgenev and Chekhov benefited from Pushkin's minimalist prosaics: his scant use of tropes, his preference for simple and straightforward syntax and (particularly Chekhov) his propensity to begin in *medias res*.

New approaches

Recent scholarship has begun to plumb the connection between Pushkin's 'life text' and his literary texts.[4] Read together, they reveal the extent to which different forms of anxiety surface throughout Pushkin's life as a frequent theme in his poetry and prose. It can be suggested that Pushkin's anxieties could have played a role in his abandoning some of his prose pieces. For example, the uneasiness about his mixed racial origin, intensified by his plans to marry, could have made it impossible for him to continue the story of his African protagonist, Gannibal, in *The Blackamoor of Peter the Great*. Pushkin's disquiet about the increasing commercialisation of literature and the corresponding rise of prose fiction could also be a strong factor in his not finishing *The Blackamoor* and, later, 'The Egyptian Nights'. Both sets of anxieties were linked by Pushkin's uneasiness about selling things that should not be sold: people, love, the fruits of artistic creation.[5] While it is always risky to divine the connection between a writer's creative psychology and biography, such speculation is worthwhile because Pushkin himself raised the issue of his black descent, first fleetingly in a footnote to chapter 1 of *Evgenii Onegin*, later when defending himself in his poem 'My Genealogy' against racist slurs cast by his literary enemies in 1830.[6] In general, commercial pressures made the late 1820s and the 1830s a period of creative anxiety for Pushkin, further exacerbated by questions of status that afflicted him as his position at court deteriorated.

I propose to probe concerns about rank and social status that form a theme in Pushkin's prose fiction. Pushkin's uneasiness about his social status, in general, and his service rank in particular is well known, and the way it makes itself evident in his poetry has been thoroughly studied.[7] His prose fiction, however, has been largely neglected. Its close examination shows that the issue of rank and status is present in virtually every piece and that it frequently constitutes the core of the narrative. Furthermore, in a substantial number of works it has clear personal significance. Manifestations of personal meaning differ, depending on what aspect of his self-image Pushkin presents in a particular work. Pushkin's many identities both in life and in literature included those of a Negro, a Russian gentleman of old bloodline, a poet and a member of high society, to name only the most important ones. Some identities brand him as an outsider, the Other; while others indicate his desire to be an accepted member of a group. Pushkin's sentiment about his Otherness was clearly ambivalent: he both highlighted and resented it. This ambivalence made him sensitive about his social standing and rank. The rest of this chapter will examine some of Pushkin's social anxieties as they manifest themselves in his prose fiction.

'An ugly descendent of negroes': Gannibal's integration into Russian culture

The Blackamoor, which fictionally sets the history of Pushkin's Abyssinian great-grandfather, Abram (Ibrahim) Gannibal, consistently foregrounds the status of his ancestor as an outsider both racially and socially. In Pushkin's reconstruction of court life under Peter the Great, Ibrahim's status as an outsider both in France and in Russia allows him to play the role of a mediator between the European and the Russian, the new and the old.[8] To fulfil his role as mediator, however, Ibrahim must be integrated, at least to some degree, into the societies in which he lives. In France, this integration is possible due to his merits: in the public sphere, he is accepted thanks to his education, intelligence and bravery; and in the private sphere, he succeeds by gaining the love of a high-society woman. In Russia, three integrative mechanisms are at work in the public sphere: the Emperor's personal favour, service and family ties. Ibrahim's integration depends on all three, and he seems to be on the road to success. However, he underestimates the importance of the private sphere, and the existing text of the novel suggests that this sets him up for failure.

Pushkin frequently evokes Ibrahim's status as Peter's favourite (that is, courtier earmarked for promotion). In the first paragraph of the novel, he calls Ibrahim Peter's godson (*krestnik*) and his favourite (*liubimets*). In the same paragraph, Peter's special treatment of Ibrahim is highlighted: the tsar abandons his usual financial prudence for the sake of his godson and generously bestows on him both money and 'fatherly advice'.[9] Pushkin continues to remind the reader about Ibrahim's status as Peter's favourite throughout the novel. Ibrahim shares the status of an outsider made prominent by Peter's favour with two other characters in the novel: the tsar's wife, Catherine, and Peter's childhood friend, Alexander Menshikov.

Ibrahim's status is also defined by his service rank. In France, he attains a considerable military rank, captain, earned in a military school and in the theatre of war. After Ibrahim returns to Russia, his designated rank of lieutenant captain is only superficially a demotion and, in fact, is an advance because he now serves in a regiment captained by the tsar himself. As a tangible sign of Peter's favour, the new rank represents a powerful tool for Ibrahim's integration into Russian society. Unsurprisingly, all Russian dignitaries immediately seek his friendship: 'The courtiers surrounded Ibrahim, each trying in his own way to show esteem for [*oblaskat'*] the new favourite' (p. 20).

Ibrahim's rank is supposed to make him a living symbol of a new kind of social hierarchy introduced by Peter: one based on merit rather than blood. Although Ibrahim rises due to Peter's favour rather than actual governmental service, Peter bestows both his love and the service rank on Ibrahim as a reflection of his merit. This is not necessarily at odds with Peter's social policy. The character of Alexander Menshikov reminds the reader of the fact that there could be worthy favourites (Catherine and Ibrahim) and unworthy ones.

The Table of Ranks and personal favour extended by the monarch normally provided opportunities for social mobility in eighteenth-century Russia; stability, on the other hand, came from family connections. The Rzhevskii household exemplifies the traditional social hierarchy of kinship (as instituted in the protocols of *mestnichestvo*) demonstrated by the order in which guests sit down for dinner. True to the custom of the day, Pushkin purposefully notes that 'the other guests sat according to the rank of their families, thereby evoking the happy old days of the order of precedence' (p. 27). It is significant that the prominence of Ibrahim's family in his native land mitigates the problem of his race for Rzhevskii: 'He is not of common birth', said Gavrila Afanasevich, '[h]e is the son of a black sultan' (p. 32). Ibrahim further strengthens his position with Rzhevskii by showing respect for the traditional clan hierarchy. Peter argues that Ibrahim's full integration into Russian society requires a union with the old Russian aristocracy through marriage, and Ibrahim accepts Peter's argument (p. 34): 'Marriage with the young Rzhevskaia will affiliate me with the proud Russian gentry, and I will no longer be a newcomer in my adopted fatherland.'

According to Pushkin's plans for the novel, Ibrahim's marriage to Natalia was to be unhappy: Natalia was to be unfaithful and bear him a white child. Ironically, the father of her illegitimate child was to be Valerian, a figure who, as orphan, ward and son of an executed state criminal, is a total social outsider and thus, in Rzhevskii's view, an unacceptable candidate for Natalia's hand. And yet, he was to win Natalia's heart and ruin Ibrahim's marriage. Ibrahim's full integration into Russian society was thus set to fail, and the failure was to be caused by his lack of success in the personal sphere.

It is well known that the life stories of the fictional Ibrahim and his historical self differ. Gannibal's and his descendents' integration into Russian culture, while ultimately successful, was even messier than Pushkin's fictitious account of it. Peter did not bless Abram's first marriage, because he was long dead by the time his godson married. Abram's first wife was not a woman from the Russian gentry, but a beauty of Greek descent who was repeatedly unfaithful to him and bore him a white daughter. Even before his scandalous divorce was granted, Gannibal cohabited with and then married a German woman who spoke no better than broken Russian, but was faithful to her black consort and gave birth to several children, Pushkin's grandfather Osip among them. Osip, in turn, did marry into a Russian gentry family, that of the Pushkins: his wife was a distant cousin of the poet's father. This first union between the exotic newcomers and the Russian gentry was not very happy: it once again included infidelities, jealousy and bigamy. It did, however, produce Nadezhda Gannibal, who once again married a Pushkin and gave birth to the poet, completing, it seems, the Gannibals' integration into the Russian social and cultural milieu. Colourful as they were, the lives of the historical Gannibals could hardly have served Pushkin's purposes in *The Blackamoor*. Their marital misfortunes cast doubt on the very success of their integration and thus on Pushkin's own place in Russian society – which could have been yet another reason for Pushkin not to finish this novel begun when he was in search of a bride.

'I am a Russian nobleman, Pushkin': the old gentry and the new aristocracy

While the Gannibal connection highlighted Pushkin's status as an outsider, his Pushkinian lineage should have placed him comfortably within the Russian privileged noble class. The Pushkins, however, were not a particularly prominent family: they did not belong to the powerful and wealthy group contemporaries dubbed 'the new aristocracy' which had risen to prominence in the previous century, in many cases thanks to their personal ties to monarchs. Pushkin attributed his family's marginality to their allegedly independent behaviour at several historical turning points in the seventeenth and eighteenth centuries, when the gentry had to take sides in the struggle for the throne. To compensate for his family's lack of present prominence, Pushkin laid claim to an old and respectable bloodline and asserted his ancestors' historical significance.[10]

Pushkin's own service rank was also remarkably insignificant, and his service career was utterly unimpressive. Upon graduation from the Lycée, he was appointed to the Foreign Ministry with the rank of collegiate secretary (tenth class), and never rose above the ninth class. In 1824, when Pushkin was ordered to live on his father's estate in Mikhailovskoe, he was dismissed from service without the usual promotion to the next rank – a sign of imperial disapproval. On 14 November 1831, at his own request, the poet was reinstated as a collegiate secretary at the Foreign Ministry. On 6 December 1831, he was promoted to the rank of titular councillor (ninth class). Pushkin's new service position brought him a yearly income of 5,000 roubles and access to the Imperial archives. On 31 December 1833, Pushkin was made 'titular councillor with the dignity of a Junior Gentleman of the Bed-Chamber (*kammerjunker*)', a courtesy title that implied greater personal favour from the Tsar than was in fact the case. The thirty-four-year-old Pushkin was deeply insulted by this undistinguished title, which, in his view, was unbecoming to a paterfamilias and renowned poet.[11] He never advanced any further.

Pushkin's awareness of the service rank system is evident in one of the *Tales of Belkin*, 'The Stationmaster'. The entire story, of course, is about differences in social status: its main character, the humble stationmaster Samson Vyrin (fourteenth class), loses his beautiful daughter Dunya to Minskii, a dashing young aristocrat and cavalry captain (seventh class). Convinced that Minskii will abandon his socially inferior lover, Vyrin travels to St Petersburg to save her, but is thrown out both from Minskii's quarters and from the apartment he keeps for Dunya. Years later Dunya shows up in her native village dressed as a *grande dame* and with three children in tow, only to learn that her father has drunk himself to death.

This inverted version of the standard fallen woman story begins with a lengthy discussion of the system of ranks in Russia. The first paragraph portrays the sorry lot of stationmasters, whose rank of fiscal clerk-of-registration (*kollezhskii registrator*) barely protects them from physical abuse at the hands of irate travellers demanding horses. It also outlines the complicated rank system that governs the dispensation of horses at post stations.

The third paragraph of the story describes the narrator's past youthful resentment of the rank system – which governs not only the dispensation of horses at post stations, but also the distribution of food at governors' dinner tables. By the time he tells the story, however, the narrator's rank has risen (the fictitious editor A. P. informs us that Belkin heard 'The Stationmaster' from titular councillor A. G. N.), and his resentment has apparently dissipated: 'Nowadays both the one and the other seem to me to be in the order of things.' He now seems to find wisdom in the rank system – or does he? He concludes wryly: 'Indeed what would happen to us if the rule convenient to all, "Let rank yield to rank", were to be replaced by some other, such as "Let mind yield to mind"? What arguments would arise! And whom would the butler serve first?' (p. 94). Such a 'defence' of the rank system actually mocks it as an absurdity that was bound to create awkward situations not only for the young A. G. N., but also, by extension, for the low-ranking Pushkin.

Another of the *Tales of Belkin*, 'The Shot', reveals Pushkin's discomfort with his social standing more directly. In this story, Silvio's opponent, Count B***, is portrayed as a representative of the 'new aristocracy'. Silvio calls him 'a young man from a rich and distinguished family [*znatnoi familii*]' and 'a brilliant child of fortune [*blistatel'nyi schastlivets*]'. He then again stresses the count's social prominence and wealth: 'Picture . . . an exalted [*gromkoe*] name, and money, more than he could count, in an inexhaustible supply' (pp. 69–70). The young man's title suggests the recent origin of both his exalted name and wealth (the first Russian count was Boris Sheremetev, who received the title in 1706, as a reward for putting down a revolt in Astrakhan).

We cannot tell whether Silvio is a middling nobleman or a foreigner (Silvio, the narrator informs us, is not his real name), but we have reason to believe that his conflict with Count B*** is as much over a difference in social standing as it is over a difference of dispositions. This supposition is supported by Silvio's behaviour as a duellist: it mimics that of many middling Russian noblemen who resorted to unconventional duelling behaviour (*breterstvo* or *bretteur* behaviour, as it was known) to force socially superior opponents to acknowledge their equal status.[12] Silvio resents Count B***'s nonchalant behaviour at the duelling site, rightly seeing it as dismissive and insulting. He wants the count to take him seriously, and to achieve this he violates the rules of proper duelling by interrupting the duel.

It seems, however, that Pushkin was not completely certain whose side to take, Silvio's or the count's, which signals his ambivalence regarding his own position *vis-à-vis* the two groups of nobility. It is telling that he distributed features of his own behaviour between Silvio and Count B***. He makes Silvio join Alexander Ypsilantis's uprising against the Turks (in which, the narrator reports, Silvio is killed) – an action Pushkin himself contemplated in the early 1820s.[13] At the same time, eating cherries under the barrel of a gun, the count's behaviour in 'The Shot', repeats Pushkin's nonchalance during his 1822 duel with the officer Zubov. Unlike Count B***, however, Pushkin withstood Zubov's shot and subsequently refused either to return fire or to reconcile – a harsher insult than the one inflicted on Silvio by Count B***, who shoots at Silvio and agrees to await the return shot indefinitely. Pushkin initially ended the story at that point (the manuscript of the first version states: 'The ending has been lost'). In this version, Silvio, like Zubov, would have been left without recourse. Two days later Pushkin added chapter 2, which reports on Silvio's retaliation.

'The Shot' was written in September of 1830 in Boldino, where Pushkin went to take possession of the nearby village of Kistenevka, allotted to him by his father on the occasion of his impending marriage. His situation thus resembled that of Count B*** as depicted in chapter 2. The fact that Pushkin was quarantined in Boldino because of a cholera epidemic that threatened him with death seems like a typically playful Pushkinian similarity. As Pushkin created his fictional character, he may have come to identify with the newly married Count B*** facing death because of youthful imprudence. The story reworks the denouement of this episode, thereby correcting his mistreatment of Zubov.

Pushkin's insulting conduct with Zubov was typical for the Kishinev period of his life. His years in Kishinev (a location that clearly was on his mind when he wrote 'The Shot') were particularly difficult for him socially. Lotman writes: 'A collegiate secretary and a versifier [*stikhotvorets*] in a world where everything was defined by rank, a person without means amidst people well provided for and spending money freely, a twenty-year-old youth amidst seasoned military officers or grand Moldavian boyars, Pushkin was a person whose dignity was constantly assaulted.'[14] One line of defence was Pushkin's perpetual readiness to duel. It is well known that his mentor in duelling affairs in Kishinev was Lieutenant Colonel I. P. Liprandi, a famous *bretteur* and Pushkin's acknowledged original both for the character of Silvio and for the story's narrator, Lieutenant Colonel I. L. P.

Not only does Liprandi split into two characters in 'The Shot', but one of them, the narrator, undergoes a strange metamorphosis in the course of the story: independent and dignified in his interactions with Silvio in chapter 1, in chapter 2 he inexplicably assumes an obsequious tone with Count B***. The narrator himself explains it with reference to current poverty: 'having grown unaccustomed to luxury in my poor corner . . . I now felt timid' (p. 72). While this might explain a momentary awkwardness, it cannot justify the narrator's servile tone throughout his brief conversation with the count, where he addresses him by title ('Your Excellency' [*Vashe siiatel'stvo*]) nine times. Moreover, he twice uses the title not as an address but as a substitute for the pronoun 'you' ('I bet Your Excellency could not hit . . .', p. 73). Such usage powerfully signals the speaker's implied lower status.

The narrator's behaviour is particularly conspicuous because there is no reason for him to feel inferior. Granted, at the time of his visit to Count B***'s estate, Lieutenant Colonel I. L. P. is retired and living in his ancestral 'poor little village' (p. 71). Nonetheless, his status as a gentleman, his respectable military rank (seventh class), and his education (Silvio, as we remember, liked to talk to him 'about different subjects', p. 68) make him the count's equal in everything but wealth. Furthermore, the narrator seems to be the only true exponent of the honour code in the story: it is against his reaction that the behaviour of the two duellists is measured. This gives him an enormous moral advantage over the count, who twice shoots at Silvio and does not endure a single shot himself.

Every first-person narrator is simultaneously the author's creation and his alter ego, and I. L. P.'s behaviour echoes Pushkin's own insecurities, both those of the Kishinev period and especially those of the time he wrote the story. About to be married and facing a cholera epidemic, he would have identified with Count B***, as I have argued. At the same time, living in Boldino, near his ancestral 'poor little village' of Kistenevka, Pushkin could not have failed to perceive the vast distance between them: unlike the count, he had no title, no service rank, no luxurious estate, no rich bride, and paltry independent income. The letters he wrote to friends when leaving for Boldino convey his concern that his royalties would not cover the cost of his wedding and impending household expenses. Pushkin symbolically purges himself of these worries by making his look-alike narrator in 'The Shot' fawn before the count. The exorcism worked: as is well known, Pushkin's involuntary sojourn in Boldino made the autumn of 1830 one of the most productive, and thus lucrative, periods of his life.

In the unfinished novel *Dubrovskii*, once again events are set in motion by a conflict between a wealthy and powerful upstart (Troekurov) and a middling nobleman (Andrei Dubrovskii). Pushkin begins by establishing the two characters' essential equality as noblemen: 'Of the same age, born of the same social class, and educated the same way, they were to some extent similar in character and disposition' (p. 146). This is how middling nobility and Pushkin himself would have wanted to see relations within the noble class. However, just as this way of thinking did not work in real life, it does not work in the novel: Troekurov accepts Dubrovskii as his equal only up to a certain point. As soon as he feels Dubrovskii has slighted him, he forgets their old friendship and begins to behave like an all-powerful and ruthless new aristocrat: he takes away Dubrovskii's village, Kistenevka (which, tellingly, is named after the village allotted to Pushkin himself in 1830).

Although Troekurov is introduced as a person 'of distinguished birth' (p. 145), Pushkin indicates that his prominence is of recent origin. As we learn from the ruling read during the court procedure that deprives Dubrovskii of his estate, Troekurov's father was of humble station: he began his career in the rank of provincial secretary (thirteenth class at the time) and eventually rose to the rank of collegiate assessor (eighth class).[15] Not only were provincial officials at the bottom of the state service hierarchy, but we cannot even be sure that Troekurov's father was a hereditary nobleman. For while the court ruling refers to the 'noble birth' of every noble person, it says no such thing about Troekurov. True, he did rise to the rank that would have secured him a place in the hereditary noble class, and Troekurov himself rose even higher, to the rank of general *en chef*, that is, full general (second class). Yet, for all his service success, Troekurov behaves like an upstart. He is boorish and enjoys flattery. Most conspicuously, he lacks the sense of honour expected from a gentleman: he agrees to take his friend's estate by means of chicanery.

In contrast, Dubrovskii is portrayed as a man of honour. A retired lieutenant of the guards (ninth class, but one should remember that the guards were the most respectable of all military services), he is independent and dignified despite his modest financial situation. He knows how to respond to an offence to his honour. In his reply to Troekurov's insulting demands he writes: 'I do not intend to tolerate jests from your serfs, nor will I tolerate them from you, for I am not a buffoon but a nobleman of ancient lineage [*starinnyi dvorianin*].' In fact, the last clause of his retort echoes the response of the nineteen-year-old Pushkin to a certain Major Denisevich who declined Pushkin's challenge to a duel because of the challenger's youth and low service rank. To this Pushkin responded: 'I am a Russian nobleman [*Ia russkii dvorianin*].' Denisevich was forced to apologise.[16] The connection is made stronger by Dubrovskii's concluding his letter with a formula that may indicate his readiness to duel: 'I remain at your disposal [*Za sim ostaius' pokornym ko uslugam*].'[17] Pushkin thus 'lends' Andrei Dubrovskii not only the name of his estate but also his own behaviour as a gentleman.

Pushkin does not have much in common with the younger Dubrovskii, the true hero of the novel and a quintessential Romantic outcast. Could this be one of the reasons Pushkin did not finish *Dubrovskii* and moved on to *The Captain's Daughter*, a novel full of personal significance? Among other things, the main character in *The Captain's Daughter*, Petr Grinev, is a poet, and one of Pushkin's goals in this novel is to examine a poet's behaviour amid social unrest.[18] In his other prose work of the 1830s, he is concerned with the poet's status in a society that did not provide a comfortable position for a writer of noble origin attempting to make a living by his trade.

'This rubbish': the poet as aristocrat and sell-out

Pushkin confronts this question most directly in 'The Egyptian Nights'. One of the two main characters in the story, Charskii, is a society man and a poet who conceals his gift, calling inspiration 'rubbish' (*drian'*), and hides from everyone when it overcomes him. He does this because, as an aristocrat, he does not fit the two prevailing institutions of literature in Russia: the system of patronage (inherited from the eighteenth century) and professional writing (taking shape in Pushkin's lifetime). Charskii cannot resolve the 'conflict between social position, literary commerce, and inspiration'.[19]

This conflict certainly had personal significance for Pushkin, who, particularly in his younger years, fashioned himself as a society man and dandy and was constantly on the alert for any attempts to treat him as a client looking for patronage. He wrote to his friend the critic Petr Viazemskii on 7 June 1824: 'None of us would want *the magnanimous patronage of an enlightened grandee*. This fell into decay [*obvetshalo*] together with Lomonosov. Our present-day literature is and has to be nobly independent.'[20] In the 1830s, without abandoning the dandy persona altogether, Pushkin came to respect the professionalism of his eighteenth-century predecessors. In his 'Journey from Moscow to Petersburg' (1833–35, published in 1841), he puts the poet and scientist Lomonosov's alleged flattery of his superiors in historical perspective and admires his occasional voicing of independence. He paraphrases Lomonosov's proud words to his patron Ivan Shuvalov: 'I do not want to be a fool either at the tables of high-born gentry or for other earthly rulers or even for the Lord God.'[21] Remarkably, Lomonosov's words are echoed in Dubrovskii's retort to Troekurov quoted above. Moreover, Pushkin would rephrase these words again, in his diary of 1834, in connection with his ill-fated title of *kammerjunker*: 'I can be a subject, even a slave, but a flunky and a jester I will not be even for the heavenly ruler.'[22] Pushkin clearly grew to perceive Lomonosov as a fellow writer and a worthy model.

Even more importantly, Pushkin came to respect professionalism. The eighteenth-century poet and literary theorist Vasilii Trediakovskii, earlier the butt of his jokes in the 1820s, receives high praise as a professional in the 'Journey' as well as in Pushkin's other writings in the 1830s.[23] Pushkin's new thinking shapes his concept of the professional writer in 'The Egyptian Nights'. Charskii's stated dilettantism no longer suits Pushkin, whereas Charskii's foil in the novel, an Italian *improvisatore*, for all his repulsiveness, embodies Pushkin's idea of a true poet. To be sure, the *improvisatore* seems to represent not only the worst case of clientage but also the commercialisation of literature in its crudest form: he sells the fruits of his inspiration directly to consumers, as if from a market stall. And yet, it is to him that Pushkin lends his own poetry: the two poems the Italian creates on demand. In contrast, we are not shown any of Charskii's poems. His refusal to acknowledge the importance of the reading public makes his writings irrelevant. It is entirely plausible to suppose that Pushkin's own similarity to the *improvisatore* unsettles the author and interferes with his finishing the piece. But in the fragment that has been written, it is the *improvisatore* who is Pushkin's alter ego.

Conclusion: a writer of prose as an insignificant person

As we recall, the first paragraph of 'The Stationmaster' discusses the sad lot of stationmasters, harassed because of their low service rank. The paragraph ends rather unexpectedly, with a statement on narrative talents of low-ranked stationmasters. They are declared better narrators than high-ranked officials: 'For my part, I must confess that I would rather listen to them than to some official of the sixth class travelling on government business' (p. 94).[24] In the third paragraph, as we recall, the narrator of 'The Stationmaster', seriously or not, hails the rank system that governs the distribution of horses at post stations and food at official dinners. He then abruptly returns to his story ('But let me return to my story', p. 94), leaving the reader to wonder how his apparent approval of the rank hierarchy reflects on his own ability as a narrator and, most importantly, on his previous statement that the hierarchy of narrative talent runs contrary to the hierarchy of rank.

As a matter of fact, in Pushkin's prose of the 1830s, none of the first-person narrators are socially prominent. The narrator of 'The Shot' is seized with a sudden social inferiority complex. The narrator of 'The Stationmaster', for all his apparent social success, remains a lowly titular councillor. The rank of the alleged narrator of the *Tales of Belkin* is not identified, but it is unlikely that this dull-minded fellow could have made a decent career in his seven years in an undistinguished infantry regiment. The narrator of the unfinished 'The History of the Village of Goriukhino' (1829–30), Belkin's double (initially, Pushkin planned to make the history Belkin's other creation), began his service as a cadet and, it seems, was able to rise only to the first officer's rank, that of ensign (fourteenth class). Even Petr Andreevich Grinev, the narrator of Pushkin's last work of prose fiction, *The Captain's Daughter*, who, like Pushkin, is of a 'good old family', is unable to rise above the very same rank of ensign. Greenleaf suggests that 'the poet in prose was one step away from the mad clerk, the next figure into which modern society would project its own sense of disorientation and self-pity'.[25] Pushkin's narrators of prose fiction, one may add, are also one step away from Gogol's pathetic heroes Aksentii Poprishchin in 'Diary of a Madman' (1835) and Akakii Bashmachkin in 'The Overcoat' (1841), both titular councillors scribbling away in mad inspiration.

As, of course, is the Titular Councillor Alexander Pushkin. In a fit of self-mockery, he gets the narrator of 'A History of the Village of Goriukhino' in trouble with higher-ranking officers for his love of writing and writers. Still a cadet, he spends a week in St Petersburg on official duty and, sitting in a café, spots 'B., the author' (p. 123). He chases after him to pay his respects, but, to his utter chagrin, he bumps into one officer after another, and every one of them stops him and demands that he stand at attention. B. disappears, and the poor cadet catches up with some solicitor instead. Chasing after B. – that is, Faddei Bulgarin, a financially successful prose writer and Pushkin's bitter enemy – and being stopped at every step by one's superiors could serve as a comic representation of Pushkin's own struggle for both respectable social status and financial success as a writer.

NOTES

1. Paul Debreczeny, *The Other Pushkin: a Study of Alexander Pushkin's Prose Fiction*, Stanford University Press, 1976.
2. Iurii Tynianov, *Pushkin i ego sovremenniki*, Moscow, Nauka, 1968, p. 162; Monika Greenleaf, *Pushkin and Romantic Fashion: Fragment, Elegy, Orient, Irony*, Stanford University Press, 1994, pp. 1–18.
3. See Boris Eikhenbaum, 'Pushkin i Tolstoi', in his *O proze. O poezii*, Leningrad, Khudozhestvennaia literatura, 1986, pp. 84–92; Barbara Loennquist, 'The Pushkin text in *Anna Karenina*', in Joe Andrew and Robert Reid (eds.), *Two Hundred Years of Pushkin*, vol. i: *'Pushkin's Secret': Russian Writers Reread and Rewrite Pushkin*, *Studies in Slavic Literature and Poetics*, vol. 37, ed. J. J. van Baak *et al.*, Amsterdam – New York, Rodopi, 2003, pp. 67–75.
4. Irina Reyfman, 'Poetic justice and injustice: autobiographical echoes in Pushkin's *The Captain's Daughter*', *Slavic and East European Journal* 38 (1994), 463–78; A. A. Faustov, *Avtorskoe povedenie Pushkina*, Voronezh, Voronezhskii gosudarstvennyi universitet, 2000, pp. 7–8, 164–242; and A. Ospovat, 'Imenovanie geroia *Kapitanskoi dochki*', *Lotmanovskii sbornik* 3 (2004), 262–64.
5. Catherine Theimer Nepomnyashchy, 'The telltale black baby or why Pushkin began *The Blackamoor of Peter the Great* but didn't finish it', in C. T. Nepomnyashchy, L. Trigos and N. Svobodny (eds.), *'Under the Sky of my Africa:*

Alexander Pushkin and Blackness, Evanston, IL, Northwestern University Press, 2006, pp. 150–71.

6. Catherine Theimer Nepomnyashchy, 'The note on curiosity in Pushkin's *The Blackamoor of Peter the Great*', *Pushkin Review* 4 (2001), 44–45.
7. Sam Driver, *Puškin: Literature and Social Ideas*, New York, Columbia University Press, 1989, pp. 67–76; Catriona Kelly, 'Pushkin's vicarious grand tour: a neo-sociological interpretation of "K vel'mozhe" (1830)', *Slavonic and East European Review* 77 (1999), 1–29.
8. Svetlana Evdokimova, *Pushkin's Historical Imagination*, New Haven, CT, and London, Yale University Press, 1999, pp. 153–54 and 169–71.
9. Alexander Pushkin, *Complete Prose Fiction*, translated by Paul Debreczeny and Walter Arndt (verse passages), Stanford University Press, 1983, p. 11. All subsequent pages from this edition are given in the text following a translated quotation.
10. *PSS*, vol. xi, pp. 160–62 ('Oproverzhenie na kritiki'); *PSS*, vol. xii, pp. 311–13 ('Nachalo avtobiografii'). See Mark Altshuller, *Mezhdu dvukh tsarei*, St Petersburg, Akademicheskii proekt, 2003, pp. 186–98.
11. For an overview of Pushkin's complaints, see N. A. Gastfreid, *Pushkin. Dokumenty gosudarstvennogo i S.-Peterburgskogo glavnogo arkhivov ministerstva inostrannykh del, otnosiashchiesia k sluzhbe ego 1831–1837 gg.*, St Petersburg, tipografiia A. Benke, 1900, pp. 38–40.
12. Irina Reyfman, *Ritualized Violence Russian Style: the Duel in Russian Culture and Literature*, Stanford University Press, 1999, pp. 80–84.
13. Iu. M. Lotman, *Aleksandr Sergeevich Pushkin Biografiia pisatelia*, Leningrad, Prosveshchenie, 1981, p. 78.
14. Ibid., pp. 86–87.
15. Pushkin inserted into the text of the chapter a copy of a real court ruling on a similar case, changing only the dates and names. See *PSS*, vol. viii, part 2, p. 164.
16. I. I. Lazhechnikov, 'Moe znakomstvo s Pushkinym', *Pushkin v vospominaniiakh sovremennikov*, 2 vols., Moscow, Khudozhestvennaia literatura, 1985, vol. ii, pp. 170–85, here p. 174.
17. *PSS*, vol. viii, part 1, p. 164. Debreczeny's translation, 'I remain your humble servant' (p. 148), does not convey this meaning.
18. Reyfman, 'Poetic justice and injustice'. On the importance of rank and name in *The Captain's Daughter*, see Ospovat, 'Imenovanie geroia *Kapitanskoi dochki*', pp. 262–64.
19. William Mills Todd III, *Fiction and Society in the Age of Pushkin: Ideology, Institutions and Narrative*, Cambridge, MA, Harvard University Press, 1986, p. 108.
20. *PSS*, vol. xiii, p. 96. The emphasis is Pushkin's.
21. Ibid., vol. xi, p. 254.
22. Ibid., vol. xii, p. 329 (entry of 10 May 1834).
23. Ibid., vol. xi, p. 254.
24. I have slightly altered Debreczeny's translation to emphasise that the narrator of 'The stationmaster' listens more than he talks.
25. Greenleaf, *Pushkin and Romantic Fashion*, p. 315.

7

OLEG PROSKURIN

Pushkin and politics

Pushkin was never political in the narrow sense of the word. He never occupied an influential governmental post, and penned no significant political treatises. Yet from the 1810s to the present day the most diverse socio-political groups have declared Pushkin their ally. He has been variously a conservative, a liberal, a gentleman revolutionary, an ideologue of peasant revolution and a stylised Orthodox monarchist. The reasons why such diverse factions strive to make Pushkin their own lie in his long-standing and unique symbolic significance in Russian culture. The most important task facing researchers today is to free the image of Pushkin as a political poet and thinker from this accumulation of later, often tendentious, stylisations.

St Petersburg: awaiting reforms

Pushkin's political views were formed in the liberal period of the reign of Alexander I. Taught by Alexander Kunitsyn, one of the most brilliant political writers in the liberal camp, Pushkin acquired at the Lycée his first ideas about the contractual nature of power, and generally about liberalism in the spirit of Charles Montesquieu, the eighteenth-century French political theorist whose work on constitutions set out a contractual relationship between absolute rulers and subjects. In Russia, the years 1817 to 1820 saw, however, a turning away from reform. It was also the period in which Russia's first secret societies came into being. Many studies often refer to the powerful influence which the ideas of Decembrism and of the activists in the Decembrist movement exerted on Pushkin during his St Petersburg period. Representing the early secret societies as an early stage in the revolutionary movement that led to the rebellion of 14 December 1825 distorts the history of political movements in Russia, creating an inaccurate perspective from which to consider the origins and evolution of Pushkin's political views. The secret societies of the 1810s (only a few of whose members went on to participate in conspiracies) were in the first instance a part of the Russian and European liberal movement. The most popular group, the Union of Philanthropy (*Soiuz blagodenstviia*), many of whose members Pushkin knew well, supported the efforts of the government to reform and to neutralise the conservative and reactionary opposition.

This was the milieu in which the young Pushkin found himself. It was in the house of the Turgenev brothers, an intellectual centre of St Petersburg, that he wrote his ode 'Liberty' ('Vol'nost''), the most important political poem of his St Petersburg period.[1] In March 1818, the Emperor Alexander made a sensational speech to the Polish Sejm in which he promised to grant Russia, too, the right to constitutional (or, in the Russian translation, 'legally free') institutions. After the Warsaw speech, calls to monarchs to organise power along constitutional lines lost their political pointedness. The ideology of the ode is in keeping with the thinking of Nikolai Turgenev in the years 1816–17, whose deliberations on constitutionalism had led him to draw a sharp contrast between an ideal 'English freedom' and the 'freedom' of the French.

In its ideology, 'Liberty' is a moderate poem in support of a constitutional monarchy. (The title itself indicates that it is an alternative to Alexander Radishchev's fiercely radical ode of the same name, composed in 1781–83.) Underlying the ode is a liberal conception of Law, based upon the doctrine of Montesquieu and political reformers, particularly the Swiss theorist Benjamin Constant (1767–1830) who in his *Principles of Politics* (1815) advocated a system of checks and balances and supported freedom of the press.[2] Law is understood as the foundation of Freedom, with its wellspring neither in the monarch nor in the people. On the one hand, Pushkin rejects the social egalitarianism professed by the Jacobin dictatorship; on the other, he aligns himself with Nikolai Turgenev in a debate which was of topical interest within the liberal camp: a debate about class equality. Another significant political poem of the Petersburg period is 'The Countryside' ('Derevnia'), written in the summer of 1819 after a visit to the family estate at Mikhailovskoe. It is closely connected with the issue of the emancipation of the serfs which was then being actively discussed. Between 1816 and 1818 several plans were presented to Alexander. Nikolai Turgenev believed that the emancipation of the serfs should unquestionably precede the granting of political freedoms. If the nobility gained political rights, they would gain with them the opportunity to put a stop to the debate about emancipation, which was not thought to be in their economic interests. For this reason, Turgenev insisted that the emancipation should take place *before* any serious political reforms were introduced and should be carried out under the aegis of an *autocratic* monarch whom the nobility dare not oppose. Turgenev's stance finds full expression in Pushkin's poem. Its ideological message is: Alexander freed the peoples of Europe from Napoleon's despotism and in so doing earned himself immortal glory; his task now is to free his own people from the yoke of 'slavery', and his glory will increase.

Since the Lycée, Pushkin had associated with dissenting Guards officers. Free-thinking hussars mixed liberalism with libertinism and indulged in criticism of the authorities, debates about a constitution and sceptical views on religion. This spirit found its fullest expression in the Green Lamp society (as discussed in Chapter 1).[3] The convivial atmosphere encouraged Pushkin to write numerous satirical and epigrammatic verses on political themes. One of the first such pieces – 'Noël' (December 1818) – is a topical re-working of a Christmas carol, following the French tradition. The extant version is a sardonic response to Alexander's famous Warsaw speech of 1818 and ironises the Emperor's promises of a constitution as nothing more than a fairytale. Boris Tomashevskii concluded that, disillusioned with Alexander, Pushkin doubted the possibility of reform and was 'gradually coming round to the idea of a revolutionary coup'.[4]

Was it really the ode 'Liberty', which was politically moderate and completely in line with Alexander's constitutional promises, which prompted such censure and persecution? In my view, what enraged Alexander was not its ideological doctrine, but the personal aspersions which could be read into it. In his so-called 'Imaginary Conversation with Alexander' ('Voobrazhaemyi razgovor s Aleksandrom', 1824/25) Pushkin would insist that 'Liberty' did not impugn the 'personal honour' of the tsar.[5] The historian Nikolai Karamzin secured from Pushkin an informal promise that he would write nothing against the government for at least two years; it was evidently supposed that he would mellow in the meantime. Pushkin's dispatch to the south became a political event which symbolised one of the last victories of liberalism at court. That is how it was interpreted by the majority of his contemporaries – an interpretation most favourable to Alexander. The Pushkin affair brought to a close the last 'liberal' period in the reign of the Emperor Alexander.

The age of European revolutions: from optimism to crisis

By exiling Pushkin in the hope that he would calm down and mature, the government inadvertently removed him to an even more liberal environment. Pushkin did not join any of the secret societies operating in the south and, what is more, appears to have been only vaguely aware of their existence. The political backdrop to Pushkin's time in Kishinev (1820–23) was a series of revolutions in Europe occurring nearby in the Black Sea region.

He watched with interest as the rebellion of the Greeks began in Moldavia in 1821 when a small army of Hellenes led by General Alexander Ypsilantis invaded and incited the locals to throw off Turkish control. A war of independence was declared in March 1821. Across Europe, as in Russia, the war was viewed romantically as a struggle between the ideals of the ancient Greeks and the occupying Turks who ruthlessly suppressed the descendants of the great men of classical Athens like Pericles, Socrates and Plato. By 1827, the Turks had succeeded in ending the unrest. Pushkin's initial response to the Greek uprising was enthusiastic. In his diary, he refers to the rebels as 'the heirs of Themistocles'. The Greeks are idealised in the spirit of classical heroism ('everyone spoke of Leonidas, of Themistocles'). In Russian society, the Ottoman Empire was regarded as the embodiment of tyranny and barbarity. By supporting the Greeks in a war with the Turks, Russia would be seen as a force for European enlightenment and freedom. Opposition circles nurtured the hope that liberals within the army would be able to exert a beneficial influence on Russia's internal politics. It was supposed that the troops heading off to war with the Turks would be led by General A. P. Ermolov, the governor-general of the Caucasus, who was popular among the liberals.

However, Alexander officially condemned the actions of the repatriated King Ypsilantis. This led to a series of events which are indirectly reflected in an important political statement made by Pushkin in the epilogue to *The Prisoner of the Caucasus*, a narrative poem which celebrates the Russian victories and the suppression of the Caucasian tribesmen (written in Odessa in May 1821). Some modern scholars have seen the epilogue to the poem as a eulogy to Russia's expansionist policies and have interpreted it as a tactical manoeuvre on Pushkin's part: 'Pushkin was possibly making a conciliatory gesture toward government officials, in the hope of winning release from his exile.'[6] This interpretation views the situation from too modern a perspective. In the first third of the nineteenth century the right of 'minor peoples' to an independent existence was not acknowledged at all, for they were not thought capable of autonomous political organisation. Thus the fate of the Caucasian peoples was seen by virtually everybody, including the most progressive political thinkers of the day, to hinge on but one issue: would they submit to Russian rule or would they be turned into an outpost of the inimical Ottoman Empire? The late composition of the epilogue is the key to its meaning. It was written in May 1821, just when the sultan, betting that Russia would not intervene in the Greek affair, issued a royal decree with a call to battle against the infidels. There followed the mass slaughter of the Greek population of Asia Minor and the islands; in April the patriarch of Constantinople was hanged. When news of the atrocities perpetrated by the Turks reached Russia, it inspired sympathy for the Greeks. The epilogue to *The Prisoner of the Caucasus* is an energetic poetic reaction to these events. Notably, General Ermolov is lauded not so much as the pacifier of the Caucasus, but more as the future conqueror of 'the East' as a whole, i.e. of the Turks ('Submit, East: Ermolov is coming!'). The epilogue is a kind of literary 'lobbying' for Ermolov to be named commander-in-chief in the coming Russo-Turkish war. It is not a piece of political propaganda conducted on behalf of the authorities, but rather an attempt to put literary pressure on them.

In 1822, the government cracked down on suspected liberals. It is notable, then, that the most outspokenly political statements and pronouncements of Pushkin's time in Kishinev were made in that very year. At this time Pushkin at last acquired a role akin to that of the local 'leader of the opposition' and his most important political text of the whole period was published under the deceptive and provisional title 'Notes on Eighteenth-Century Russian History' ('Zametki po russkoi istorii XVIII veka').[7] The text apparently summarises the arguments and discussions in which the officers of the general staff had been engaged. This 'historical' work has strong contemporary overtones: the history of Russia from Peter to Paul is seen as the key to understanding the present day and the future course of her domestic and foreign policies. Characteristically, it interprets the actions of Peter the Great as the actions of a Napoleon, a figure who despises mankind. Typical of Pushkin's stance at this time is his highly critical attitude towards the 'aristocracy', by which he meant all the nobility as an undifferentiated sociological unit. If asked to choose between the aristocracy and despotism, Pushkin would choose despotism because it created the conditions conducive to the obliteration of class boundaries, the spread of enlightenment and freedom for the people. Peter's despotism laid the foundation for ending serfdom, whereas a victory for the aristocracy would block reform.

Certain features that first appear in this period will come to be important in Pushkin's political outlook in the 1830s. Early traces of historical pessimism emerge in reaction to the failed European revolutions, which had found no widespread support among 'the people'.[8] The search for alternative models of political thought coincided with Pushkin's transfer to Mikhailovskoe.

Mikhailovskoe (1824–1826): the formation of a new historico-political outlook

Pushkin's new conception of politics was honed in an atmosphere of near isolation intellectually. Among Pushkin's reading at that time were the *Annals* of Tacitus, which leave their mark on the central work of the Mikhailovskoe period, the tragedy *Boris Godunov* (1824–25). Although set in the seventeenth-century Time of Troubles, its contemporary relevance is unmistakable. Tsar Boris, whose path to the throne began with the murder of the rightful heir, inevitably called to mind Alexander, who ascended to the throne by indirectly sanctioning the murder of his father. In Pushkin's interpretation, Boris's reforming ventures end in failure and popular disenchantment that lead to civil war (the Time of Troubles). The reasons Pushkin puts forward for the tragedy of Boris's reign reflect the transitional and contradictory nature of his political stance at that time. On the one hand, the reason for Boris's failure is the nefarious start to his rule with a murder that, because it flouts the law, brings with it a series of atrocities as moral punishment. At the same time, alongside moral evaluation enshrined in the law, history passes judgement on the political course of rulers. Boris, according to Pushkin, adheres consistently to a policy of 'suppressing' the hereditary nobility by humiliating and intimidating the descendants of the most ancient lines and acting against their political and economic interests.

Made aware of a secret society when his friend Ivan Pushchin visited him in January 1825, Pushkin undoubtedly contemplated a second Time of Troubles to come in Russia once Alexander's reign had come to an end. Pushkin's reading of Tacitus would have led him to expect an uprising in Russia supported by the humiliated nobility and inspired by the idea of a false tsar (hence the figure of the false Dmitrii, the Napoleonic usurper of his play). Thus a major change in Pushkin's ideology can be discerned. The markedly 'anti-aristocratic' position which he occupied in the 1810s and early 1820s is replaced by a different view: it is no longer the authorities, but rather the humiliated nobility which stands as a potential ally of the people. This view was a reworking of two others: Karamzin's view of the nobility as the natural mediator between the monarchy and the people; and the views held by former opponents in the liberal camp to which Pushkin had become more sympathetic.

For Pushkin, nobility of lineage ought to guarantee nobility of character, intellectual independence and personal honour. A man in possession of these qualities is capable of standing up to despotism. In a polemical exchange of letters with Pushkin, the Decembrist poet Konstantin Ryleev championed the principles of bourgeois democracy that could follow in the aftermath of a military coup. Pushkin did not believe that revolution would succeed in Russia (he saw bloodshed and unrest as the only possible outcomes of rebellion). Consequently, he viewed the autocratic monarchy as a stable institution in a Russia capable of internal change as guided by intelligent advisors. He maintained that co-operation between intellectual noblemen and the monarchy would be possible if the authorities showed respect for the intellectual (the monarch's equal), as a kind of cultural-political force.

Pushkin was soon given the opportunity to put this new political utopia to the test, when Alexander I died and was succeeded on the throne by Nicholas I, an event marked by the uprising of 14 December 1825.

The beginning of Nicholas's reign: attempts at an alliance with the government

Pushkin was unaware that many of the conspirators had admitted that his writings shaped their liberal convictions. In the tense atmosphere after the uprising it was also reported that new anti-government poems ('songs') written by Pushkin were in circulation. On 19 July 1826, a week after five of the conspirators were executed, a special agent was sent to the Pskov district with an open (that is, with no name stated) warrant with which to arrest Pushkin, should the report about the new poems be substantiated. Happily for Pushkin, it was not. Nevertheless, in the summer of 1826 his fate hung in the balance, without his realising it.[9]

On 8 September, Pushkin was received by Nicholas personally in the Chudov Palace in the Kremlin. Mystery surrounds the hour-long conversation. Natan Eidel'man's reconstruction of the interview can be accepted with a few modifications.[10] Pushkin was asked whether he would have been on Senate Square if he had been in St Petersburg on 14 December. He answered: 'Certainly, your Highness, all my friends were in the conspiracy, and I would have found it impossible to break with them. Only my absence saved me, and I thank Heaven for it.'[11] This admission attracted much tendentious interpretation during the Soviet era. Iurii Lotman doubted that Pushkin would have criticised the Decembrists at any length. Yet all the evidence suggests that the conversation did indeed focus on his differences of opinion with them, and these were the reason for his 'pardon'.[12]

After the Decembrist revolt, Pushkin attempted to enter into 'contractual' relations with the monarch as an autonomous party, in accordance with his newly-formed conception of the independent writer-nobleman.[13] In the course of the interview, the emperor for his own part became convinced of the huge impact of Pushkin's political verse, and he decided to exploit his pen for his own ends. At the end, the tsar solemnly announced his 'pardon', announcing his intention to act as Pushkin's 'first reader' and censor. This unprecedented gesture was seen by Pushkin (and later by his friends) as an unheard-of kindness; the kindness subsequently became a string of complications that made Pushkin perpetually subjected to the supervision of General Benckendorff and the intrigues of the Third Section.

A test of Pushkin's loyalty was promptly arranged. On Nicholas's orders, Pushkin was 'invited' to compose a 'Memorandum on National Education'.

He wrote the essay with the utmost caution, making skilful use of official discourse, and of quotations from and paraphrases of the 'Manifesto' of Nicholas I, but at the same time it was a work of great boldness. Adroitly turning the tenets of 'His Majesty's manifesto' to his advantage, Pushkin insists that the foundation upon which the state rests ought to be enlightenment. He attempts to separate the propagandistic and reforming activities of a group such as the Union of Philanthropy (with its strategy of peaceful co-operation with the government and the creation of the conditions in society necessary for the realisation of its plans for reform) from the Decembrist conspirators, who wanted to change 'the force of things' by armed uprising and who brought the country to the edge of civil war.

The exact nature of Pushkin's utopian hopes and the extent of his idealism at this moment becomes clear from the poem 'Stanzas' ('Stansy', 1826), which was addressed to Nicholas. It takes on a special meaning in the light of his 'Memorandum'. The poem is based upon an implicit parallel between Peter I and Nicholas I. The mythologised image of Peter as the ideal monarch was potent in the Russian literary and political tradition. To compare a new monarch to Peter the Great was a customary part of the Russian ode, since his image is central to the conception of enlightened monarchy. In Pushkin's case, there was a particular point to be made by aligning himself with this tradition: he proclaimed in public for the first time that autocracy was the most suitable form of government for Russia; only autocracy had the strength and the opportunities necessary to overcome society's inertia and carry out the reforms which were vital to the country. The fact that autocracy can stand '*above* the Law', once identified by Pushkin as a failing, is now seen as an advantage because it gives the Sovereign the right to be more merciful than the Law. It is as though Pushkin is calling on the emperor to take further steps in that direction and show new mercies to the conspirators who had been condemned on the basis of harsh laws.

But the political message of 'Stanzas' is not limited to an appeal for mercy. The poem establishes a parallel between contemporary history and an event from Peter's reign in which the nobleman Dolgorukii, while critical of the tsar, opposed the openly rebellious guardsmen (*strel'tsy*). Clearly this vignette stands as analogous to the opposition between the rebels of 14 December and a figure like Nikolai Turgenev, the moderate constitutionalist and deviser of economic plans. Indeed, it is no coincidence that the second stanza of the poem contains textual echoes of formulations used in the 'Memorandum on National Education' with reference to Turgenev. When he drew this implicit parallel between Turgenev and Peter's celebrated comrade, the honourable and independent grandee, Pushkin was not simply speaking of the importance of pardoning Turgenev, but was also hinting at the benefit of involving the former opponent of the government in the activities of the state. Thus Pushkin formulates his model of ideal power as he saw it at that time. Involving independent people in the institutions of power ought, on the one hand, to make allies of opponents and, on the other, to guarantee the dynamism of the new government, protecting it from stagnation. To a certain extent 'Stanzas' expressed the position of a group of intellectuals to whom Pushkin was close – both liberal (enlightened) conservatives (such as Zhukovskii) and moderate liberals (such as Viazemskii) – who endeavoured to lessen state terror and nudge the government's course in the direction of reform.

Pushkin published 'Stanzas' in the first issue of the journal the *Moscow Herald* in 1828. His ideas failed to strike a chord largely because his contemporaries' ignorance of the 'Memorandum' made the poem obscure. Many liberal contemporaries interpreted the poem as an act of sycophancy that tarnished his reputation.[14] He was obliged to justify himself and explained his position in the verse-epistle 'To Friends' ('Druz'iam', 1828). The poem emphasises those aspects of Nicholas's policies, both foreign and domestic, which were of greatest importance to Pushkin because they had inspired in him hopes of action: the start of the war with the Turks, and the development of a plan for the emancipation of the serfs. On all these points, a contrast was implied between the active and energetic Nicholas and the inert Alexander. The poem presents a strong case for the view that mercy is the most important feature of the aristocrats' 'ruling powers' (an aspect of the poem which is directly related to the plight of the victims involved in the rebellion). It also explains the mission of the poet as Pushkin understood it at that time: as a comrade to the monarch, called upon to assist in the beneficial reforms and the labours of the state. To the poet is partially extended the role of an independent assistant to Nicholas's government.[15] However, Pushkin's hopes that his voice would carry some weight in government decisions proved to be fruitless. Any pretensions Pushkin had to the role of a free ally of the sovereign and the government were, of course, utterly futile. But Pushkin had yet to fathom the extent of the government's antagonism and continued to contemplate an enhanced political role for the nobility. The essence of Pushkin's historico-political views on the matter is reflected in a series of drafts written in 1830, and especially in the drafts for the article 'On the Nobility' ('O dvorianstve'). Inspired in many respects by the ideas of Constant, who had insisted on the necessity of a house of peers, Pushkin proclaimed the nobility 'to be first and foremost a particular kind of political institution which ought to be granted corresponding social advantages that would safeguard its political mission'. Essentially, Pushkin synthesised the old ideas belonging to the aristocratic wing of the early secret societies in Russia with the recent ideas of moderate European liberalism.

No matter the importance of these ideas to Pushkin, they failed to gain acceptance by Nicholas and his circle for two reasons. First, Nicholas, who was working towards the bureaucratic centralisation of absolute power, generally denied the nobility the right to any sort of autonomous political activity. Second, any idea linked to the ideas of the July Revolution in France was bound to provoke nothing but suspicious ill will from Nicholas.

A Russian Tory

Pushkin watched political events both foreign and domestic with alarm. He had grave misgivings about Russia's intervention in 1831 to restore Russian control after an uprising broke out in Poland at the end of 1830. A more general revolt was possible and, in 1833, when the Russian harvest failed disastrously, a peasant uprising stirred. At this time his thinking focused on two questions: how to prevent a revolt, and how, if the need arose, to deal with it. Most of his political prose of the period is also devoted to these issues.

One of Pushkin's most important political texts from this time is the unfinished article usually printed under the editorial title 'Journey from Moscow to Petersburg'. It was begun in St Petersburg in December 1833, immediately after the completion of his work on the history of Pugachev. At this time Pushkin followed events in Europe closely. He was less concerned by the 'new order' in France than by events in England, particularly the parliamentary reforms of 1832 and the victory of the Whigs, which had brought to power the leaders of the mercantile and industrial middle classes. 'Journey from Moscow' contains strong criticism of the outcome of this victory – the dramatic development of capitalist relations in Great Britain. Parliamentarianism – at one time so attractive to Pushkin – now reveals to him its ugly side. The bourgeoisie is responsible for the exploitation and pauperisation of the proletariat, for social hypocrisy and so on. Such is the basis of Pushkin's criticism of bourgeois democracy, the reverse side of which is said to be 'repellent cynicism'.

Pushkin sympathised with the Tories who had lost power in Britain, and he developed a kind of 'Russian Toryism', characterised by an apologia for the landowning classes, an overstatement of the extent to which the interests of landowners and peasantry coincided, and an idealisation of the state of the Russian peasantry. He acknowledges the need for change, for improved relations between the classes, and indeed for an improvement in the lot of the peasantry itself, but he stresses that the changes should come about gradually, without upheaval. The government is expected to support the interests of the nobility ('society'), on the grounds of its supposedly special role in Russian history. Arguably, Pushkin was not really addressing the sovereigns of Europe, but the monarch of Russia, warning him that any deviation from the task of 'always being ahead' was fraught with revolutionary consequences. If it diverges from the principle of political priority, the state itself will be primarily responsible for its own troubles. As in the *History of the Pugachev Rebellion*, Pushkin has a second addressee – society (particularly liberal society). He explains to its members that an alliance with the government is their only way forward. Notably, when talking of the nobility here, Pushkin plays down somewhat the depth of the division between the new aristocracy and the hereditary nobility. He does so partly as a tactical concession, partly because he reasoned that in the face of a massive domestic threat any disputes should be forgotten and the unity of the class should serve to guarantee its safety from rebellions and revolutions.

Return to opposition

One of the central themes of Pushkin's writing at this time is the relationship between literature and power. The theme is developed in a series of articles intended for *The Contemporary* (1836). Foremost among them is the article 'Alexander Radishchev' (not passed by the censor), which on the one hand continues the critique of political radicalism which had been begun in the 'Journey from Moscow', and on the other embarks upon a critique of the state of politics under Nicholas. According to Pushkin, Catherine's government had apparently itself sought an alliance with right-thinking literary intellectuals, which rendered Radishchev's opposition baseless. Pushkin wished to contrast Catherine's rule with the present one,[16] which no longer 'felt the need' for the assistance of enlightened and right-thinking people.

At this point Pushkin revived his ideas about the special political role of Russia's ancient nobility. He criticises the Romanov government more harshly than ever before for 'levelling out' the classes. Having talked about it openly with the tsar's brother, Grand Prince Mikhail Pavlovich, he made a note of their conversation in his diary (which from 1834 onwards begins to read as a chronicle of life at court and among the aristocracy).

Pushkin's new conception of the Romanovs and of empire was embodied in his preparatory work on the history of Peter, to which he devoted himself in earnest only in 1835 (the extant synopses and material date to the period between January and December of that year). As he familiarised himself with the sources, the image of Peter which had been idealised by tradition underwent a complete transformation in Pushkin's mind. He began to see the titan Peter primarily as a despot and an 'impatient, autocratic landowner'. Compiling synopses of the source material, he notes the similarity between Peter and Ivan the Terrible, which had been acknowledged with some satisfaction by the monarch himself. He takes every opportunity to emphasise Peter's role in the suppression of the nobility as an autonomous political force. For Pushkin, who cherished notions of the high calling of the nobility, Peter was a 'wrecker' of dreams. As a result of his research, Pushkin starts to have doubts that his history of Peter can ever be published.

The utopian dream of independence finds expression in many ways in Pushkin's creative output in the final years of his life. He writes a series of pieces for *The Contemporary* which treat the independence of the writer from various angles. In an article about Voltaire's unpublished correspondence, the conclusion of which undoubtedly has an autobiographical subtext, Pushkin condemns the worthlessness and petty-mindedness of a great writer who grovels before the powers-that-be. The most important consequence of Pushkin's 'opposition' in general political terms was that he distanced himself from the formation of Nicholas's official ideology of the 1830s, the so-called 'official nationhood' (*ofitsial'naia narodnost'*). It was inspired and created by the education minister S. S. Uvarov, who in 1834 formulated its three-part slogan: 'Orthodoxy, Autocracy and Nationhood'. Uvarov sacrificed the concept of the nobility as an intermediary between the ruler and the people for the concept of class unity under the aegis of the monarchy. Using all manner of ploys, he was able to induce many of Pushkin's friends and allies, from Zhukovskii to Pogodin, to support the idea. He failed on just one score: he could not secure the co-operation of Pushkin himself. Uvarov's idea of the complete engagement of the individual with the state was at odds with Pushkin's idea of independence and personal honour, which had gained a new sociological colouring in Pushkin's thinking in the mid-1830s (an apologia for the independent class of the ancient nobility as an intermediary).

NOTES

1. See M. A. Tsiavlovskii, 'Khronologiia ody "Vol'nost'"' in his *Stat'i o Pushkine*, Moscow, Akademiia nauk, 1962, pp. 66–81.
2. Boris Tomashevskii, *Pushkin. Kniga pervaia (1813–1824)*, Moscow, Akademiia nauk, 1956, vol. i, pp. 159–72 ('Politicheskaia doktrina "Vol'nosti"').
3. For seminal reconstructions of the history of the group and its ideas, see P. E. Shchegolev, *Iz zhizni i tvorchestva Pushkina*, Leningrad, Khudozhestvennaia literatura, 1981, pp. 39–67; and B. L. Modzalevskii, *Pushkin i ego sovremenniki. Izbrannye trudy (1898–1928)*, ed. A. Iu. Balakina, St Petersburg, Iskusstvo, 1999, pp. 9–66. These studies provide a wealth of invaluable material but present too radical an image of the Green Lamp.
4. Tomashevskii, *Pushkin*, vol. i, p. 176.
5. *PSS*, vol. xi, pp. 23–25.

6. Susan Layton, *Russian Literature and Empire: Conquests of the Caucasus from Pushkin to Tolstoy*, Cambridge University Press, 1994, p. 102.
7. N. Ia. Eidel'man, *Pushkin i dekabristy*, Moscow, Khudozhestvennaia literatura, 1979, pp. 110–13.
8. In the so-called Alekseev anthology, Pushkin's 'Observations' appear next to a manuscript copy of 'The declaration of the Courts of Russia, Austria and Prussia', which had been signed in Ljubljana on 30 April (new style: 12 May) 1821. The declaration asserted the view that it was natural that the European revolutions had failed because local populations were bound to support outside intervention against disruptive revolutionary movements: 'They saw these warriors as the defenders of their freedom, not as the enemies of their independence.'
9. See Modzalevskii, *Pushkin i ego sovremenniki*, pp. 12–32, and N. Ia. Eidel'man, *Stat'i o Pushkine*, Moscow, Novoe literaturnoe obozrenie, 2000, pp. 381–402.
10. Reprinted in Eidel'man, *Stat'i o Pushkine*, pp. 166–212. See also P. E. Shchegolev, 'Imperator Nikolai I i Pushkin v 1826-om godu', in his *Perventsy russkoi svobody*, Moscow, Sovremennik, 1987, pp. 308–38.
11. P. I. Bartenev (ed.), *Russkii arkhiv*, Moscow, Izdatel'stvo pri Chertkovskoi biblioteke, 1867, col. 1065–8, contains a report made by Khomutova, based on her diary entry about her meeting with Pushkin on 26 October 1826.
12. The most important points of the conversation are summed up by the French historian Paul Lacroix, *Histoire de la vie et du règne de Nicholas I*, 6 vols., Paris, 1864–71, vol. ii, pp. 398–99.
13. For a thorough critical analysis of Pushkin's behaviour during the first half of 1826, see P. Miliukov, *Zhivoi Pushkin (1837–1937): kritiko-biograficheskii ocherk*, 2nd edn., Paris, n.p., 1937, pp. 49–53. Miliukov persuasively shows how utopian and flimsy Pushkin's plans were.
14. The most interesting example is the polemic response to 'Stanzas' in P. A. Katenin's poem 'Staraia byl'' ('An Old Story'), which has been investigated superbly by Tynianov.
15. Nicholas, who had read the poem, but who had clearly not understood its true political message completely, decreed: 'Cela peut courir, mais pas être imprimé.' As a result, the poem was published only after Pushkin's death.
16. The 1830s in general saw a certain mythologisation of Catherine's reign, which comes to the fore especially clearly against the background of the extremely harsh comments Pushkin made about her in the early 1820s. This mythologising tendency became an important part of the cultural and political stance adopted by writers in Pushkin's circle.

8

SIMON DIXON

Pushkin and history

Four years Pushkin's senior, Leopold von Ranke began his career as an obscure Prussian schoolmaster and ended it with an uncontested reputation as the nineteenth century's most distinguished historian. Published in 1824, Ranke's first book, *Histories of the Romanic and Germanic Peoples*, led to his appointment as a supernumerary professor at the University of Berlin in the following year. Since 1825 also marked Pushkin's first sustained engagement with a historical subject – his tragedy, *Boris Godunov* – let us begin by comparing these two great contemporaries. Although it is tempting to regard them as polar opposites in their approach to the past, Pushkin and Ranke each deserve a place on the spectrum of European historical writing prompted by the political demands and philosophical insecurities of the French Revolutionary era. As Goethe declared, 'Anyone who has lived through the revolution feels impelled towards history. He sees the past in the present and contemplates it with fresh eyes.'[1]

Ranke lived to the age of ninety, by which time he had published some forty-five volumes of formidable historical scholarship: nine more were to follow by 1890. Though Pushkin devoted much of the last decade of his short life to work on historical subjects, he completed but a single *History of Pugachev*, finished at Boldino in the autumn of 1833 and published a year later. Many of his most significant ideas about the past were expressed in a variety of fictional genres that Ranke would have dismissed as inherently inauthentic. Inspired partly by Shakespeare, *Boris Godunov* was written in the shadow of Nikolai Karamzin's incomplete *History of the Russian State* (twelve volumes, 1818–29). Karamzin's death in 1826 left a vacuum in Russian intellectual life that Viazemskii compared to that left in poetry by Byron and in contemporary history by Napoleon.[2] Since Pushkin could scarcely hope to fill the void merely by retracing the master's steps, much of his subsequent historical writing focused on a period Karamzin had left untouched and which Pushkin had already sketched in some acerbic 'Notes on Eighteenth-Century Russian History' in summer 1822 (see Chapter 7).

The epigraph – 'By Peter's iron will / Russia is transformed' – signalled that *The Blackamoor of Peter the Great* (1827) was intended as a commentary on the Petrine reforms as a whole. When the theme proved too ambitious for the anecdotal evidence on which it was based, the novel was soon abandoned. Narrower in both scope and significance, the epic narrative poem *Poltava* (1828) never achieved the recognition that Pushkin thought it deserved. Undeterred, he immersed himself in the historical debates that filled Russian journals – a glowing review of Ranke's first two books appeared in Mikhail Pavlov's journal *Atenei* in 1828 – and developed his long-standing interest in the work of the key French Romantic historians. Pushkin parodied the journalist Nikolai Polevoi's unsophisticated imitation of their methods, and those of Ranke's teacher, Barthold Georg Niebuhr, in an incomplete 'The History of the Village of Goriukhino' written in the summer of 1831.

By that time, his fascination with the relationship between past and present had been boosted by the need for money to support his marriage. So he followed up his petition to publish a political and literary journal, *The Contemporary* (*Sovremennik*), with a second, related request:

> Permission to engage in historical research in our state archives and libraries would correspond even more with my pursuits and inclinations. I do not dare and do not wish to assume the title of Historiographer after the unforgettable Karamzin; but I could in time fulfil my long-held wish to write a History of Peter the Great and his successors down to the Emperor Peter III.
>
> (*PSS*, vol. xiv, p. 256, to A. Kh. Benckendorff, not later than 21 July 1831)

Though this work remained unfinished at the time of his death, Pushkin completed *The Bronze Horseman* at Boldino in 1833, and worked on a fictional treatment of the Pugachev rebellion in parallel to his scholarly history. Though *The Captain's Daughter* (1836) was a unique confection, incorporating elements of both the *Bildungsroman* and the Russian fairytale, Pushkin openly acknowledged his generation's debt to Sir Walter Scott: 'In our age we understand by the word *novel* a historical epoch developed within an invented narrative' (*PSS*, vol. vii, p. 72).

While it was inconceivable to Ranke to question the supremacy of his critical approach to manuscript sources, Pushkin never regarded any single way of writing about the past as superior to others. On the contrary, he reproved Polevoi, a disciple of the 'novelistic' methods of French Romantic historians inspired by Scott, for having 'fanatically denied the existence of any other history' (*PSS*, vol. xi, p. 121). Since it was a part of the purpose of his experiments with genre to show that the same events could be experienced by different people in radically different ways, Pushkin's underlying pluralism of approach is matched by a multiplicity of perspectives that makes it perilous to identify heroes in his historical writings. Mocking the pretensions of scholars who posed as Olympian moral arbiters in 'The History of the Village of Goriukhino', Pushkin left his readers to resolve for themselves the tensions he placed before them and warned that even the most carefully considered research could generate only provisional conclusions. The *History of Pugachev* begins with an admission that it is incomplete and open to future correction, rather as Pimen's monologue in *Boris Godunov* had predicted that a monk in some later age would 'rewrite' (*perepisat'*) – rather than merely 'copy out' – his chronicle.[3]

The most important tension in Pushkin's historical writings was that between rulers and their subjects. No student of eighteenth-century Russia could doubt that the state had been the driving force in its development. Pushkin repeatedly acknowledged the point, laying particular emphasis on the government's vanguard role in matters of education and enlightenment. But since it was equally plain that the tsars' most glorious achievements – the construction of St Petersburg and the expansion of the empire – had been made at the cost of thousands of Russian lives, he was fascinated, too, by the scale of the sacrifice imposed on a people who followed the government 'always lazily, and sometimes unwillingly' (*PSS*, vol. xi, p. 244). *The Bronze Horseman* represents the classic literary treatment of the devastating social consequences that transpired when a visionary leader sought progress through coercion. But Pushkin was equally preoccupied with the dangers of popular passivity, an issue he had highlighted in a controversial stage direction at the end of *Boris Godunov*: 'the people remain speechless' (*narod bezmolvstvuet*). As befitted a writer who found the 'principal charm' of Scott's novels in their capacity to bring to life the 'contemporary, domestic' aspects of bygone eras rather than invest them 'with the dignity of history' (*PSS*, vol. xii, p. 195), Pushkin explored the problem not so much through the history of social movements as through the private lives of imaginary individuals.

Since such humble subjects lay largely beyond Ranke's field of vision, Pushkin, again paying tribute to Scott, drew on a wider range of sources than Ranke was prepared to contemplate. Pushkin worked assiduously, if fitfully, in the archives, reproducing documents verbatim in both his fiction and the *History of Pugachev*. Yet his technique was unorthodox even when transcribing manuscripts – he imitated Peter I's handwriting in his copy of one of the tsar's letters – and he never believed that manuscripts alone could convey a vivid sense of the past.

A sense of place was also crucial. Educated at the Lycée at Tsarskoe Selo, Pushkin had grown up in the shadow of Catherine II's favourite summer palace, already a shrine for her posthumous admirers in 1814 when he recited 'Recollections in Tsarskoe Selo' ('Vospominaniia v Tsarskom Sele') in the presence of Derzhavin, the most celebrated poet of her age: 'Every step here arouses in the soul / Memories of former years' (*PSS*, vol. i, p. 79). Tsarskoe Selo provided the setting for both 'I feel regret for the great woman' ('Mne zhal' velikie zheny', 1824) and the touching denouement of *The Captain's Daughter*, marked by a date replete with significance for its author: 19 October 1836, the anniversary of the Lycée. The spell cast by Tsarskoe Selo contributed to Pushkin's lifelong urge to visit sites of historic importance. Exiled in the south in December 1821, he was disappointed not to see the camp where Charles XII of Sweden had fled after his defeat at Poltava in 1709, but delighted to get inside the fortress at Izmail, whose storming by Suvorov in 1791 had been immortalised by Byron in *Don Juan* (Canto VII). When Pushkin came to write his history of the rebellion of 1773–74, it was natural to seek permission to conduct research in Orenburg province, where an aged Cossack woman showed him into one of the very huts in which Pugachev had lived.

The need to record the oral testimony of survivors from Catherine's reign seemed particularly acute at a time when most of the era's written legacy seemed destined to remain permanently beyond public scrutiny. Alarmed by the empress's reputation for licentiousness, Nicholas I repeatedly refused to sanction publication of more than a fraction of the sources under his control. These included Catherine's own memoir, in which she explosively implied that Tsar Paul, Nicholas I's father, was the illegitimate son of Sergei Saltykov.[4] Pushkin nevertheless acquired a copy, transcribed from a clandestine version almost certainly lent to him by Alexander Turgenev, which sent Grand Duchess Elena Pavlovna 'out of her mind' when he lent it to her in 1835 (*PSS*, vol. xii, p. 336). Pushkin took similar pleasure from regaling friends with a wide range of anecdotes about the most notable Russian figures of the eighteenth century. While some of these stories were drawn from published collections, many were culled from his own personal contacts. He had been particularly captivated by his wife's great aunt, Natalia Kirillovna Zagriazhskaia (1747–1837), daughter of the Ukrainian chieftain (*hetman*), Kirill Razumovskii. This aged livewire – one of a dwindling band of relics of an increasingly lost world – supplied Pushkin with most of the irreverent historical anecdotes that make up his *Table-Talk* (1835–36). The act of recording Zagriazhskaia's reminiscences prompted him to consider his own potential contribution to the historical record. Equivocal in his attitude to tsarist power, Pushkin feigned illness rather than attend the ceremony at which the sixteen-year-old tsarevich took an oath on reaching the age of majority at Easter 1834. Yet such absenteeism was not without its costs: 'From one point of view, I greatly regret that I did not see the historic scene and that it will be impossible for me to speak of it as a witness in my old age' (*PSS*, vol. xv, p. 130).

Pushkin's openly experimental approach to historical writing, his catholic range of sources, and his interest in private as well as public dimensions of the past, all reflected the informal institutional context in which he worked. The rigorous standards and specialist qualifications fostered by Ranke's seminar at the University of Berlin reached Moscow only in the 1840s under the aegis of his pupil, Timofei Granovskii, professor of world history at Moscow University, a liberal who debated Russia's historic path with socialist thinkers of the next generation such as Alexander Herzen. Russian universities in Pushkin's time were relatively underdeveloped and exerted only a limited influence on writers who operated primarily within overlapping networks of friends, patrons and a fickle commercial market. Viazemskii acknowledged Pushkin's friend and collaborator, Mikhail Pogodin, as a mind worth reckoning with *despite* his university affiliation. So although Pushkin kept himself abreast of developments in Western historical scholarship, his own judgements were formed independently, in conversation and correspondence with intimates and acquaintances, rather than under structured professorial guidance. That is one reason why his opinions were so trenchant. Already in 1824, Pushkin found French historians 'not a bit inferior to the English', by which he meant the Scottish Enlightenment historians, David Hume and William Robertson. 'If precedence is worth anything, then remember that Voltaire first set out on a new road and brought the lamp of philosophy into the dark archives of history.' Among nineteenth-century names, Pushkin singled out Pierre Edouard Lémontey as 'a genius': 'Read his *Survey of the Reign of Louis XIV* [1818] and you will place him higher than Hume and Robertson. Rabaut de Saint Etienne is rubbish' (*PSS*, vol. xiii, p. 102).

Only in the sense that he hoped to benefit financially from his work can Pushkin be regarded as a professional historian. By any other criterion, comparisons with Ranke reveal him as an amateur, rather than a professional, a poet, not a scholar. The one work in which he claimed to have 'set fiction aside' was the *History of Pugachev*: 'I fulfilled the duty of a historian in all conscience: I searched for truth zealously and gave an account of it without duplicity, without trying to flatter either Power or any fashionable mode of thought' (*PSS*, vol. xv, p. 226). Reviewing the book for the journal *The Northern Bee* (*Severnaia pchela*), Baron Rozen complimented his friend on his success: 'That our great poet was able not to be a poet in his History is precisely why he deserves the highest praise, and demonstrates how well he understands the immutable bounds of each of the fine arts.'[5]

Yet the boundaries between history and literature were surely more porous in the 1830s than Rozen allowed. For all their technical sophistication,

Ranke's histories were as accessible to the educated reader as they were to trained scholars. As consummate a stylist as Guizot or Macaulay, his mature works combined a novelist's powers of characterisation with the structural skills of a dramatist.[6] And if the greatest historians were masters of literary creativity, then fiction by no means precluded the quest for impartiality. Discouraging his Russian critics from searching for 'allegories, hints [and] *allusions*' in *Boris Godunov*, Pushkin lamented their failure to 'understand how a dramatic author could completely renounce his own way of thinking and transmigrate completely to the age he is depicting' (*PSS*, vol. xi, p. 68). Urging the dramatic poet to be 'dispassionate, like fate', Pushkin insisted that it was 'not his business to justify or accuse, to prompt speeches. His business is to resurrect a past age in all its truth' (*PSS*, vol. xi, p. 181). Here was a clear anticipation of Ranke's claim, in his 1854 lectures 'On the epochs of modern history', that every past age deserved to be studied on its own terms.

Not surprisingly, Pushkin proved unable to stick to his own self-denying ordinance on allusions. In April 1831, not long after the publication of *Boris Godunov*, Pogodin recorded a four-hour argument in which he defended the tsar against Pushkin's attacks.[7] Yet even when ambition exceeded execution, the sincerity of Pushkin's search for authenticity is not in doubt. He found that the essence of tragedy lay not in imitation of life but rather in 'verisimilitude of situations and truth of dialogue' (*PSS*, vol. xiii, p. 197). Plausible characterisation lay at the heart of all his most successful historical writing. And in the cause of psychological truth, he was willing to perpetrate all manner of anachronisms. As Viazemskii pointed out, there is probably no historical foundation for the scene in *The Blackamoor of Peter the Great* in which the tsar meets Ibrahim at Krasnoe Selo: 'but it is true psychologically, which is more important. It did not happen, but it could have happened; it corresponds to Peter's character, to his impatient and fervent nature, to the simplicity of his manners and his character.'[8] By contrast, critics warned that Ranke's scrupulous accuracy was no guarantee of objectivity. No Lutheran as devout as Ranke could hope to satisfy the Catholic historian, Lord Acton: 'few have committed so few mistakes', yet 'none is a more unsafe guide. The whole is untrue, but the element of untruth is most difficult to detect.'[9]

Descended from a line of Protestant pastors, Ranke saw God as a 'holy hieroglyphic' that only a historian could decipher, and history as a divine 'eternal poem' which it was 'the historian's task to read and translate'.[10] Pushkin shared his sense that historical events were connected by a hidden pattern that could be comprehended even if it could not be directly proved. But whereas Ranke portrayed the historian's task as a sacred calling, the superstitious Pushkin preferred the language of divination. The representation of medieval Novgorod at the opening of Karamzin's historical tale *Marfa Posadnitsa* (1803) impressed him as an outstanding example of historical intuition: 'What a scene! What historical authenticity! How well the diplomacy of the free Russian city is divined [*ugadana*]!' (*PSS*, vol. xi, p. 182). The vocabulary of fortune telling – a fashionable pastime for the Russian elite in the 1820s and 1830s as Pushkin showed in chapter 5 of *Evgenii Onegin* – is similarly crucial to his rejection of the notion of inevitability in history. 'Do not say: *It could not have been otherwise*', he warned in a review of Polevoi's second volume:

> If that were true then the historian would be an astronomer, and the events of the life of mankind would be predicted in calendars like solar eclipses. But Providence is not algebra. The human mind, as the common people's expression has it, is not a prophet but a guesser [*ugadchik*], it sees the general course of things and can deduce from it profound suppositions, often justified by time, but it cannot foresee *chance* – that powerful, instantaneous weapon of Providence. (*PSS*, vol. xi, p. 127)

Pushkin certainly emphasised the power of the unpredictable as a corrective to the French Romantics' inflexible teleology. But does this make his *History of Pugachev* a 'polemically archaized' challenge to 'the very notion of historicism'?[11]

Historicism is a dangerous word because it has come to acquire two radically different meanings. Much of the recent interest in Pushkin's treatment of chance and necessity has been designed to undermine implausible Soviet claims that he conceived of history as a progressive movement driven by social conflict. It was precisely the notion that history was ineluctably advancing towards some predetermined goal that Karl Popper attacked in *The Poverty of Historicism* (1957). Ranke, however, understood historicism to mean the opposite of this. Since, in his eyes, every historical period was 'immediate to God', he believed that every historical phenomenon had its own distinctive identity and that it was the historian's task to reveal its essence. That is what he meant by his celebrated aspiration, expressed in the preface to his first book, to show 'how, essentially, things happened' (*wie es eigentlich gewesen ist*). To grasp the essence of a particular historical period was precisely what Pushkin was trying to do in both his studies of the Pugachev rebellion. And his methods are surely more modern than archaic. Though 'strange coincidences' are shown to have affected the fate of both fictional characters and historical personages, it is also clear that Pushkin seeks to offer a rational explanation of cause and effect not only in the *History of Pugachev*, but also in *The Captain's Daughter*. In both works Pugachev embodies a historical process rather than accident, and both works aim to elucidate the events of the rebellion in terms of an underlying pattern of history.[12]

Closely related to Pushkin's belief in a general course of things was his Romantic conviction that every era has its own distinctive spirit of the age. He chided those who failed to keep pace with that spirit (*PSS*, vol. viii, p. 55) or whose thinking and character seemed stuck in the past (*PSS*, vol. xiii, p. 15). By the same token, he was hostile to any attempt to force the pace of history. The impatient critique of serfdom, published in 1790 by the writer and philosopher Alexander Radishchev and immediately suppressed by Catherine the Great, struck him as an obvious case in point. 'Of course, great changes must still take place,' Pushkin acknowledged in his 'Journey from Moscow to St Petersburg' (1834), 'but one should not hurry time, which is active enough on its own. The best and most enduring changes are those which occur solely as a result of the improvement of morals, without forcible political shocks, terrible for mankind' (*PSS*, vol. xi, p. 258). The hero Grinev expresses the same thought in *The Captain's Daughter*, exhorting his descendants to 'remember that the best and most enduring changes are those which stem from an improvement in moral behaviour, without any violent upheaval'.[13]

Sentiments such as these exposed Pushkin to charges that the imperial patronage bestowed upon him on his return from exile had forced him to sacrifice his youthful liberalism on the altar of Restoration conservatism. Reading *Poltava* in exile in Cheltenham, Nikolai Turgenev took its triumphalist tone as evidence of Pushkin's capitulation to the prevailing cult of Peter the Great. Pushkin couched his riposte to charges of sycophancy under the guise of praise for Karamzin, who, unable to contemplate writing his *History* in a private capacity, had returned to state service in order to embark on the work. Noting that Alexander I could hardly have been expected to free an extremist writer from censorship, Pushkin stressed that Karamzin had remained faithful to his imperial patron without compromising his own integrity: 'the *History of the Russian State* is not only the creation of a great writer, but also the feat of an honourable man' (*PSS*, vol. xii, p. 306). In stark contrast, Nikolai Polevoi's *History of the Russian People* (1829), a work driven by the dictates of passing fashion, had been 'written without meaning, without research, and without any conscience' (*PSS*, vol. xii, p. 286).

A second way of stemming his anxieties about toadyism was to create a persona for himself at the head of a long line of ancestors who, despite having been 'insiders' involved in some of the most significant events in Russian history, had nevertheless preserved a degree of detachment verging on dissent. This was the 'mutinous' Pushkin clan referred to by Tsar Boris. 'To take pride in the glory of one's ancestors is not only permissible but necessary', Pushkin insisted in summer 1827 at the time of his abortive attempt to construct a historical novel around the person of his maternal great-grandfather, Abram Petrovich Gannibal (*PSS*, vol. xi, p. 55). While the 'outsider' credentials of a former African slave were hard to question, Pushkin resorted to outright falsehood in claiming that his paternal grandfather had been gaoled in 1762 as a supporter of the deposed Peter III.[14]

This preoccupation with his own lineage reflected Pushkin's wider interest in the history of the Russian nobility. Three short drafts written between 1830 and 1834 suggest that he contemplated a full-scale study, never begun. If any feature of his work deserves to be called archaic, it is the defensive note that sounded in Pushkin's historical writings as loudly as it had in Nikolai Novikov's *Ancient Russian Library* (1773–75). In this series (which Pushkin possessed in the twenty-part second edition of 1788–91), Novikov had been anxious to publish descriptions of Muscovite noble genealogies in order to counter charges of barbarity levelled against Russians in the abbé Chappe d'Auteroche's *Voyage en Sibérie* (1768). More than fifty years later, Pushkin drew particular attention to Chappe's book among the many writings by foreign travellers in eighteenth-century Russia and still felt impelled to remind his fellow countrymen that 'disrespect for one's ancestors is the first sign of barbarity and immorality' (*PSS*, vol. viii, p. 42):

> An educated Frenchman or Englishman holds dear every line of an old chronicle in which his ancestor's name is mentioned – an honourable knight who fell in some battle or other, or returned from Palestine in such-and-such a year – but the Kalmyks have neither a nobility nor a history. Savagery, baseness, and ignorance have no respect for the past, grovelling only before the present.
>
> (*PSS*, vol. xi, p. 162)

Concerned that the Muscovite aristocracy had been usurped by wealthy parvenus in the age of Catherine II – a theme which recurs repeatedly from the 'Notes on Eighteenth-Century Russian History' to 'To the Grandee' ('K vel'mozhe', 1830) – Pushkin highlighted the damage done to the national memory by the rise of a metropolitan service nobility divorced from its popular roots: 'The nobility's family memoirs should be the people's historical memoirs. But what sort of family memoirs can one expect from the children of a collegiate assessor?' (*PSS*, vol. viii, p. 55).

In the Pugachev revolt, Pushkin had found a subject with a precise geographical location, a circumscribed time-span, and an uncontroversial sequence of events marked by an identifiable beginning, middle and end. None of these boundaries was easy to define when he turned his attentions to the Petrine era. *The Blackamoor of Peter the Great* resolves the question of geography by means of a simple binary contrast. The 'austere simplicity' of Peter's Russia – 'one vast workshop, where only machines moved, where every workman, a cog in an established process, was busy about his task' – is set against the ultimate symbol of European decadence, the corrupt and unproductive court of Louis XIV.[15] Yet so uneasily did the vision of Peter as a humble craftsman sit alongside the sacralised image in *Poltava*, in which Peter plays Christ to Mazeppa's Judas in the manner of an eighteenth-century panegyric sermon, that John Bayley thinks it 'sacrilegious' to seek to make the tsar the subject of a historical novel. Domestication was tantamount to vulgarisation, 'and respect itself became almost patronising'.[16] Chronology proved even harder to handle. Peter's innovative 'assemblies' – elite social occasions at which the presence of women was required for the first time in Russian history – could be contrasted readily enough with the patriarchal culture of the Muscovite boyars, treated far from unsympathetically in the novel. But if Peter was 'simultaneously Robespierre and Napoleon (The Revolution incarnate)' (*PSS*, vol. xii, p. 205), when could his reforms be said to end? One reason why *The Blackamoor of Peter the Great* remained incomplete is surely that a plausible resolution was inconceivable: as *The Bronze Horseman* showed, the tsar reformer was still a living presence in early nineteenth-century Russia. Similar problems of perspective frustrated Pushkin's attempts to write a conventional history of Peter's reign. He confessed as much to the lexicographer, Vladimir Dahl, who guided his fieldwork in Orenburg in the summer of 1833:

> Up to now I still cannot understand and comprehend intellectually that giant: he is too huge for us short-sighted ones, and we are still too close to him – one has to move away two centuries – but I understand him emotionally; the longer I study him, the more astonishment and reverence deprive me of the means of thinking and judging freely.[17]

Though he vowed ultimately 'to make something out of this gold', Pushkin's contemporaries, conscious of his playful sociability and incurable passion for conversation, doubted his capacity to see through to the end such a substantial project.[18] Pogodin and Alexander Turgenev spurred him on with references and copies of manuscripts in private hands. Yet Pushkin greeted a long reading list with a degree of bewilderment, admitting that most of the books on the list were shamefully unfamiliar to him. Though he promised to do his best to acquire them, he was pessimistic about the prospects: 'What a field, this modern Russian history! And when you think that it is virtually uncultivated and that apart from us Russians, no one can undertake [the work]! But history is long, life is short, and human nature is lazy (Russian nature in particular)' (*PSS*, vol. xvi, p. 168). By the time of his death, Pushkin had yet to find a guiding idea through which he could control the vast pile of notes he had taken from Ivan Golikov's *The Deeds of Peter the Great*, published originally in 1788–89. Pogodin lived up to Pushkin's image of him as a 'pure German' by suggesting to Viazemskii that these notes should be published as they stood as a priceless *Nachlass* for future generations. The suggestion went unheeded and only fragments of what became known as the *History of Peter* appeared in print before the twentieth century.

Pushkin could doubtless have coped with the disappointment since he had always been as keen to make history as to write it. Alexander Ypsilantis's 'brilliant' leadership of the Greek uprising in 1821 had shown what could be done: 'Dead or a conqueror, from now on he belongs to history – twenty-eight years old, an arm torn off, a magnanimous goal! – an enviable lot' (*PSS*, vol. xiii, p. 24). Though such swashbuckling exploits were beyond him, Pushkin could never extinguish his own personality in writing about the past, as Ranke sought to do. Determined to bequeath his own distinctive legacy to posterity as Russia's national genius, he consistently stressed the distinctiveness of Russia's historical development. Unique in themselves, Pushkin's historical writings nevertheless formed part of 'one of the greatest intellectual revolutions of the modern era':[19] the European phenomenon in which history usurped philosophy as the leading discipline in the humanities in the first half of the nineteenth century, and interpretations of the past replaced reason, nature and religion as the crucial justification for political action in the present. Pushkin dismissed Radishchev, a disciple of the *philosophes*, as 'a true representative of semi-enlightenment' because his mind had been inhibited by 'ignorant contempt for all the past; feebleminded amazement at his own age; blind bias toward novelty; particular, superficial knowledge, adapted to everything in random fashion' (*PSS*, vol. xii, p. 36). At the dawn of a new millennium, it is a warning worth heeding.

NOTES

1. Quoted by James J. Sheehan, *German History 1770–1866*, Oxford University Press, 1989, p. 544.
2. P. A. Viazemskii, *Zapisnye knizhki (1813–1848)*, ed. V. S. Nechaev, Moscow, Nauka, 1963, p. 135.
3. See Andrew Baruch Wachtel, *An Obsession with History: Russian Writers Confront the Past*, Stanford University Press, 1994, pp. 82–83.
4. See Simon Dixon, 'The posthumous reputation of Catherine II in Russia, 1797–1837', *Slavonic and East European Review* 77 (1999), 649–79, esp. 654–56.
5. Quoted in T. J. Binyon, *Pushkin: a Biography*, London, HarperCollins, 2002, p. 478.
6. See Peter Gay, *Style in History*, London, Jonathan Cape, 1975, pp. 59–76.

7. Nikolai Barsukov, *Zhizn' i trudy M. P. Pogodina*, St Petersburg, tipografiia M. M. Stasiulevicha, 1890, vol. iii, p. 247.
8. Quoted in Svetlana Evdokimova, *Pushkin's Historical Imagination*, New Haven, CT, and London, Yale University Press, 1999, p. 148.
9. Quoted in Herbert Butterfield, *Man on His Past: the Study of the History of Historical Scholarship*, Cambridge University Press, 1955, p. 87.
10. Quoted in Gay, *Style in History*, pp. 79, 81.
11. Alexander Dolinin, 'Historicism or providentialism? Pushkin's *History of Pugachev* in the context of French Romantic historiography', *Slavic Review* 58 (1999), 291–92.
12. See Evdokimova, *Pushkin's Historical Imagination*, pp. 74–84, esp. p. 83.
13. Alexander Pushkin, *The Queen of Spades and Other Stories*, translated by Alan Myers, ed. Andrew Kahn, Oxford University Press, 1997, p. 147.
14. See M. G. Al'tshuller, *Mezhdu dvukh tsarei: Pushkin 1824–1836*, St Petersburg, Akademicheshii proekt, 2003, pp. 186–98.
15. Pushkin, *The Queen of Spades and Other Stories*, pp. 211–12, 222.
16. John Bayley, *Pushkin: a Comparative Commentary*, Cambridge University Press, 1971, p. 129.
17. Quoted in Binyon, *Pushkin*, p. 418.
18. N. M. Smirnov, quoted in V. S. Listov, '"Istoriia Petra" v biografii i tvorchestve A. S. Pushkina', in A. S. Pushkin, *Istoriia Petra*, ed. V. S. Listov, Moscow, Iazyki russkoi kul'tury, 2000, p. 18.
19. Thomas Nipperdey, *Germany from Napoleon to Bismarck 1800–1866*, translated by Daniel Nolan, Princeton University Press, 1996, p. 442.

9

MIKHAIL GRONAS

Pushkin and the art of the letter

Pushkin's letters are among the most widely read and cited in the Russian epistolary tradition. In reviewing an edition of Voltaire's correspondence, Pushkin himself gave a psychological rationale for a fascination with an author's sub-canonical works:

> Every line of a great writer becomes precious to posterity . . . We are involuntarily struck by the thought that the hand which traced these humble figures, these insignificant words, also wrote great works, the objects of our studies and raptures, in the same script and, perhaps, with the same pen.[1]

A writer's letters (along with other sub-canonical types of writing, such as diaries, notebooks and marginalia) occupy a liminal space on the border of conventional literary and linguistic categories.[2] Letters are written, but it is the oral nature of the genre that is emphasised in the very first lines of traditional manuals on letter writing: 'A letter is a conversation between those who are absent . . . To write a successful letter, imagine that you are in the presence of the one who will read you, that he is hearing the sound of your voice.'[3]

The need 'to imagine that you are in the presence' of the addressee erodes the borders of individual authorship. In no other type of writing does an author have such strong obligations towards the reader and addressee: a shared frame of reference has to be established, the reader's opinions taken into account and reactions anticipated. Pushkin was a past master of adjusting to the stylistic expectations of his correspondents, even to the point of mimicking their epistolary 'voices'. But the real addressee may not (only) be the person whose name appears in the salutation; a letter may be intended for eventual publication, or for circulation in a relatively open group of acquaintances, or addressed to a closed group of friends engaged in an epistolary game.

Are letters documentary or literary? If documentary, then not in the same sense as a birth certificate or a photograph – and it would be very naive to treat letters as a direct and unprocessed source of biographical information without taking into account authorial intentions and strategies of self-presentation. If literary, then again, obviously not in the same sense as a short story or a novel.

One approach to Pushkin's letters is to 'go back' from the letters to the author; that is, to use the letters as material for reconstructing biographical details, the political and cultural context that shaped his personality, or the evolution of his political opinions and literary views.[4] An opposite approach is to 'go forward' from Pushkin's letters to his literary works, to trace the parallels between the stylistic and aesthetic evolutions within these two domains. Representatives of this approach often treat Pushkin's letters as a 'creative laboratory' that he used to try out literary innovations before employing them in prose.[5] Finally, one can also 'stay with' the letters and treat Pushkin's correspondence in its entirety as an autonomous object, valuable in its own right.[6] This is the approach I will be using in this essay, only occasionally venturing into what might have preceded the letters in 'pre-epistolary' historical or psychological reality or followed from them in the 'post-epistolary' domain of the literary works.

Networks

The letters that I am going to discuss can be treated as a communicative network, not unlike the internet today. At the same time, letters form a social network.[7] In the nineteenth century, one's letters document and materialise one's social relations, and when one is absent from one's customary social arena (as the exiled Pushkin was), they become the only available medium of social interaction.

In all, 847 of Pushkin's letters have survived. Pushkin was meticulous about preserving drafts or extant copies for sentimental value, but also, in some cases, for future use in literary work or polemics and, especially later, for the sake of accountability in business dealings and affairs of honour.[8] The intensity of his epistolary activity varied throughout the years, peaking in the periods of his enforced absences: first, from his St Petersburg and Moscow friends (the exile of 1820–26) and then from his wife in the 1830s.

During the first of these periods, Pushkin's epistolary output is comparable to the volume of his literary production of the time. In the years before his return from exile, Pushkin recreated in epistolary form not just the severed ties with his friends, but the whole tapestry of social and intellectual connections which he had developed before going into exile. One key to Pushkin's centrality in Russian culture lies precisely in his centrality on the map of early nineteenth-century intellectual networks, as documented in his correspondence. If such a map were visualised, Pushkin would be found at the intersection of the most important groups and movements of the time. Pushkin's letters to members of these groups employ the distinctive repertoire of topics and stylistic conventions characteristic of each group as a whole.

This 'feel for the network' is already apparent in one of Pushkin's early, pre-exile letters addressed to Pavel Mansurov, a fellow member of the Green Lamp, a society of politically minded bon vivants. Mansurov had left for military service, and Pushkin is filling him in on what has transpired in his absence:

> As your historian I shall tell about our fellows. Everything is going as before: the champagne, thank God, is lusty – the actresses likewise – the former gets drunk up, and the latter get f[ucked]. Amen. Amen. That's as it ought to be. Iuriev, thank God, is well of the c[lap]. I have a little dose which is clearing up; that is fine, too. N. Vsevolozhskii is gambling; the air is thick with chalk! Money is scattered all around! [The actress] Sosnitskaia and [the playwright] Prince Shakhovskoi are growing fat and stupid – but I am not in love with them. Nevertheless, I have been loudly applauding them both – him for his bad comedy, and her for her mediocre acting. Tolstoy is sick – I shall not say of what – as it is, I already have too many c[ocks] in my letter. The Green Lamp's wick needs trimming – it looks as though it may go out – and that is a pity – there is oil (i.e., our friend's champagne). Are you writing, will you write me, my pal, my nithe fewow? Tell me about yourself and about the military settlements. I need all this – because I love you – and hate despotism. Good-by, little Paw. Cricket A. Pushkin.[9]

Within the space of a paragraph, Pushkin manages to produce a rapid survey of the social network 'at work', from which one can easily reconstruct the symbolism of the group (the Green Lamp), its values (licentious hedonism and political liberalism), its habitual occupations (sexual escapades, gambling, carousing and theatregoing), and the general atmosphere (the youthful exuberance of a playful brotherhood). True to the spirit of the Green Lamp, Pushkin inserts a political declaration. But he saves it ('I hate despotism') for the last line in order to maximise the bathetic contrast between a lofty conclusion and the preceding report on the young radicals' venereal diseases. This play on contrasting stylistic registers (note also the peculiar placement of 'Amen. Amen.'), lisping parody ('nithe fewwow' for 'nice fellow'), generous use of obscenities, and conversational freedom in changing topics align this letter with the epistolary tradition of Arzamas. In fact, Pushkin signs the letter with his Arzamasian nickname: Cricket. Fellow Arzamasians (such as the intellectuals Mikhail Orlov and the Turgenev brothers and, most importantly, the poets Vasilii Zhukovskii and Petr Viazemskii) were to become his lifelong correspondents.

Although ever sociable, the exiled Pushkin never developed a single deep and fruitful intellectual connection which could sustain a long-lasting epistolary contact. It was by keeping alive his old metropolitan connections, building upon them and restructuring them, that Pushkin gradually created a new epistolary network, one centred around himself, which would eventually become 'the Pushkin circle'. The appearance of this network was not just a manifestation of the early nineteenth-century cult of friendship. Rather, it was dictated by the objective logic of the cultural field, by discrepancy between Pushkin's rapidly growing importance and his temporary geographical remoteness. Russia is famously over-centralised: it was difficult to have a meaningful impact on cultural life without being present oneself in Moscow or St Petersburg. However, through his epistolary presence the exiled Pushkin managed not just to participate in this life, but actually to influence literary and publishing life, remaining central to the cultural field.

The epistolary network provided Pushkin with both an immediate knowledge of the cultural context and the means by which to influence and transform the field. Through his correspondents, Pushkin was able to acquire immediate professional feedback on his new works and to gauge public sentiment. 'Tell me, my dear fellow, is my *Prisoner* [*of the Caucasus*] making a sensation? *A-t-il produit de scandale?* [. . . .] How's my Onegin / doing? Making a stir?' (*LAP*, vol. i, p. 104. To Lev Pushkin, October 1822). These are the typical questions with which Pushkin bombarded his correspondents. The latter kept him informed about the latest literary developments both in Russia and abroad, ensuring that the exiled Pushkin's cultural competence never lagged. Thus, with Petr Viazemskii, his most frequent correspondent in this period, Pushkin conducts detailed line-by-line analyses of his own and Viazemskii's new poems; in letters to Viazemskii and the writer Alexander Bestuzhev, Pushkin engages in literary polemics over Romanticism and the composition of the Russian literary canon. Viazemskii and his Lycée friend the poet Anton Del'vig kept Pushkin informed on all the latest literary novelties. Viazemskii, Pushkin's younger brother Lev, the classicist and publisher Nikolai Gnedich and, especially, the poet and critic Petr Pletnev serve as Pushkin's publishers and literary managers: on Pushkin's behalf, they interact with censors and bargain with book distributors. His correspondence of the period also serves as an epistolary literary magazine and an epistolary newspaper as well, a source of political news and high-society rumours. Finally, Pushkin uses the network to improve his social standing and political reputation: it is partly through his and his friends' carefully orchestrated epistolary efforts that he is eventually pardoned and allowed to return from exile.

Upon his return in 1826, Pushkin was once again able to communicate directly with most of his old friends and acquaintances. His new epistolary networks were more specialised, often by-products of Pushkin's professional activities, such as co-ordinating the contributors to his literary magazines, *The Literary Gazette* and *The Contemporary*. Finally, after his marriage in 1831, a network of two – Pushkin himself and his wife Natalia Goncharova – eclipsed all the other social configurations in significance. In the seventeen months of their separation, Pushkin wrote to her seventy-eight (surviving) letters, compared to the seventy-eight he wrote to his second most frequent correspondent, Viazemskii, over the twenty years of their acquaintance.[10]

Channels

A map of the network does not yet give a full understanding of how it works. This requires an analysis of the epistolary channels themselves: what particular relations were at work between sender and addressee, how access to the message was regulated. Our contemporary conventions presuppose the unambiguous privacy of everyday epistolary transmissions. But letters that are accessible to the public, such as the postings on an internet message board, constitute separate genres. In Pushkin's epoch, this distinction was blurred and the precise character of the 'addressee' was more ambiguous.

Familiar letters, especially those written within the Arzamas tradition, were literary artefacts intended for passing around among friends as a form of publication. Why waste the sophisticated humour and stylistic mastery of an Arzamasian letter on a single recipient? Thus, Pushkin often wrote to his friends anticipating a wider distribution. This was not a rule, however, but a possible outcome which had to be effected with tact and care. Determining what one can share and with whom required considerable social skills: an inattentive or unskilful recipient could cause a communication failure by sharing a letter with the wrong person.

The following exchange of three letters between Pushkin, his brother Lev and Pletnev illustrates the considerable effort that Pushkin made to remedy the consequences of a misaddressed communication. In an 1822 letter to his brother, Pushkin is discussing a variety of new literary pieces, among them a recent poem by Pletnev, and offers a frank opinion about it in an offhand manner: 'He [Pletnev] has no feeling at all, no vivacity – his style is as pale as a corpse. Give my respects to Pletnev – not his style – and assure him that he is our Goethe' (*LAP*, vol. i, p. 100: 4 September 1822). The second sentence seems to imply a warning against sharing this – quite scathing – judgement with Pletnev.

But either by an oversight or out of mischief, Pushkin's feckless brother showed the letter to Pletnev, who greatly valued Pushkin's opinions in matters of taste. The distressed Pletnev replied with a poetic epistle in which he purports to prefer Pushkin's candid judgement to the flattery of the 'crowd'. Pushkin, however, took it as a reproach and masterfully used the next epistles to manipulate the psychology of his addressees and defuse the tension. Pushkin's second letter to brother Lev begins with a scolding: 'If you were in reach, my charming one, I would pull your ears. Why did you show Pletnev my letter? If in a friendly conversation I allow myself to make harsh and ill-considered judgments, they must remain between us' (*LAP* vol. i, p. 104: October 1822). Pushkin does not mean to say that private letters must remain private: rather, he reprehends his brother for contextual insensitivity. Note, however, that the adjectives 'harsh' and 'ill-considered' sound too objective and 'adult', coming after the playful 'my charming one' and 'I would pull your ears' of the first line. One suspects that Pushkin is deliberately manipulating the communication channel, hoping that Lev will once again share his letter with Pletnev. This suspicion grows as the letter progresses: 'Incidentally, Pletnev's epistle is perhaps the first piece which has been prompted by fullness of feeling. It sparkles with true beauties. He has been able to take advantage of his position, which was favourable against me; his tone is bold and noble.' Whatever the actual degree of sincerity, Pushkin's expression of a newfound fondness for Pletnev's poetry betrays a shift in psychological perspective. Nowhere else in his correspondence with his brother Lev does the young Pushkin use such an objective and unimpassioned tone when evaluating a literary work. The almost imperceptible shift here indicates that Pushkin is turning from the recipient (Lev) to the real addressee (Pletnev).

As Pushkin and Pletnev had never previously exchanged letters, Pushkin had yet to find the 'stylistic key' to fit his new correspondent. Pushkin decides to write to Pletnev direct. This letter has survived only in the form of a rough draft. As a rule, Pushkin used drafts for literary letters intended for wider circulation or eventual publication, official letters and letters carefully calculated to produce a desired psychological effect on the addressee.[11] The letter to Pletnev definitely belongs to this last category:

> Your position is too favorable against me . . . I do not repent of my momentary injustice – it gave rise to an [~~beautiful present~~] unexpected beauty in poetry. But if [~~not~~] you are angry with me, your verses, [~~as mu~~] however [~~beautiful~~] charming, will never console me. Of course you would forgive my ill-considered lines, if you knew how often I am subject to so-called spleen [~~about which it is difficult~~]. In these minutes I am wroth at the entire world, and no poetry stirs my heart. Do not think, however, that I [~~would~~] [~~would not esteem~~] do not esteem your indisputable talent. [~~I value your opinion~~][~~I am not completely deprived~~

> ~~of taste~~] The feeling for the elegant has not become completely [~~utterly~~] dull in me [~~I value~~] [~~I do not want to gain the character of~~] – and when I am in complete possession of myself – your [~~pure~~] harmony, poetic precision, nobility of expression, beauty of structure, harmoniousness, the purity in the finish of your verses captivate me, like the poetry of [~~my favourite poets~~] those I love most.[12] (*LAP*, vol. i, pp. 105–06: November or December 1822)

Pushkin's position here is indeed unenviable. He needs to convince Pletnev that his initial scathing remarks were induced by spleen, although – as Pletnev no doubt could recall – the rest of that ill-fated letter was quite cheerful. Pushkin also needs to persuade his correspondent that he is now being sincere in his praises – although, again, Pletnev could certainly recall Pushkin's cynical recommendation to Lev: 'assure him [Pletnev] that he is our Goethe'.

The number of corrections show Pushkin struggling diffidently to be credible and persuasive. Since he wishes to avoid the appearance of flattery, praise should not come too easily: '~~beautiful present~~' sounds too trite, and is replaced by the more exact 'unexpected beauty of poetry'. The phrases '~~I value your opinion~~' and '~~I am not completely deprived of taste~~' include the pronoun 'I', implying an unnecessary personal involvement: they are replaced with an impersonal construction. We do not know whether Pushkin's painstakingly composed letter 'worked'. But we do know that this letter initiated Pushkin's long-lasting correspondence with Pletnev, who eventually became one of his closest friends.

The dissemination of letters among friends was an acceptable infringement of Pushkin's privacy. Far less acceptable was the behaviour of the postal authorities and the secret police who regularly opened and inspected his letters as part of their routine surveillance. Pushkin had two options: either to use the regular mail and risk certain inspection or when possible to send a letter with a travelling friend or acquaintance.

The medium of communication was bound to influence the message. In letters sent by mail, Pushkin largely avoids risky political matters, or uses allegorical allusions unintelligible to outsiders. Tsar Alexander I is often referred to as August(us) – a hint at the exiled Pushkin's personal mythology, in which he plays the role of Ovid. Political changes are described in terms of weather: 'warm' stands for a relaxation in the regime, 'cold' for a retrenchment. Pushkin even develops a metaphoric code for talking about these two types of transmission. Letters sent with private carriers and free from perlustration are associated with wearing careless dress. The following is a typical coded complaint about surveillance from a letter to Viazemskii: 'Dear one, I am fed up with writing to you, because I cannot appear to you in my dressing gown, unbuttoned, and with drooping sleeves' (*LAP*, vol. i, p. 263: second half of November 1825). Letters sent by regular mail, and therefore intended for the authorities, are described as 'wearing official attire': 'Enclosed is a letter to Zhukovskii in a three-cornered hat and shoes' (*LAP*, vol. i, p. 107: 7 March 1826).

While surveillance irked Pushkin, he used it to his own advantage as a way to manipulate the authorities. After the Decembrist rebellion and accession of Nicholas I, Pushkin hoped for a quick end to his exile. By way of instigating this he sent the authorities a message about his newfound loyalty and political trustworthiness through letters sent to his friends. A good example of this manipulative strategy (of the 'hat and shoes' kind) is a letter he addressed to Vasilii Zhukovskii. Pushkin expected Zhukovskii to show it to Nicholas I, the real addressee. Here is a characteristic passage, in which it is obvious that Pushkin is actually talking to the tsar: 'The accession to the throne of the Sovereign Nikolai Pavlovich gives me joyful hope. Perhaps His Majesty will see fit to change my lot . . . I have no intention of insanely opposing the generally accepted order of things, and necessity' (*LAP*, vol. i, p. 307: 7 March 1826).

Surveillance and interception often annoyed Pushkin without raising his indignation. However, when the police intercepted a letter he sent to his wife in 1834, Pushkin became furious. Pushkin never overreacted when the rules of the game had been observed: the familiar letter was intended for circulation and the government was entitled to some measure of control over communications. However, because family stood at the apex of Pushkin's hierarchy of networks in the 1830s, its privacy deserved to be defended against intrusions from state and society. Thus, Pushkin is essentially protesting against a breach of trust: treating a letter to family as a letter to a friend constituted a violation of the rules of communication.

Goals

Pushkin's insistence on the difference between familiar letters and family letters brings us to a discussion of epistolary typology. Even a cursory look at the passages quoted in this essay gives an idea of the versatility and stylistic heterogeneity of his correspondence. Let us return for a moment to two of the letters discussed above: the 1819 letter to his fellow Green Lamp member Mansurov and the 1822 letter aimed at encouraging Pletnev. Although they both belong to the (loosely defined) genre of the familiar letter, it is difficult to imagine two more different performances. The obvious difference in content is not the point. What is more important is the difference in structure and function: the letter to Mansurov races from topic to topic more or less chaotically and aims at creating the illusion of an unrestrained oral exchange; the letter to Pletnev presents a carefully drafted, slow-paced and coherent argument, focused on a single topic, and aims at being rhetorically effective.

In other words, the letter to Mansurov is conversational, and the letter to Pletnev is literary. While this opposition is often treated as a binary one, it is more useful to speak here of a series of epistolary modes that vary along a spectrum of orality and literariness determined by specific communicative goals. Within Pushkin's conversational letters one notices the presence of at least two such modes: a 'chatter' mode, a free-wheeling and noncommittal exchange on many subjects at once; and a 'learned discussion' mode, a more literary exchange (often a debate) on a more or less unified intellectual topic. These two modes are of course not mutually exclusive, and in many instances Pushkin switches between them within the same letter.

'Chatter' letters are closest to the oral pole of the spectrum. Their primary communicative goal is to exchange information or to make requests and inquiries, and the quantity of the content supersedes concerns of structure. In such letters Pushkin addresses as many topics as possible, spending a few short sentences on each, and connecting the topics (if at all) by associative links or puns.[13]

Pushkin's letters to his wife constitute a sub-variety of the chatter letter. The illusion of spoken conversation is still present – and even further strengthened by extreme concision, use of colloquialisms, and fractured syntax. However, the topics in these letters are much more structured because they serve a more specific communicative goal: to give his wife a full and detailed picture of his life without her. During their temporary separations, Pushkin constantly worried about her lack of experience in high society and was obsessed about her fidelity. By giving her the full details of his daily life and, probably, receiving similarly detailed letters from her, he was able not just to keep in touch, but to participate actively in and control his wife's and his family's everyday affairs. These letters are often more or less chronological reports on his actions and concerns, alternating with rumours and occasional anecdotes, and an almost continual barrage of advice and warnings. Their function is similar to that of a diary or a notebook and, indeed, some topics and phrases from Pushkin's diary in this period also turn up in the letters to his wife.

If the chatter mode serves for the exchange of information, the discussion mode facilitates the exchange of opinions. 'Discussion letters' are less oral and oscillate between the epistolary recreation of a learned conversation (usually between two male friends) and journal polemics. As a rule, discussion letters served as a medium for Pushkin's epistolary literary criticism, which took up a considerable part of his correspondence, especially during the exile. In fact, Pushkin more than once reused fragments from such letters in his critical articles. Pushkin's epistolary critical discussions included line-by-line analyses of his friends' poems (e.g. Viazemskii's 'Narva Waterfall' [*LAP*, vol. i, pp. 244–46]), reactions to new literary works (such as Pushkin's express-review of the playwright Alexander Griboedov's *Woe from Wit* in a letter to Alexander Bestuzhev [*LAP*, vol. i, pp. 200–01]), and arguments on the comparative value of writers. By contrast with the chatter letters, discussion letters usually went through one or two drafts without losing their conversational tone.

If Pushkin's letters served him as a creative laboratory for new literary devices, then it is in his conversational letters that many such innovations originated before migrating to major genres. In the 1820s, Pushkin the Romantic was primarily interested in the literary potential inherent in the stylistic eclecticism of the epistolary 'chatter' and its compositional freedom, a swift succession of loosely linked themes and topics. The following piece of advice on novel writing given to a fellow writer, the Decembrist Alexander Bestuzhev, shows that by 1825 Pushkin was conscious of the new stylistic energy contained in familiar letters: 'take on a novel, and write it with all the freedom of conversation or of a letter, else the style will keep on slipping into Kotzebuese . . . I love poetry without a plan better than a plan without poetry' (*LAP*, vol. i, p. 265: 30 November 1825). Pushkin was the first to follow his own advice, and, according to one convincing hypothesis, used the familiar correspondence as one of the sources for the poetics of the seemingly 'planless' *Evgenii Onegin* and its ever digressive and unrestrained authorial persona.[14]

Conversational letters (both 'chatters' and 'discussions') presuppose not only the imaginary presence of the addressee, but also his or her active participation in the exchange. An opposing class of Pushkin's letters may be termed rhetorical. These letters do not presume and do not seek the addressee's participation, nor do they imitate a conversation; rather, they aim at affecting the addressee, influencing his or her mood, opinion or behaviour. Pushkin's apologetic letter to Pletnev is just such a rhetorical letter in the guise of a conversational discussion letter because, as we have seen, Pushkin was primarily interested in making amends and assuaging his correspondent rather than communicating his literary opinions.

Rhetorical as well are Pushkin's few surviving letters aimed at insulting his enemies, such as the fateful one sent to Baron van Heeckeren on 26 January 1837, which led to Pushkin's death (for the context see Chapter 1). Just one sentence from this letter will suffice to demonstrate the rhetorical virtuosity of Pushkin when infuriated: 'Like an obscene old woman, you would go and lie in wait for my wife in every corner, in order to tell her of the love of your bastard, or the one so called, and when, ill with syphilis, he was kept at home, you would say that he was dying of love for her' (*LAP*, vol. iii, p. 818).[15] The whole letter was carefully worded to ensure the inevitability of a duel with either the Baron himself or his adopted son. Not one word is wasted. 'Obscene old woman', insulting in itself, is a hint at the rumours of homosexual relations between van Heeckeren and d'Anthès; 'your bastard' – a hint at more gossip; 'or the one so called' implies scornful unwillingness even to go into these rumours; 'ill with syphilis', not weak in itself, is a rhetorical rhyme to 'dying of love' in the next clause; 'kept at home' de-personifies d'Anthès as an object to be kept.

Pushkin's epistolary declarations of love are also rhetorical, since in writing them he obviously meant above all to affect the feelings of the recipients. He wrote both his hate letters (the one to van Heeckeren above) and his love letters in French, which, among other functions, served as the epistolary language of his addressees.[16] Pushkin and his fellow literati perceived French as a more developed and cultivated language, rich in a ready idiom of abstract concepts and psychological realities. In addition, writing in French provided Pushkin with a bridge to the epistolary tradition of the French Enlightenment and Romanticism. Pushkin's love letters are among his most literary. The following letter to an unidentified woman, which has only survived in this unfinished draft, ranges from exquisite suggestiveness in the manner of *Les Liaisons dangereuses* (for instance, the letters sent to Anna Kern during his northern exile), to psychological introspection learned from the first-person narrator of Benjamin Constant's novel *Adolphe*:

> I am not writing to defy you, but I have had the weakness to confess to you a ludicrous passion, and I wish to explain myself frankly with regard to it. Do not pretend anything – that would be unworthy of you – coquetry would be a frivolous cruelty and moreover quite useless. I shall not believe in your anger, either, any more – wherein can I offend you? I love you with such tender rapture, but with such care not to be over-familiar, that not even your pride can be wounded by it. If I had any hopes, I would not have waited until the eve of your departure to make my declaration. You must attribute my avowal to a state of exaltation which I could no longer master, and which ended in my fainting away. I ask nothing, I do not know what I want myself – nevertheless I you . . .[17] (*LAP*, vol. i, p. 115: June or July 1823)

Though I have deliberately refrained from suggesting links between Pushkin's letters and his literary works, it's hard not to notice the parallel one of his most canonical texts. The initial phrase of the letter recalls the beginning of Tatiana's letter to Onegin: 'I write to you – what would one more?' (*Evgenii Onegin*, Chapter 3). To open a letter with a statement about writing itself is to indicate one's heightened self-consciousness. In this letter, every movement of the soul has to be fully sensed and explained; the analysis of the passion precedes, and even replaces, its expression. Every statement must be qualified or conditioned; there is not a single simple sentence: the text as a whole is unimaginable in oral form. The reactions of the addressee are contemplated – 'coquetry would be a frivolous cruelty'; 'I shall not believe in your anger' – but not to make her come alive on the page, as in the 'chatter' and 'discussion' letters; rather than recreating his addressee's response, Pushkin tries to anticipate – and even influence – the emotions and feelings that she will be experiencing while reading the letter. The compositional layout of the surviving fragment still gives an idea of the logical coherence of the whole. The letter could be rewritten as a chain of syllogisms structured around a single rhetorical purpose. The letter thus belongs to the literary end of the spectrum.

Viewing Pushkin's letters as documents brings us closer to his personality; viewing them as literary texts gives us reading pleasure. Is there an aesthetic counterpart to a scholarly focus on the letters as a network? I think the answer is yes, and this specific 'network' pleasure is integral to our experience of reading an author's letters. It consists in a feeling of our own embeddedness and participation in society's never-ending work of linking and communicating.

NOTES

1. 'Voltaire', in *The Critical Prose of Alexander Pushkin with Critical Essays by Four Russian Romantic Poets*, ed. and trans. Carl Proffer, Bloomington, IN, Indiana University Press, 1969, p. 194.
2. For an overview of approaches to these 'inconvenient' genres see Irina Paperno, 'What can be done with diaries?', *Russian Review* 63 (October 2004), 561–73.
3. A definition from *Grande Encyclopédie du XIXe siècle*, quoted in Cécile Dauphin, 'Les manuels épistolaires au XIXe siècle', in Roger Chartier (ed.), *La Correspondance: les usages de la lettre au XIXe siècle*, Paris, Fayard, 1991, pp. 209–42, here p. 229.
4. For a typical biographical reading of the period, see V. V. Sipovskii, 'Pushkin po ego pis'mam', in N.D. Chechulin (ed.), *Pamiati L. N. Maikova*, St Petersburg, ODP, 1902, pp. 454–68.

5. The view of Pushkin's letters as a 'creative laboratory' begins with Russian Formalists. See Grigorii Vinokur, 'Pushkin-prozaik', *Kul'tura iazyka*, Moscow, Federatsiia, 1929, pp. 286–303; and Abram Lezhnev, *Pushkin's Prose*, Ann Arbor, MI, Ardis, 1983, pp. 190–206.
6. See Irina Paperno, 'Perepiska Pushkina kak tselostnyi text (mai – oktiabr' 1831)', in *Uchenye zapiski Tartuskogo universiteta* 240:2 (1977), 71–81.
7. For a general theory of intellectual networks see Randall Collins, *The Sociology of Philosophies: a Global Theory of Intellectual Change*, Cambridge, MA, Belknap Press, 1998, pp. 19–74.
8. Boris Modzalevskii estimates that only about one third of Pushkin's letters have survived. See Modzalevskii, 'Predislovie', in A. S. Pushkin, *Pis'ma*, vol. i: *1815–1825*, Moscow, Leningrad, Gosizdat, 1926, pp. iii–xlviii.
9. *Letters of Alexander Pushkin*, translated by J. Thomas Shaw (henceforward *LAP*), Madison, WI, University of Wisconsin Press, 1967, 27 October 1819.
10. As noted by Ianina Levkovich, 'Pis'ma Pushkina k zhene', in A. S. *Pushkin, Pis'ma k zhene*, ed. Ia. Levkovich, Leningrad, Nauka, 1986, pp. 87–107, here p. 89.
11. See Ia. Levkovich, 'Iz nabliudenii nad chernovikami pisem Pushkina', in *Pushkin: Issledovaniia i materialy*, vol. ix, Leningrad, Akademiia Nauk SSSR, 1979, pp. 123–40.
12. In the translation of this letter in *LAP* the crossed out words are skipped. They are translated here from Modzalevskii, in Pushkin, *Pis'ma*, vol. i, p. 41.
13. See William Mills Todd III, *The Familiar Letter as a Literary Genre in the Age of Pushkin*, Princeton University Press, 1976, pp. 166–71.
14. Todd, *The Familiar Letter*, pp. 188–92.
15. Original in French.
16. See Irina Paperno, 'O dvuiazychnoi perepiske pushkinskoi pory', *Uchenye zapiski Tartuskogo universiteta* 358 (1975), 148–56; and E. Maimin, 'Frantsuzskaia rech' v pis'makh Pushkina k Viazemskomu', in *Sbornik trudov SNO filologicheskogo fakul'teta: Russkaia filologiia* 5 (1977), 22–32.
17. Original in French.

10

WILLIAM MILLS TODD III

Pushkin and literary criticism

Context

In his twenty-three years of public literary life, which included active participation in two periodicals, *The Literary Gazette* (1830–31) and *The Contemporary* (1836–37), Alexander Pushkin published only fifty-two prose pieces on literary subjects, many of them just a paragraph in length. Serious scholarly editions of his work include nine unfinished articles intended for *The Contemporary* and over sixty critical fragments from his notebooks. Yet Pushkin was nothing if not critical. From his first published work, 'To a Poet-Friend' (1814), to the last lines he penned before his fatal duel (27 January 1837), a letter of encouragement to the writer Alexandra Ishimova, Pushkin indefatigably engaged in the analysis and judgement of literary works and literary life.[1] In ways both bold and subtle, his verse and prose works, regardless of genre, obsessively reflect upon literary instances, fads and traditions. Nikolai Gogol's haunting characterisation of Pushkin's work, 'in every word there is an abyss of space',[2] may be partly understood in terms of the explicitly and implicitly critical quality of Pushkin's writing.[3] None of his works illustrates this more comprehensively than *Evgenii Onegin*, in which the author-narrator's unfolding encounters with critics, with literary fashions, with genres and with the expectations of his readers make the verse novel nothing less than a critical autobiography.

Short as Pushkin's career was, it witnessed major shifts in all aspects of literary life. He wrote his first poems and made his first literary alliances at a time when the very language of literature was a subject of open debate; it would remain a subject of critical concern throughout his life. English and German literature began to offer foreign models more attractive than the French and Classical ones which had prevailed as Pushkin began to write. Authorship became an incipient profession, as authors began to be remunerated for their original works, not only for translations and editorial activity, and concomitant issues of authorial status wracked heretofore amateur literary circles. In 1828, Russia's first copyright law began to protect intellectual property. Also in 1828, a seemingly more liberal censorship code replaced the restrictive 'Cast Iron Statute' of 1826. Such relative bestsellers as Karamzin's *History of the Russian State* (1818), Pushkin's Southern poems and Faddei Bulgarin's *Ivan Vyzhigin* (1829) began to tempt writers away from previous ways of literary life, centred in schools, at court, in the learned academies and universities, and in the salons of Moscow and St Petersburg. The reading public began to expand, as did the number of bookstores and periodicals which could serve it. In Pushkin's childhood the most popular journal, Karamzin's *Herald of Europe*, had a circulation of 600 copies; Pushkin lived to see Osip Senkovskii's *Library for Reading* enjoy a circulation ten times as great.

In his letters, conversations, imaginative writing and critical prose Pushkin not only took cognisance of these changes, he sought to make sense of them, and he took strong (if evolving) positions. Pushkin was far from the most prolific critic of his time (Nikolai Polevoi, Faddei Bulgarin, Nikolai Grech, Osip Senkovskii and Vissarion Belinsky surpassed him in gross tonnage and critical visibility). Others, such as Moscow's 'archival youth', the young noblemen serving in bureaucratic sinecures (including the writers V. F. Odoevskii, S. P. Shevyrev and D. P. Venevitinov) and their successors in the older capital, had greater philosophical ambitions and direct access to German philosophical aesthetics, which reached Pushkin indirectly, through the mediation of French and Russian critics. But Pushkin's status as 'national poet', already proclaimed in the 1830s, gives his critical comments weight and invites us to search for their relation to his own unsurpassed creativity. In this chapter, I will survey his coming of age as a critical intelligence and outline his responses, always engaging and engaged, to the changing literary landscape of his time.

Early criticism: the Lycée and familiar circles

Pushkin arrived at the Imperial Lycée in Tsarskoe Selo already proficient in French and informed about the literary issues of the day. His travelling companion and uncle, Vasilii Pushkin, a Francophile salon poet, proved an appropriate guide to the matter and manner of literary debate in early nineteenth-century Russia: his uncle's scabrous comic poem 'The Dangerous Neighbour' (1811) would compromise the works of literary opponents by making them reading material in a brothel. Although Tsarskoe Selo was not so close to St Petersburg as Pushkin would have liked, he was hardly cut off from current literary events during these formative years. Visiting poets from the capital and literate dragoons quartered nearby kept the adolescent close to the controversies of the day about literary language and literary genres and helped imbue him with the growing restlessness of the educated, westernised nobility ('society', as it called itself).

The school curriculum was itself less than inspiring, and Pushkin excelled only at Russian and French literature, neglecting his other subjects, such as German, Latin, political economy and history. But he did acquire solid grounding in the rhetoric, poetics and poetry of the Russian and French eighteenth century. His Russian teacher, N. F. Koshanskii, himself an author of rhetorical manuals, bored his students with his lists of terms and their definitions.[4] The pupils were encouraged to write, and they produced short-lived journals and miscellanies. They also acquired a sense of literary traditions, genres and techniques. This background in writing, analysing and editing counterbalanced the casual liveliness of the St Petersburg salons.

When Pushkin left the Lycée in 1817, he was fully able to participate in the capital's salons and groups. His poetic precocity earned him a place in the polite world for which literature had become a favourite diversion. Literature provided appropriately entertaining genres for social occasions, as verse, word games like *bouts-rimés*, and epigrams were read at balls, suppers and other assemblies. Young ladies of fashion kept albums in which friends and admirers would write gallant verse, compliments and madrigals. Polite society distributed and criticised literature, a function only partially fulfilled by Russia's unstable and still immature periodical press. Criticism in this milieu functioned differently from the way it does in an age of mass literacy and mass reproducibility. In the early nineteenth century it was less a matter of helping a public to choose between and understand individual works but was rather something exchanged between friends and fellow amateur writers (in conversation, verse epistles or familiar letters) or else levelled against opponents in satires, parodies, epigrams and comedies. Some of the most acute critics of the time, such as Karamzin, rejected the criticism of living Russian authors for fear of discouraging Russia's incipient literature or polluting it with the sordid activities which they recalled from eighteenth-century France and England's notorious Grub Street, where impoverished writers and hacks lived.[5]

Within familiar groups, such as the Arzamas society to which Pushkin, his uncle, Zhukovskii, Batiushkov, Viazemskii, Karamzin and other prominent writers belonged, letters and epistles followed the tradition of friendly criticism, instilled in them in such schools as the Lycée, and they could dissect their friends' works in a sensible, hard-headed manner, anticipating that their own works would be treated similarly. Specific comments on style and convention, perceived as pedantic in public criticism, were perfectly permissible in a conversation or letter. Pushkin would continue to observe this convention into the 1820s. He could be highly critical of Zhukovskii's verse and ideas, but he loyally defended his friend against public criticism: 'I do not quite agree with [Bestuzhev's] stern sentence against Zhukovskii. Why should we bite the breasts of our wet nurse? Because we have cut our teeth? Whatever you say, Zhukovskii had a decisive influence on the spirit of our literature; moreover, the style of his translations will forever remain the model.'[6]

Pushkin's 1818 verse epistle 'To Zhukovskii' shows the possibilities and limitations of this in-group criticism (translated by James Falen):

When reaching for the world of dreams,
Your lofty spirit all afire,
Impatiently upon your knees
You hold with restless hand the lyre.
When in the magic dark you see
Fleet visions pass before our eyes,
And inspiration's chilling breeze
Makes all your hair in dread arise, –
You're right, you sing for just the few,
And not for jealous connoisseurs
Or all that wretched carping crew
Who love to parrot what they've heard,
But only for the loyal friends
Of sacred truth and talent's ends.
Good fortune doesn't shine on all,
Not all were born to wear a wreath,
But blest who hears the subtle call
Of lofty thought and poet's speech!
Who took delight in beauty's spell
When beauty hovered near
And understood the joy you felt
With joy as hot and clear.[7]

For readers in the know, this is an elegantly precise and succinct characterisation of Zhukovskii's life (personal misfortune, role at court, increasing baldness), critical reception (harsh responses to his popular ballads, ability to evoke the emotions), and writing (fantastic visions, terrifying characters, ecstatic tone, melodic versification). It deftly hints at Zhukovskii's court writings, six issues of a collection *Für Wenige* (*For the Few*, 1818), written for the Prussian-born grand princess he was tutoring, an activity of which many of Zhukovskii's friends disapproved. It does so by turning the 'few' into those truly able to appreciate Zhukovskii's gift, his literary friends. And it concludes by even more deftly capturing the essence of Zhukovskii's innovation in verse diction, his precisely imprecise psychological and emotional epithets. A twenty-first-century reader with access not only to Zhukovskii's complete works but also to scholarly studies of his life, language and poetics can appreciate Pushkin's critical achievement in this epistle, as could Zhukovskii, Batiushkov and the other poets of their circle. But this is a far cry from the sort of public criticism which could educate the growing readership for serious Russian literature.

New considerations: Pushkin's criticism in the 1820s

During the years of his Southern and Northern exile, Pushkin would continue to fill notebooks, letters and imaginative works with critical commentary on the literature and literary debates of the time. But the times, as noted above, were changing. New possibilities for public literary life were opening with the reign of Nicholas I, and Pushkin, like others, could dream, inspired by such European models as the public man of letters (Benjamin Constant, René de Chateaubriand), the rebellious titan (Byron), the respected and influential historical novelist (Scott). 'Happiness was so possible, so close', as Tatiana would tell Onegin, happiness in the writer's case being remuneration for his work, public status, prestige. From the standpoint of his own success with the Southern poems, Pushkin became increasingly aware of literary life as a whole, as an institution.

Pushkin went public with his reflections in an article innocuously entitled 'Fragments from Letters, Thoughts, and Comments'. One of his first, and most important, published critical pieces, it appeared in an almanac, *Northern Flowers for 1828* (published 1827), which was edited by his Lycée friend, Anton Del'vig. Almanacs, an early Russian form of periodical literature, were small-format annual collections of lyric poems and prose fragments together with a critical overview of the year in literature. For the most part any money that they earned went to the editors and publisher, not to the contributors, who were typically polite-society amateurs. At their best they gave people of fashion a handy means to prepare for salon conversations. The title and structure of Pushkin's piece, a seemingly loose set of thirty paragraph- or sentence-length fragments, parodies a piece that his feckless uncle had published the year before. But the parody soon turns to a target much larger than Pushkin's ultimately harmless uncle Vasilii Pushkin.

The piece turns out to be nothing less than a history of secular Russian literature, told in terms of institutions and principal actors, and culminating in the struggles of Nikolai Karamzin to establish authorial status. Karamzin – sentimental poet, salon figure, salaried editor of a journal, and official historiographer at the court of Alexander I – wins credit for synthesising positive aspects of the patronage system (freedom from censorship at the emperor's orders), the salons (status in polite society), and the incipient literary trade (commercial success). At the same time, Pushkin shows how Karamzin avoids their pitfalls: compromise with the truth, insufficient dedication to major projects, and loss of dignity:

> The appearance of *The History of the Russian State* caused much commotion and made a powerful impression (as well it should have). Three thousand copies sold out in one month, which not even Karamzin himself had expected. Society people rushed to read the history of their fatherland. It was a new discovery for them. Ancient Russia, it seemed, had been discovered by Karamzin, as America had been by Columbus. For a time nowhere did anyone speak of anything else. I must confess, it is impossible to imagine anything more stupid than the judgements of society that I heard; they were enough to break anyone of the desire for fame . . . In the journals they did not criticise him; none among us was in a position to analyse and evaluate Karamzin's huge creation . . . Almost no one said thank you to this man who had closeted himself in his study during the period of his most flattering successes and had devoted twelve whole years of his life to silent and tireless labours. The notes bear witness to Karamzin's broad learning, acquired by him at that age when for ordinary people the circle of education and knowledge has long been closed and occupational cares replace striving for enlightenment. Many forgot that Karamzin published his *History* in Russia, in an autocratic state and that the tsar, having freed him from the censorship, imposed upon Karamzin by this sign an obligation to be as modest and moderate as possible. I repeat, *The History of the Russian State* is not only the work of a great writer, but the feat of an honest man.[8]

Commercial success, an enlightening impact on the public and personal independence – to name them in the order in which they appear – join in this lonely and heroic achievement. Lest the reader miss the point, Pushkin places the passage toward the end of a series of fragments that show the disadvantages of patronage:

> It happened that Trediakovskii was thrashed more than once . . . Volynskii had ordered an ode for some festival from the court poet Vasilii Trediakovskii, but the ode was not ready, and the fiery State Secretary punished the negligent versifier with his cane. (*PSS*, vol. xi, p. 53)

The disadvantages of the salons and their hostesses:

> Notice how they sing fashionable romances, how they distort the most natural lines, thwart the metre, and destroy the rhyme. Listen to their literary judgements and you will be amazed at the distortedness and even crudeness of their concepts . . . Exceptions are rare. (*PSS*, vol. xi, p. 52)

And the disadvantages of literary commerce, including publicity-conscious professionals, who rely on their advertisers' ignorance of Russian:

> The traveller Ancelot speaks of some grammar [Grech's], yet unpublished, that ratifies the rules of our language; of some novel [Bulgarin's], still in manuscript, that has made its author famous . . . What an amusing literature!
>
> (*PSS*, vol. xi, p. 54)

The exaggerated fragmentariness of Pushkin's essay itself pays tribute to the magnitude of Karamzin's achievement, realised, Pushkin insists, at no cost to Karamzin's personal dignity. But the fragments show how badly Russia lacked the criticism that could mediate between writers and their public, informing the public of literary developments and conveying to the writer a focused sense of the public's interests and expectations.

By the mid-1820s, Pushkin was becoming keenly aware of these deficiencies. Taking issue with Alexander Bestuzhev, the co-editor of the successful almanac *Polar Star*, Pushkin railed: 'It is precisely criticism that we lack . . . We do not have a single commentary, not a single critical book . . . nothing that can establish some sort of public opinion, nothing that can be counted a code of taste' (*PSS*, vol. xiii, pp. 178–79). Without intelligent, principled help in the selection and reception of literature, a reader can remain unaware of much that is appearing, undisposed toward new developments, and subject to crudely commercial or ideological manipulation. This was precisely the prospect that faced Russian literature of the late 1820s, as works of disparate foreign and native movements filled the bookstores and journals. Mere bibliographical notices in the Russian journals could no longer suffice, as Pushkin noted (*PSS*, vol. xiii, p. 178; *PSS*, vol. xi, p. 89), nor could vulgar exchanges of epithets (*PSS*, vol. xi, p. 151), outright abuse (*PSS*, vol. xi, pp. 123–24), clever jokes (*PSS*, vol. xii, p. 178), satiric comments, the mutual admiration of friends, proof-reader's comments (*PSS*, vol. xi, p. 89), 'unliterary' ad hominem accusations (*PSS*, vol. xi, p. 166) and 'several separate articles full of bright thoughts and pompous wit' (*PSS*, vol. xi, p. 167).

Whither criticism? Pushkin as critic and metacritic in the 1830s

Even more instructive than this incisive and comprehensive list of failings are Pushkin's positive attempts to define a role for criticism. His notebooks for the years 1830–31, when he was actively contributing to Del'vig's *Literary Gazette*, are filled with attempts to create a viable public criticism. No fragment is his final word on the subject; they served, rather, as dialogues with himself, with his society and with his culture.

One possibility that Pushkin entertains is simply to print the debates within the familiar groups. As one of the parties in an imagined 'conversation on criticism' puts it:

> If all the writers who deserved the respect and trust of the public would take upon themselves the labour of directing public opinion, soon criticism would become something different. Wouldn't it be interesting, for example, to read Gnedich's opinion on Romanticism or Krylov's on the present elegiac poetry? Wouldn't it be pleasant to see Pushkin analysing a tragedy by Khomiakov? These gentlemen are closely connected with each other and probably exchange comments with each other on new works. Why not make us participants in their critical conversations?' (*PSS*, vol. xi, p. 90)

Yet as Pushkin well knew, much of this conversation involved the exchange of satiric observations, specific comments on turns of phrase, and mutual admiration of a sort that might encourage writers, but could not serve the needs of the Russian reader, especially with these examples, which demonstratively ignore the prose genres that were beginning to take their place on fashion's reading table. It takes the reader for granted in ways that the author of *Poltava*, a brilliant narrative poem but commercial failure, could no longer afford to do.

A subsequent attempt to define criticism reads like something from one of his Lycée textbooks, slightly updated with its animus against base commerce:

> Criticism is the science of revealing the beauties and shortcomings in works of art and literature.
>
> It is founded on a perfect knowledge of the rules, by which the artist or writer is guided in his works, on a profound study of models, and on the active observation of remarkable contemporary phenomena.
>
> I am not speaking of impartiality – whoever is guided in his criticism by anything but a true love for art is descending to the level of the crowd, which is slavishly governed by base, mercenary motives.
>
> Where there is no love of art, there is no criticism. 'Do you wish to be a connoisseur of the arts?' asks Winckelmann. 'Try to love the artist, seek the beauty in his creations.' (*PSS*, vol. xi, p. 139)

This fragment addresses the vital problem of critical ethics – here one recalls Bulgarin's confession that he did not always read what he reviewed – and the conjunction of conventions, models and new phenomena that conditions the developing codes of literature. But, like Pushkin's previous fragment, it does not allow for the critic's interaction with the reading public. There the reader was permitted merely to overhear the writer's discussions; here a Romantic contempt for the everyday interests of the 'crowd' promises no attempt to engage those interests and to mediate between them and the poet's artistic choices. Yet it was precisely this growing distance, physical and psychological, between poet and public that criticism was now called upon to span.

A third approach to the criticism that Pushkin followed in his notebooks reacted more realistically to the shortcomings of Russian literary life in the 1830s, yet permitted the critical dialogue and principled criticism that he sought to define in the other fragments. This involved 'anti-criticism' or polemics, something that Karamzin and Zhukovskii had avoided when they edited the *Herald of Europe* earlier in the century. 'Such "anti-criticism"', wrote Pushkin, 'would bring a twofold benefit: the correction of mistaken opinions and the spread of sensible conceptions about art' (*PSS*, vol. xi, p. 132). Here, in theory, the writer or critic could address both the public and the literary situation, but too often in practice, including Pushkin's own, the dialogue became not an exchange of educated opinions, but of harsh personal attacks, necessary and effective with a public that would not distinguish a work from its author and with writers who outwardly 'preserved a reverence for concepts sacred to humanity', as Pushkin put it, mimicking Bulgarin's grandiloquence (*PSS*, vol. xi, p. 129). The exchanges between Pushkin and Bulgarin in the late 1820s and early 1830s are among the most savage in the history of Russian criticism.[9]

As Pushkin became increasingly involved in Russian journalism, helping with Del'vig's ill-fated *Literary Gazette*, editing the last volume of Del'vig's almanac *Northern Flowers*, and founding his own journal, *The Contemporary*, Pushkin's persona became more moderate. He rarely addressed specific works, although he called such events as Viazemskii's translation of Constant's *Adolphe*, Nadezhda Durova's memoirs and Gogol's *Evenings on a Farm near Dikanka* to the attention of his readers. His work as a public critic followed the lines established in his notebooks, letters and articles of the 1820s: defining crucial terms, commenting on literature as an institution, and attempting to set some ethical guidelines for literature as a public activity.

Pushkin's critical concepts are more remarkable for their conciseness and historical grounding than for their originality and theoretical profundity, and one sees little of the intricacy here that one sees when he develops irony in *Evgenii Onegin*, multiple historical perspectives in *The Captain's Daughter*, generic border-crossing in *Boris Godunov*, or incipient realism in *The Bronze Horseman*. He addressed, however briefly, many of the contested ideas of his time, seeking to relate them to contemporary European (usually French, sometimes English) discussions and to his broad reading in Classical and European writing. A representative sample shows his ambition to reduce complicated aesthetic and cultural issues to easily graspable concepts or distinctions:

> Taste – 'consists not in the unreasoning rejection of some word or turn of speech, but rather in a sense of proportion and appropriateness'
> (*PSS*, vol. xi, p. 52)
>
> Good society – 'can exist not even in the highest circle, but everywhere there are honest people, intelligent and educated' (*PSS*, vol. xi, p. 98)
>
> Morality in poetry – 'to depict weaknesses, errors, and human passions is no more immorality than anatomy is murder' (*PSS*, vol. xi, p. 201)
>
> Innovation – 'The mind is as inexhaustible in its *grasp* of concepts as language is inexhaustible in its joining of words. All words may be found in the dictionary, but books, appearing by the minute, are not mere repetitions of the dictionary. A *single thought* by itself can never represent anything new; *thoughts* can be infinitely varied' (*PSS*, vol. xii, p. 100)
>
> Romantic poetry – 'those [genres] which were unknown to the Ancients and those in which the previous forms changed or were replaced by others'
> (*PSS*, vol. xi, p. 36)
>
> National essence (*narodnost'*) – 'a way of thinking and feeling, a multitude of customs, beliefs, and habits which belong exclusively to a certain people'
> (*PSS*, vol. xi, p. 40)

Pushkin gives historical and national contexts for all of these terse definitions, thus clarifying them and making them readily applicable. Lengthy articles could be written – and have been written – on his use of such terms, but more because he used them in different contexts than because he wrote on them at length in any given critical or imaginative work.[10]

We have already seen Pushkin's concern with such institutional issues as authorial status, public criticism and the literary language. Increasingly he became aware of the problem of reaching the public, which seemed larger, increasingly diverse, and more likely to be distant from the two capitals than it had in the 1810s and 1820s. This involved, first of all, finding and holding readers. Already in 1827 Pushkin had warned M. P. Pogodin, the high-minded editor of *The Moscow Herald*, 'the misfortune is that it has too little trash', and, indeed, the journal, oriented towards poetry and German philosophical Romanticism, held a mere 300 subscribers. Pushkin went on to characterise a relatively successful rival: 'his criticism is superficial or unjust, but the manner of his incidental thoughts and their expression are sharply original; he thinks, angers, and makes one think and laugh' (*PSS*, vol. xiii, p. 341).

Pushkin would not himself seize this less than high ground in editing *The Contemporary*, and circulation suffered for it, but he refused to join – at least directly – in condemning Senkovskii's *Library for Reading* for its unprecedented commercial success and for its breezily entertaining criticism, irresponsible as it often was. On the contrary, when Gogol wrote a condemnation of Senkovskii's journal for *The Contemporary*, 'On the movement of journalistic literature in 1834 and 1835', Pushkin assumed the guise of 'A. B.', a self-styled 'humble provincial', to comment on literary journalism from the perspective of one of the new readers. In this letter to his own journal, Pushkin defends wit and variety, the historical richness of the literary language, and the European orientation of Russian literature. Defending Senkovskii's journal against Gogol's attacks, A. B. also defends the questions Gogol raises about the state of Russian and European literature. With amiable civility this fabricated letter to the editor seeks to encourage public debate, public criticism and the spread of enlightened curiosity, suggesting that they are attractive not only in the capitals, but in the provinces as well.

A third tendency in Pushkin's late criticism, after defining critical concepts and assessing Russian literary life, concerns what we might call professional ethics. When Russian literature was a court activity, a school exercise or a salon entertainment, behaviour could be regulated by the decorum and etiquette of these limited spheres of face-to-face interaction. As literature began to become a profession, however, and not just a 'craft' (*remeslo*), as Pushkin had called it when he first started to receive payment for his verse (*PSS*, vol. xiii, pp. 88, 93), it was very much in need of a new understanding of ethical behaviour for all participants, especially writers, editors, censors and critics. Court etiquette, loyalty to friends or noble honour would no longer suffice, although a member of the gentry, such as Pushkin, could never entirely lay them aside. In a series of essays published in *The Contemporary* or drafted for it, Pushkin set out to explore the boundaries of ethical behaviour in literature intended to reach the public through print media. The articles I mention all concern French literature; the Russian censorship, believing that 'anti-criticism' would upset and confuse the public, would not have permitted Pushkin to criticise contemporary Russian literary ethics so sharply. The first essay, 'The opinions of M. E. Lobanov on the spirit of literature, both abroad and at home', defends the dynamism of imaginative literature against naive censorship, restrictive and proscriptive, puncturing the factual inaccuracy, flawed logic and pompous style of Lobanov's attack on modern French literature. Among other arguments, Pushkin demonstrates that political revolutions and literary revolutions do not historically coincide (*PSS*, vol. xii, p. 70). A second essay in literary ethics, 'On Milton and on Chateaubriand's translation of *Paradise Lost*', addresses authorial dignity and the ethics of representation. In it, Pushkin lauds Chateaubriand for undertaking a scrupulous translation as a commercial venture, preferring to support himself with literary work to currying favour with the new French regime. Two younger French authors, by contrast, earn Pushkin's critical ire for treating Milton in an inaccurate and demeaning fashion in their imaginative works. Pushkin condemns Alfred de Vigny's novel *Cinq-mars* for 'absurd incongruities' (*PSS*, vol. xii, p. 141), and he finds Victor Hugo's Romantic tragedy *Cromwell* irritatingly bereft of 'historical truth and dramatic verisimilitude' (*PSS*, vol. xii, p. 140). Another essay, this time a review of Voltaire's correspondence, becomes a harsh analysis of the writer's behaviour, particularly at the Prussian court. Pushkin's conclusion reflects in sombre fashion upon the perils of public literary life (*PSS*, vol. xiii, p. 81): 'What may we conclude from this? That genius has its weaknesses, which console mediocrity, but grieve noble hearts, reminding them of human imperfection; that the real place for a writer is in his study, and that, finally, independence and self-respect alone can raise us above the trifles of life and the storms of fate.' Pushkin understood well the high cost of celebrity from his own experience in society, at court and on the printed page. And he understood that an immature public would interweave the poet's private life, his public persona and the personalities of his literary creations to the detriment of authorial dignity.

Pushkin's bitter personal experience as a pioneering professional writer, in turn, lends animus to these essays in literary ethics. Pushkin's criticism, here as elsewhere, is part and parcel of his attempt to make literature a worthy occupation, an activity valuable as an expression of the imagination and, in its own ungovernable ways, a cultural and social force.

NOTES

1. In later years Pushkin would return to the iambic hexameters of this first published poem for further reflection on literary life: 'Epistle to the Censor' ('Poslanie tsensoru', 1822), 'Second Epistle to the Censor' ('Vtoroe poslanie tsensoru', 1824), 'My ruddy critic' ('Rumianyi kritik moi', 1830), and 'From Pindemonte' ('Iz Pindemonti', 1836) are salient examples.
2. N. V. Gogol, *Polnoe sobranie sochinenii*, 14 vols., Moscow, Nauka, 1937–52, vol. viii, p. 55.
3. N. F. Filippova, *Kritik-poet Aleksandr Sergeevich Pushkin*, Moscow, Nasledie, 1998, takes admirable cognisance of the many loci of Pushkin's critical observations but neglects Pushkin's critical obsession with literary institutions and mores, to which he devoted many of his most enduring reflections.
4. B. M. Tomashevskii, *Pushkin. Kniga pervaia (1813–1824)*, Moscow, Leningrad, Akademiia nauk, 1956, pp. 675–719.

5. N. M. Karamzin, *Izbrannye sochineniia*, 2 vols., Moscow, Leningrad, Izdatel'stvo Khudozhestvennaia literatura, 1964, vol. ii, p. 176.
6. *PSS*, vol. xiii, p. 135. Letter of 25 January 1825 to K. F. Ryleev.
7. A. S. Pushkin, *The Complete Works of Alexander Pushkin*, 15 vols., Norfolk, Milner, 1999–2003, vol. i, p. 275. Readers without Russian will find English translations of Pushkin's critical articles and fragments in volume xiii of this edition and in Tatiana Wolff (ed. and trans.), *Pushkin on Literature*, rev. edn., Stanford University Press, 1986. Carl R. Proffer (ed. and trans.), *The Critical Prose of Alexander Pushkin with Critical Essays by Four Russian Romantic Poets*, Bloomington, IN, Indiana University Press, 1969, is a useful, but less complete selection.
8. *PSS*, vol. xi, p. 57. Translations are my own unless otherwise stated.
9. For an analysis of Pushkin's part in the exchange, see J. Thomas Shaw, 'The problem of the "persona" in journalism: Pushkin's *Feofilakt Kosichkin*', in his *Pushkin: Poet and Man of Letters and his Prose*, Los Angeles, Charles Schlacks Jr, 1995, pp. 205–30; for an analysis of Bulgarin's part, together with documents, see A. I. Reitblat (ed.), *Vidok Figliarin: Pis'ma i agenturnye zapiski F. B. Bulgarina v III Otdelenie*, Moscow, Novoe literaturnoe obozrenie, 1998.
10. For brief surveys see John Mersereau, 'Pushkin's concept of Romanticism', *Studies in Romanticism* 3:1 (1963), 24–41; V. B. Tomashevskii, *Pushkin: Kniga vtoraia, materialy k monografii (1824–1837)*, Moscow, Leningrad, Akademiia nauk, 1961, pp. 106–53; and N. L. Stepanov, 'Pushkin-kritik', in V. E. Evgen'ev-Maksimov *et al.* (eds.), *Ocherki po istorii russkoi zhurnalistiki i kritiki. Vol. I: XVIII vek i pervaia polovina XIX-ego veka*, Leningrad, LGU, 1950, pp. 415–33.

II

THE PUSHKINIAN TRADITION

11

BORIS GASPAROV

Pushkin in music

Among modern poets set to music, Pushkin occupies an unparalleled position. According to the Russian scholar Valerii Kikta, in opera alone there are no fewer than 141 works based on Pushkin's œuvre, including one rock opera (*Tsar, Saltan* by V. Sokolov, 1980) and excluding works that take Pushkin as their subject. *The Gypsies*, for instance, has inspired no fewer than eighteen operas – among them, Rakhmaninov's *Aleko* (1893), *Tsygany* by Rimskii-Korsakov's disciple V. Kalafati (1941), *Gli zingari* by Ruggerio Leoncavallo (1912) and *Zigäunen* (1883) by Walter von Goethe (the poet's grandson) – plus a half a dozen ballets. The first of over sixty Pushkinian pieces for the musical theatre, the ballet *Ruslan and Ludmila, or the Overthrow of Chernomor, the Evil Sorcerer* by Friedrich ('Fedor Efimovich') Scholz, appeared in 1821 just as Pushkin achieved his first success. The early Soviet period celebrated the centennial of his death with the opera *Pushkin's Death* (*Gibel' Pushkina*) by G. Kreitner (1937), while in the post-Soviet period Pushkin has already inspired *The Captain's Daughter*, a ballet produced in 1998 by the former 'chairman' of Soviet music, the octogenarian Tikhon Khrennikov, and the ballet *Alexander and Natalie* (*Aleksandr i Natali*, 1990) by V. A. Pikul', a product of more frivolous times. A host of cantatas, programmatic symphonic and chamber compositions, and numerous pieces of incidental music for films and stage productions, also form part of this musical corpus. The collective output of about 500 authors of 'romances' (art songs) and choruses based on Pushkin's lyrical poetry numbers in the range of several thousand pieces.

The list of 'Pushkin' composers features such curious entries as Friedrich Nietzsche, the author of the songs 'A winter evening' and 'Incantation' (the latter arranged for the voice and the orchestra by Alfred Schnittke, 1984), and a nineteenth-century Kazakh poet and composer of folkloric bent, Abai (Kunanbaev), the author of the 'Onegin cycle' of songs. It also includes virtually all Russian composers of stature (with perhaps the only exception of Scriabin), as well as quite a few western ones, among them Felix Mendelssohn,

Franz Liszt, Witosław Lutosławski and Benjamin Britten. Below the exotic and the sublime lies a wasteland of compositions by indigenous authors of a minor and minuscule standing whose activity amounts to nothing less than a national pastime.

Musical Pushkiniana is both an obvious product of and significant factor in the Pushkin cult central to the Russian cultural tradition. The bulk of critical works about Pushkin in music, often prompted by new compositions, were published around the Pushkin anniversaries in 1899, 1937 and 1999 and were inevitably eulogistic.[1] Early studies of the problem of Pushkin in Russian music appeared at the turn of the nineteenth century in connection with the first widely celebrated Pushkin anniversary of 1899.[2] Even the remarkable Pushkin 'Jubilee' of 1921 (see Chapter 12) was not left without a musicological echo in the form of a collection of essays, *Orfei* (Petrograd, 1922), that included B. V. Asafiev's remarkable 'At the source of life. To the memory of Pushkin' ('U istokov zhizni. Pamiati Pushkina').

Pushkin's exceptional popularity among musicians seems to be taken for granted as highly positive. This essay will argue, however, that the relation between Pushkin the poet and Pushkin as a stimulus to musical composition has been far from straightforward. First and foremost, the history of musical incarnations of Pushkin's œuvre is the history of its displacements – displacements into different historical and aesthetic epochs, different genres, and above all, into a musical tradition that has an inner logic of its own. As a rule, the transposition of works of verbal art into music creates effects of displacement.[3] In Pushkin's case, however, the effect goes deeper. The habit of setting Pushkin's words and characters to music has been so entrenched that over time it coalesced into a musical tradition of its own. In appropriating Pushkin musically, the challenge faced by each successive generation of composers stemmed more from their awareness of the work of their predecessors than from their direct 'dialogue' with Pushkin's poetry. Musical Pushkiniana emerged as a powerful means by which each generation strove to define itself *vis-à-vis* the preceding tradition and to express aesthetic and philosophical sensibilities of its own time. The nature of the displacement is considerably different in regard to the two principal musical genres in which Pushkin's works were used on a massive scale – works for musical theatre, on the one hand, and songs based on Pushkin's lyrical poetry, on the other.

Opera and Pushkin

When a notable opera on a Pushkinian subject appears, its perception is inevitably affected by the public's intimate familiarity with its literary counterpart. Until it becomes itself a firmly established cultural fact, a Pushkin opera inevitably creates a shock by disrupting cultural expectations. Complaints about the 'desecration' of a hallowed literary text appear with the inevitability of a cultural ritual. One can cite as the most famous examples of this popular critical genre Turgenev's letter to Tolstoy (15 November 1878) about Tchaikovsky's *Evgenii Onegin* ('Undoubtedly remarkable music . . . But what a libretto!'), or N. Strakhov's rebuke to Musorgsky (in a 'letter to the Editor' published in Dostoevsky's *The Citizen*) for the 'unceremonious' treatment of Pushkin's *Boris Godunov* in his opera. Mikhail Bulgakov captured the essence of this attitude in his *Master and Margarita* when he made Bezdomny's futile chase of the Devil proceed under the persistent accompaniment of a 'literary-musical' radio broadcast of *Evgenii Onegin* blasted by street loudspeakers; a 'heavy bass singing about his love to Tatiana' sounds in this context like the voice of hell itself.[4]

This attitude entirely misses the point because an opera is not about Pushkin's 'words' but about his narrative. The displacement of the literary prototype does take place, but it stems primarily from the fact that Pushkin's characters and situations reappear in an opera written in a different historical epoch, by an artist who reflects the aesthetic and psychological sensibilities of his own time. Tchaikovsky himself, when pressed by the Imperial Theatre to compose *The Queen of Spades*, expressed his distaste for Pushkin's story in which he initially saw nothing more than a shallow anecdote. Tchaikovsky eventually wrote his great expressionist opera after his brother's libretto, which carefully removed all the reticent irony and nonchalant bantering of its literary prototype, infusing it with period melodrama instead.[5]

Let me illustrate this point about how musical adaptations adjusted literary works to the contemporary context by treating just a few outstanding operas after Pushkin's works. Tchaikovsky's *Evgenii Onegin* (1877–78) and Musorgsky's *Boris Godunov* (1868–72) project Pushkin into the epoch of psychological novel. When Tchaikovsky decided to write an opera after *Evgenii Onegin* in 1877, many questioned his choice of what was widely regarded at the time as a superficial and obsolete literary work; among those who made this point most severely was César Cui (1835–1918), one of the founding members of the New Russian School (the 'Mighty Kuchka' or 'The Five') in 1856. This view did not prevent him from writing three Pushkin operas of his own (*The Prisoner of the Caucasus*, *Feast in the Time of Plague* and *The Captain's Daughter*). Tchaikovsky's treatment of Pushkin's narrative recalls characters and situations typical of Turgenev's novels. Within this new cultural space, familiar situations acquired different meaning. Tatiana's letter, and Onegin's failure to respond to it, are recast into a situation typical for novels of the 1850s and 1860s: a spirited woman boldly declares her love to a male hero unable to meet this challenge, who reveals a weakness that portends his eventual moral and physical demise. Tchaikovsky invests all his lyrical genius in Tatiana's letter where she is the embodiment of sincerity itself. The music displaces the rhetoric of her letter where old-fashioned language reflects the world of sentimentalist novels that had been fashionable in the time of her mother's youth.[6] Tchaikovsky's opera makes the conflict between the sentimental and Romantic generations all but irrelevant, replacing it with the conflict between the heroine's 'true feelings' and the hero's inner emptiness – a picture that stands in full agreement with the psychological world of Turgenev's and Goncharov's novels.[7]

Musorgsky harmonises Pushkin's drama with the different pitch of the realist novel as practised by Dostoevsky. What distinguishes his version of Boris's 'crime and punishment' from Pushkin's is its introspective character. Pushkin followed the historical account of Karamzin, which was unequivocal about Boris's guilt. By contrast, Musorgsky plunged his narrative into Dostoevskian ambiguities. His Boris does assume guilt for the tsarevich's death, but it remains unclear whether he committed or merely condoned the terrible crime, or deems himself morally culpable as a beneficiary of the murder. At first glance, the crucial scene in which Boris sees the apparition of the slain tsarevich covered in blood, looks like proof of his involvement in the murder. What triggered this hallucination, however, was the ringing of the clock in Boris's chamber. Musorgsky's music recalls the ringing of the bells from the Coronation scene, a vivid reminder of the moment when Boris agreed to become tsar, and thereby condemned himself to pangs of conscience.[8] We see a character crushed by his inner drama, no matter what relation it had to the reality.

Pushkin and song

Narrative musical works tend to treat the literary prototype macroscopically, from the point of view of character and situation. By contrast, a song takes a microscopic attitude towards its poetic text, dealing primarily with the meaning and style of the text word by word. We can say that an opera's principal relation to its literary prototype is that of an interpretation, while a song's task is to give a musical expression to its lyrics.

It is a tenet of scholarly literature about Pushkin's songs that his lyrical poetry serves as a vital source of inspiration because of its inherent 'musicality'. According to this argument, the best composers reciprocate by creating music that gives Pushkin's poetic images a new life. Critics, however, consistently ignore the phenomenon of mass musical production associated with Pushkin's texts: an ocean of mediocre and routine musical pieces hides behind the few best works.[9] Given the hallowed association of Pushkin and music, such lack of critical frankness is understandable. To the best of their means, most composers felt compelled to enter the tradition of treating Pushkin's poetry musically. It is particularly interesting to explore how the appropriation of Pushkin in art songs influenced the development of this musical genre, on the one hand, and what impact, if any, that process might have on the perception of Pushkin's lyrical poetry, on the other.

For all the enormous variety of the corpus, the history of the Pushkinian romance can be roughly divided into three major epochs. The first period roughly coincides with Pushkin's creative span, that is, from the 1820s, when the first 'Pushkin songs' appeared, to the early 1840s. These years saw the formation of the Russian art song, a process in which Pushkin's poetry played a major role. In the second phase, which extends to the early twentieth century, the Russian art song, as a counterpart of the German *Lied*, reached full maturity. Once again, the contribution of Pushkin's poetry to this process was overwhelming; yet one senses tentative signs that composers began to struggle with a tradition that had by that time become virtually a musical compulsion. The third epoch covers most of the twentieth century. As the rate of production of Pushkin art songs in the high nineteenth-century tradition plateaued, the fixed patterns that composers followed, while somewhat enlivened by modernist innovations, began to sound increasingly banal. The best Pushkin songs of this epoch reveal a deliberate effort either to depart from or to play with the existing tradition; their music assumes a secondary – that is, self-reflective and referential – character. Finally, beginning with the generation of the 1960s, one can observe (with a few exceptions) a remarkable reticence among leading composers toward the genre of the 'Pushkin song'.

The golden age of the popular song

The 1820s and 1830s were the golden age of the Russian popular urban song. Performing 'urban' romances eventually became a pastime among all social classes in cities. This type of romance featured a simple strophic structure, harmony based on a few basic chords, and an unabashedly emotional solo vocal line seconded by a light-textured accompaniment. The accompanying instrument might vary from a keyboard to the balalaika, but the most favoured one was the Russian seven-string guitar. The choice of the lyrics, often drawn from contemporary poetry of diverse artistic levels, leaned heavily toward the sentimental and favoured a stylised folkloric colour.

Out of this fertile ground the art song, also known as 'romance', emerged. What distinguished these romances from their popular predecessors was primarily a sophisticated musical language that used more complex and varied harmonies, an enhanced role for the accompaniment (and as a consequence, a preference for the piano), and a wider variety of sub-genres and use of topoi. In general, because an art song was a crafted rather than spontaneous expression of emotion in song, it showed a higher degree of aesthetic self-awareness. In popular song a single musical stanza was typically repeated as many times as required by the lyrics. In the romance the design is more complex: the music of each stanza contained variations that follow the words' meaning more closely. What unifies the variations are devices such as a recurring motif, or a single harmony through the whole piece, or the addition of an identical piano introduction and conclusion as a frame.

A gradual transition from the popular song to the art song was the result of creative efforts of a *pléiade* of talented amateur and semi-professional composers, most important among them Aleksei Verstovskii (1799–1862), Alexander Aliabiev (1787–1851), Nikolai Titov (1798–1843), Alexander Varlamov (1801–48) and Alexander Gurilev (1803–58), whose art thrived in the 1820s and 1830s. This development culminated in Mikhail Glinka's (1804–57) romances of the 1830s and early 1840s. Pushkin's poetry proved to be crucial to this process.

Although the combined sentimentality and native colour favoured in the early romances were in short supply in Pushkin's mature lyrics, his early poetry offered the first generation of romance composers a rich palette of colours. Among Pushkin romances of the 1820s and 1830s, the dominance of the exotic immediately strikes the ear. Verstovskii wrote the 'Gypsy Song' (after Zemfira's 'The old husband, the fearsome husband' from *The Gypsies*, 1827), 'Moldavian Song' ('Chernaia shal'', 1823), and 'Spanish Song' ('Gishpanskaia pesnia. Nochnoi struit zefir', 1827). Glinka's insatiable hunger for diverse musical colours tapped a rich vein in Pushkin's poetry. He composed two Pushkin songs on Spanish topoi, 'I am here, Inezilla', ('Ia zdes', Inezila', 1834) and 'The Night Zephyr' ('Nochnoi zefir', 1838), 'The flame of desire is burning in my blood' ('V krovi gorit ogon' zhelaniia', 1838), a song in the mode of Biblical Orientalism, a 'Georgian song' entitled 'Don't sing, O beautiful maiden' ('Ne poi krasavitsa', 1828), as well as 'Mary' ('Meri', after Pushkin's 'From Barry Cornwall', 1849). Another domain of Pushkin's œuvre that proved to be universally attractive was, predictably, his love poetry and early elegies, where the expression of elegant melancholy was uncomplicated by philosophical meditation.

Pushkin's versatility in creating vivid motifs challenged composers to expand their artistic aspirations for the romance. Composers of the first 'Pushkin generation' extended the modest scope of their musical language, previously confined to a limited assortment of musical expressions of conventional nativism, by reaching to the exotic. For instance, in Nikolai Titov's

'The Talisman' ('Talisman', 1829) the music scarcely deviates from generic patterns in melody and harmony; one can imagine it as a pleasant accompaniment to virtually any poem in trochaic tetrameter. When, however, the music reaches the key word 'talisman', the harmony jumps from the E flat to the C flat major – a device that, while relatively rare in 1830, would later become a commonplace mystical stroke in the works of such composers as Liszt or Rimskii-Korsakov. This momentary touch of magical Orientalism interrupts a pretty but indifferent musical recitation, providing a connection to the meaning of a particular word. In a similar vein, Verstovskii strove in his 'Spanish Song' ('Gishpanskaia pesnia', 1827) to recreate the poem's exoticism. In the song, the picture of a sumptuous Spanish night that opens the poem is adumbrated musically with a bolero-like rhythm in the accompaniment; the suitor's amorous exhortations are supported by arpeggios imitating the sound of a guitar. Verstovskii's 'Moldavian Song' showed artistic ambition of another kind, also prompted by the lyrics. The song is cast as a musical ballad, a form of narrative song that flourished as a literary and musical genre in the nineteenth century that usually drew its subjects from history and legend. The setting of the narrative is strophic, unfolding in units made up of the same number of lines, rhyme scheme and metre. Within the use of recurrent features there is considerable musical variation in a way that recalls Schubert's balladic 'Erlkönig' (1815). While Verstovskii's heavy borrowing from Schubert resulted in a somewhat comic effect when applied to Pushkin's 'Moldavian' melodrama, his song signified a decisive departure from rudimentary repetitions of a single musical stanza in favour of a varied yet coherent musical narrative.

Despite their overt simplicity, the sophistication of Glinka's songs far surpassed anything achieved by his predecessors. Perhaps the main secret of the unique charm of Glinka's romances lies in the fact that, although artfully constructed, they never lose the transparent sparseness of musical texture and a directness of expression verging on the naive, signatures of the popular song. Glinka's stylised simplicity resembles that of Schubert, although his musical language has more of the Italian (most especially, the influence of Rossini) than German in it. Verstovskii and others strove to expand the modest realm of the popular song toward something more aesthetically ambitious. Glinka's songs, on the contrary, hide their mastery of the artistic detail behind an unpretentious façade of a salon impromptu. In this, they are congenial to the artfully constructed casualness and simplicity of Pushkin's lyrical poetry. Glinka's 'The flame of desire is burning in my blood' ('V krovi gorit ogon' zhelaniia,' 1838) after Pushkin's poetic setting of *The Song of Songs* employs sultry chromaticisms, or changes in harmony that depart from the principal scale, as the sign of the passionate Orient. This unabashedly conventional feature requires only a few touches in the accompaniment. Moreover, generic Orientalism is fused here with another convention – that of a waltz as clearly suggested by the metre and the texture of the piano part. While the subject of Glinka's song is not an exotic Biblical figure, the musical exoticism that accompanies his entrance into modern ballroom enhances his allure. Against the rotation of the waltz, chromaticism creates a subtly jarring effect, done virtually without any emphasis and with a truly Pushkinian nonchalance.

The score of Glinka's 'Where is our rose?' ('Gde nasha roza?', 1837) occupies just one page (Nikolai Medtner's, by comparison, takes twice as much space). It is an exercise in musical negativity of rare sophistication. The opening rhetorical question about the vanished rose is cast in an unusual metre (5/4); its hesitant pace underscores the void sound of a few scattered intervals in the accompaniment. The banality of its hypothetical statements ('Don't say: Such are the joys of life! Don't say: This is how youth withers!') is expressed by musical phrases whose melody and harmony are completely generic; yet the 5/4 metre, by injecting a hesitant pause on the odd beat at the end of each phrase, 'negates' their superficial conclusiveness. A very brief dramatic moment, featuring a dissonant and chromatic harmony, follows on the words 'Alas! I regret it . . .' However, as the poem's subject turns from the withered rose to the blooming lily, the indecision of the odd metre gives way to the exuberant, waltz-like 3/4 time. The song reverts to the conventional mode.

The Pushkinian song post-Glinka

Throughout the second part of the nineteenth and the early twentieth centuries, the romance in general, and Pushkin romances in particular, became increasingly complex as a musical language in its relationship with the poetic text. The process can be seen as similar to the way in which German *Lieder* were evolving at the same time from Schubert to Schumann, and Brahms to Hugo Wolf. The late nineteenth-century romance loses virtually all connections with a more populist concept of a song, and becomes a fully fledged genre of art music. Its harmonies, replete with chromaticisms and sharp tonal shifts, are on a par with instrumental music of the time, while its melody becomes an increasingly complex and on occasion flexible, musical declamation. Musical discourse now unfolds as an intense dialogue between the voice and the piano, the latter often expressing shifts of emotions in broad strokes while the vocal line follows closely the meaning of the words.

Despite this trend, the range of Pushkin's poems set as lyrics remains relatively narrow and confined to established preferences. The prevalence of the exotic, the amorous and the elegiac remained as decisive among the second generation of Pushkin romances as in the previous epoch. New versions of 'The Flower' and '*Thou* and *you*' by Rimskii-Korsakov together with Cui's 'I loved you' ('Ia vas liubil', 1899) appear alongside other pieces in a similar mode like Borodin's 'For the shores of your distant homeland' ('Dlia beregov otchizny dal'noi', 1888), Glazunov's 'The Dream' ('Snovidenie', 1898), and Cui's 'The Burned Letter' ('Sozhzhennoe pis'mo', 1885–86). Long before Ravel's *Jeux d'eau*, song composers employed the device of the continuous, refined arpeggio in order to imitate the flow of water as in Cui's 'The Statue in Tsarskoe Selo', ('Tsarskosel'skaia statuia', 1899) and Glazunov's 'Nereide' ('Nereida', 1887–90), or to suggest the motion of light clouds as in Rimskii-Korsakov's 'The light flock of clouds disperses' ('Redeet oblakov letuchaia griada', n.d.). For the most part, composers were content to build on the extant musical image of Pushkin by projecting it on a more complex and diverse musical language.

The musical expression of Pushkin's exoticism reaches its most sophisticated moment with Mily Balakirev's 'Georgian Song' ('Ne poi krasavitsa', 1862), which remains undoubtedly one of the most remarkable achievements of Russian musical Orientalism. A far cry from the token Orientalism of the early romances, this song resounds with sharp, repeated melodic phrases in the bass (also known as ostinato) which recreate the sounds of an oriental drum, and punctuate the complex vocal line replete with intricate chromaticisms and ornamentations. Ironically, the rich oriental trappings of Balakirev's musical portrait of the Georgian maiden are hardly authentic since Georgian music is predominantly written in the diatonic scale (as opposed to the chromatic scale) in which each letter name for a note has only one pitch as embodied in the white keys of the piano keyboard and does not include semitones, like sharps and flats. This nuance did not escape Glinka who had chosen a simple diatonic tune (authentically Georgian) for his version of the 'Georgian song'.

With its greater sophistication of expression, the mature romance should be better equipped to capture, and perhaps even enrich, the meaning of the poetic word. The reality, however, is not that simple. For the very power of the musical element led to its domination of poetic meaning and prosody. Consequently, while the musical picture presented in a romance was animated, its relationship to the poem on its own was highly attenuated. Musical settings turned Pushkin's elliptical foreshadowing of meaning into more immediate images. Pushkin's poetic diction, which, despite its overt 'melodiousness', is in fact quite sober and often relies on tiny prosodic details, faced the danger of being drowned in conspicuous gestures of musical rhythm and texture.

Consider as a case in point Anton Rubinstein's 'The Night' ('Noch'', 1864), one of the most popular among the 'second generation' of Pushkin romances. The song is held together by an elaborate accompaniment whose pace gradually intensifies as the drama mounts. There are instances when the music follows Pushkin's words with remarkable closeness: a sudden tense chromaticism appears on the word 'languid' (*tomnyi*), a melancholy note is struck on the words 'my sad candle'. Yet as a whole the song shows how the composer's artistic individuality and the music's inner logic supersede the texture and the meaning of words. The poem's movement is fluid in the extreme; it proceeds in a fast succession of images, ending inconclusively, with abrupt exclamations. In contradistinction to this, Rubinstein's musical discourse abounds in emphatic reiterations; virtually every line is rendered in two versions, the first more dramatic, the second letting the tension subside in an elaborate cadence – a device reflecting the composer's penchant for neoclassical symmetries. While the poem ends in a chain of elliptic exclamations, the romance concludes with an elaborate coda that gradually brings the flow of the music to a complete halt. The well-organised unity of the music contradicts the precipitous unpredictability of the poem's flow.

For the nineteenth century, Rimskii-Korsakov's 'The Prophet' ('Prorok', 1897) represented a rare attempt to address those aspects of Pushkin's poetry outside the habitual domain of the exotic and amorous. The romance faithfully follows the more sensational aspects of the poem's message, as well as its solemn Biblical mode. Stern, archaic-sounding unisons depicting the Prophet's dwelling in the 'gloomy desert' suddenly give way to the ethereal lightness of arpeggios as the six-winged Seraph appears. When the Seraph begins his initiation rites, the music, while retaining its ethereal pace, becomes more dramatic, culminating with stark dissonances on the words 'And he clove my bosom with his sword.' The song's triumphant climax – God's words addressed to the Prophet – is rendered by bright strokes of archaically sounding diatonic chords soaring over a powerful descending sequence of octaves in the left hand. The figures of the Prophet in the 'gloomy desert', the Seraph and God are cast in relief as musical pictures. Yet the sensual immediacy of the poem's musical rendition, while enhancing the descriptive power of each separate image, also takes away the ambiguities and understatements that are imprinted in its poetic discourse. Rimskii-Korsakov's Seraph is ethereal, his God is epically magnificent, and his Prophet is stern and stalwart. The overt meaning of the words seems to match the musical expression; however, their stylistic texture tells a different story. The poem's saturation with archaisms (*persty*, *otverzlis'*, *zenitsy*, *prazdnoslovnyi*, *vizhd' i vnemli*) looks natural as a sign of its Biblical mode. What is less predictable is the way Pushkin juxtaposes Slavonicisms with expressions borrowed from the vocabulary of elegiac poetry. These discordant registers, which are harmonised by the uncanny virtuosity of Pushkin's poetic diction, in the song send a message of the contradiction that interferes with the original fresco-like picture of the Prophet anointed to his hallowed mission.

By offering a succession of musical images organised by specifically musical means of identification and variation, a song gives us something that the poem does not and cannot do. When the Prophet hears tremors in the heaven and discerns the life underwater and underground, the music, while rendering all these images, never loses sight of the Seraph's presence; his signature motif (the arpeggios) persists through all the transformations. We never forget about the Seraph's mystical lightness while following his increasingly violent actions. The poetic discourse is incapable of such simultaneity. The music lives its own life that is distinct from that of the poem.

That a song and a poem are two distinct works of art is obvious. What seems less obvious is the fact that their mutual projection does not necessarily benefit understanding of either of them. An inherent contradiction exists between the words and the music. The relation between a poem and its musical rendition is that of either/or. One has to cast away the vividness of the musical image in order to appreciate more subtle and complex aspects of the verbal meaning. Similarly, one must forget about the poem *as a poem*, that is to say, a verbal discourse in all complexity of its dimensions, in order to appreciate the song as a musical artefact. Drawn into the element of music, the poem turns into the song's lyrics – an internal matter of the music, a part of its own aesthetic organism. Paradoxically, this contradiction can be sensed most acutely in the cases of highest artistic achievement, both poetic and musical. Although a great poem has a magnetic attraction to composers, the complex and subtle inflections that inhere to the verbal text often escape complete musical expression. By the same token, the more powerful the music, the more distinctly it shapes its own message, sidelining at least some of the poem's own properties.

With respect to Pushkin's poetry, this inherent contradiction could have become particularly acute as the romance advanced towards the utmost richness and individuation of musical expression. Musorgsky and Tchaikovsky, the two most prolific and inventive Russian song composers of the second half of the nineteenth century, both showed a remarkable reticence towards Pushkin's poetry as a vehicle for their song music. Musorgsky's only Pushkin song – 'The Night' ('Noch'', 1864) – belongs to his juvenilia, although he rearranged it later. With its straightforward 'nocturnal' image rendered by rich piano tremolandos, it is no match for the accomplished artistry of Rubinstein's piece. Avoiding Pushkin in their song writing constituted a rare point of coincidence between Musorgsky and Tchaikovsky, whose distaste for each other's music and personality is well known.

The late nineteenth-century romance achieved its climax in songs by Sergei Rakhmaninov. In his romances, the piano usually assumes the dominant role; it creates an uninterrupted flow of musical images echoing the meaning of the words, while the vocal line proceeds in declamatory phrases, often separated by extensive piano interludes. Typical examples of this technique can be seen in such songs as 'Nereide', 'Arion', and 'Have you seen the maiden on the cliff?' – all unified by the 'aquarian' topos, which gives the piano rich opportunities to combine the pictorial and the expressive element. The effect is almost Wagnerian; a song turns into a miniature musical drama.

The late nineteenth century and beyond

The powerful development of the art song in the second half of the nineteenth century created a fertile ground for imitators. In the Soviet period, there was no shortage of ethereal arpeggios representing the murmur of water (A. Vlasov, 'To the fountain of Bakhchisarai'), or of a poignant imitation of small bells clinking conveying the melancholy of a Russian *Winterreise* (T. Khrennikov, 'Winter road', 1935). The tradition of Pushkin romances became in fact a heavy burden to composers in search of a new way to set Pushkin's lyric creatively.

Many composers, notably Nikolai Medtner (1875–1951), Dmitrii Shostakovich (1906–75) and Georgii Sviridov (1915–98), treated Pushkin's work with a sparseness reminiscent of Glinka, or even of the pre-Glinkian romance. A typical twentieth-century Pushkin romance becomes a self-conscious replay of its 'naive' early predecessor; one can easily recognise traditional turns of musical speech, yet these well-worn formulas take a modernist twist that gives them fresh, sometimes paradoxical meaning. Once again, a parallel can be drawn with the development of German *Lieder*, where the stylised simplicity of Mahler's songs emerged against the backdrop of the utmost expressive intensity the genre had achieved in the works by Brahms and Hugo Wolf.

Much credit for this development should be given to Nikolai Medtner. Written for the most part in emigration between the wars, Medtner's romances have only recently and deservedly come into vogue. His songs revisit virtually all the hackneyed subjects of musical Pushkiniana. Moreover, Medtner's musical discourse conspicuously displays evident debts to his predecessors. His setting of 'The Night' (1918–19) vaguely recalls Rubinstein's version. His song 'I love you' (1915) retains distinct traces of the pleasant if indifferent melody of Sheremetev's well-known piece, and his setting of 'The Rose' ('Roza', 1913) clearly alludes to Glinka's song. Yet conventional idioms of melody, harmony and piano texture now become exaggerated. While the melody will make the expected leap at a climactic moment, it goes too far and pushes the music off the 'right' tonality as the piano's conventional chords suddenly lose tonal stability and sound harshly assertive. The effect is disturbed, almost hysterical. The song subverts the smoothness of the traditional discourse of the romance from inside, by respecting conventions, and exposing hidden skeletons in the process.

It is the exotic element of Pushkin that remains a staple in twentieth-century songs. But this mannerism is leavened with new-found irony. Instead of the former lush musical ambiance, the exaggerated employment of traditional exotic sonorities now produces an exuberant chaos. Such is Medtner's 'I am here, Inezilla', in which each couplet is accompanied by a prolonged refrain 'La-la-la-la', whose music transparently alludes to the sensuous 'Seguidilla' of Bizet's *Carmen*.

For all the difference of Shostakovich's style from Medtner's, his treatment of Pushkin shows some remarkable similarities. Shostakovich's 'Farewell' ('Proshchanie', 1952) begins in an almost ideally diatonical C major; virtually no chromaticism appears through the whole first stanza. The light and uniform texture of the accompaniment recalls the amateur, early nineteenth-century romance. Slowly and gradually, as the farewell employs a succession of dramatic images – death, widowhood, fading away from memory – the accompaniment dissolves into a discontinuous succession of chords without a stable tonal centre. As the poem arrives at the concluding image of embracing one's friend whose arrest is imminent, the harmony, through a succession of chromatic shifts, finally arrives at C major once again.

The Pushkin romance increasingly becomes a rarity in the last third of the twentieth century. Both Shostakovich and Prokofiev never returned to Pushkin after writing their short cycles of Pushkin romances by the year of Pushkin's anniversary of 1937. Many leading composers of the post-war generation, such as Alfred Schnittke, Sofia Gubaidulina, Sergei Slonimskii, Boris Tishchenko, Rodion Shchedrin, have written no songs after Pushkin's poems.

It seems that the genre of the 'Pushkin song' can be now observed in its entirety, as a tradition that has come full circle in its development. From this perspective, one can pose the question once again: what, if any, has been the impact of the Pushkin romance on his poetry? The answer to this question may be paradoxical. Once again, I would like to suggest caution toward a straightforward impression that the music enhances and enlivens the meaning of the poetic word. It does not; rather, it creates vivid images of its own, which depart from their poetic counterparts and go their own way as determined by the nature of musical expression and the logic of musical development. To be truly appreciated, a song must be freed from the mesmerising presence of Pushkin's poetic voice that it allegedly strives to recreate. The rich tradition of Pushkin romances needs to be observed for its own intrinsic features, and from the inner perspective of its own historical development.

Yet if viewed as an independent artistic creation, a counterpart of rather than a derivation from Pushkin's poems, songs may reveal something about the nature of Pushkin's poetry after all, if only by way of a negative example. A dynamic, expressively rich song, by virtue of its very existence as a counterpart of a poem, highlights something in the latter that it cannot and should not capture.

What is most characteristic for Pushkin's poetry, particularly in his lyrical poems, is its trans-sensual quality – the elusive fluidity of meaning and dizzying ellipses through which it conveys its message. Paradoxically, this quality of Pushkin's poetic word can be defined as musicality, albeit in a way more fundamental than merely a superficial sonority. Like instrumental music, a poem by Pushkin suggests more than it says, and excites with rich promises that remain never fully realised. The sonorous harmony of Pushkin's poetic diction and clarity of his images stand like a shining screen that makes the transcendent quality of his words only more elusive. Paradoxically, a musical portrait of Pushkin's lyrical poetry takes away its fundamental 'musicality' by giving it a rich, directly appealing sensual texture. The tradition of Pushkin songs owes its richness and popularity not to its adherence to its hallowed literary prototype but, on the contrary, to its inherent tensions with Pushkin's poetic word.

NOTES

1. Examples include A. N. Kriuger, *Pushkin v muzyke*, Moscow, Sovietskii kompozitor, 1936, and V. A. Kiselev, *Pushkin v romansakh i pesniakh ego sovremennikov*, Moscow, n.p., 1936.
2. M. M. Ivanov, *Pushkin v muzyke*, St Petersburg, Suvorin's typography, 1899; S. K. Bulich, *Pushkin i russkaia muzyka*, St Petersburg, 1900.
3. Caryl Emerson, *Boris Godunov: Transpositions of a Russian Theme*, Bloomington, IN, Indiana University Press, 1986, part 4.
4. Asafiev was the first to suggest that people tended to replace the novel's characters and situations with those they recall from the opera. See B. V. Asafiev, '*Evgenii Onegin*: liricheskie stseny Chaikovskogo', in his *O muzyke Chaikovskogo*, Leningrad, Izdatel'stvo Muzyka, 1972, p. 76.
5. The tale's image as an anecdote found its musical expression as well – in an operetta by F. von Suppé (*Die Kartenschlägerin*, 1862), while its 'French' connection was

pursued by F. Halévy (*La Dame de pique*, after Mérimée's rendition of the story, 1850).

6. Caryl Emerson, 'Tchaikovsky's Tatiana', in Leslie Kearney (ed.), *Tchaikovsky and his World*, Princeton University Press, 1998, pp. 216–20; Kadja Grönke, 'On the role of Gremin: Tchaikovsky's *Evgenii Onegin*', in Kearney (ed.), *Tchaikovsky and his World*, pp. 220–34.
7. Boris Gasparov, *Five Operas and a Symphony: Word and Music in Russian Culture*, New Haven, CT, Yale University Press, 2005, chap. 3.
8. Richard Taruskin, *Musorgsky: Eight Essays and an Epilogue*, Princeton University Press, 1993, chap. 4 and 5.
9. V. A. Vasina-Grossman, *Russkii klassicheskii romans XIX-ogo veka*, Moscow, Academy of Sciences, 1956, p. 84, which addresses only Pushkin's well-known romances.

12

ROBERT P. HUGHES

Pushkin and Russia Abroad

The charge of social and cultural energy inherent for Russians in the figure of Pushkin and his legacy was released in the diaspora of the 1920s and 1930s with extraordinary force and consequence. The staggering dislocations of war and revolution caused the mass exodus of Russians from their native land in the five years following 1917. It has been plausibly argued that social upheavals over a period of time exert a substantial influence on the self-definition of given communities, and in this case both the émigrés and the Russians at home redefined themselves culturally. Inevitably, Pushkin's experiences of exile and the trauma of his violent death in 1837 had special resonance among the newly dispossessed. The first wave of emigration, especially in the deportations of 1922, carried with it a disproportionate number of the highly educated cultural elite determined to preserve not only their Russian identity, but to create a culture abroad. Language and literature contained the dynamic energy to invigorate such a project, for which Pushkin was its unifying symbol.

Pushkin had come to embody for Russians an intense vitality, especially since the historic anniversary observances of 1880, and the potency of Pushkin's name was continually reaffirmed in Russia Abroad during the period between the twentieth century's two world wars.[1] The discussion that follows is bracketed by the Pushkin celebrations of 1924 and 1937 and is focused on activities in Paris, the capital of Russia Abroad. They took place within the framework of a social, cultural and educational entity soon linked directly to the name of Pushkin, the so-called Day of Russian Culture (*Den' russkoi kul'tury*). A Day of Russian Enlightenment, as it was first called, was organised by Russian émigrés in Estonia in 1924 and then elaborated in Berlin, Prague and Paris beginning in 1925, when it was decided to make the Day coincide with Pushkin's birthday. It became the national holiday of Russia Abroad. A glance at any chronology of events in even minor centres of the diaspora reveals the frequency and variety of occasions associated with this unique institution, which was intended to unite the expatriates and to preserve a heritage seen as threatened by the Bolsheviks.

In a sense, this émigré event was inaugurated in St Petersburg during the civil conflict that followed the Bolshevik Revolution. Late in 1920, traumatised by the perceived and potential loss of cultural values and menaced by the new state, the remnants of the intelligentsia, the artistic, cultural and intellectual elite still living in the beleaguered former capital, arranged for February 1921 a series of events to commemorate Pushkin's death.[2] A formal 'Declaration' of the intent to observe, nationwide, the date of Pushkin's death was issued; in the event, the observances were soon shifted to the poet's birth date in June, laying the foundation for similar enterprises and rituals both in Soviet Russia and in Russia Abroad. A beacon in parlous times, Pushkin's life was celebrated by some leading voices. Mikhail Kuzmin's poem 'Pushkin' (1921), a distant response to Lermontov's 1837 elegiac ode written on Pushkin's death, insisted on the poet's eternal vitality. The formalist critic Boris Eikhenbaum, in his 'Problems in Pushkin's poetics', called for the smashing of the 'boudoir knick-knack' that Pushkin had become; and he insisted that the real Pushkin could now be more clearly recognised after the distancing effects of recent literary, social and political revolutions. Much less optimistic were Alexander Blok and Vladislav Khodasevich (poets, respectively, of the Symbolist and post-Symbolist generations), whose fervid statements have been reprinted and discussed ever since. The historic and prophetic message of Blok's 'On the Calling of the Poet' ('O naznachenii poeta', 1921) dealt with a poet's intrinsic conflict with bureaucracy and censorship, accusing them of robbing the poet of the 'peace and freedom' essential to creativity. Khodasevich's essay 'The swaying tripod' ('Koleblemyi trenozhnik', 1921) predicted for Pushkin another 'eclipse' in the 'post-Petrine, post-Petersburg' era; and he deplored the barbarisation of culture that obscured for Russians the true stature of Pushkin. Already a leading poet of the post-Symbolist generation at the turn of the 1920s, Khodasevich (1881–1939) assumed prominence as a touchstone for Pushkin studies in Russia Abroad.

Pushkin and the literary life of the diaspora

By the beginning of 1924, Russia Abroad was firmly established and had been re-energised by the late influx of 1922–23. The émigrés had initially gravitated to the major European cities: the Baltic capitals; Berlin, where the diaspora flourished between 1921 and 1923; and, naturally, Prague, Sofia, Belgrade and Warsaw, all located in countries where kindred Slavic languages were spoken; and most of all, Paris, home to the largest expatriate

Russian community. As it became increasingly clear that a return home was unlikely, the need for maintaining Russian identity and celebrating Russian achievements, indeed Russian culture itself, was apparent. Cultural organisations, publishing houses, a periodical press and educational institutions were established. This was a task undertaken by the émigrés not only for themselves but, in their eyes, for Russia itself. Pushkin was surely the single greatest manifestation of Russian values. The 125th anniversary of his birth was marked in June 1924 by an unusual number of celebrations in the several centres of emigration. Commemorating Pushkin had become a way of perpetuating those values.

In what may be called Russia Abroad's metropolis by the mid-1920s, the Paris community was the locus of spirited activity. Lecture series by scholars like Grigorii Lozinskii and the Dostoevsky specialist Konstantin Mochul'skii were given. Periodicals and publishing houses paid special attention to Pushkin. The writer Aleksei Remizov (1877–1957) appeared with his widely admired and oft-repeated rendition of Pushkin's *The Tale of the Fisherman and the Fish* (*Skazka o rybake i rybke*). Russian music associated with Pushkin was widely performed. The first of many such convocations, a solemn gathering at the Sorbonne in Pushkin's memory was sponsored by the People's University and the Union of Russian Writers and Journalists on 12 June 1924. Speeches were delivered by representatives of the Russian and French literary and academic worlds. Particularly refreshing and almost universally acclaimed was the analysis by Khodasevich of Pushkin's lyric poetry which advertised, as it were, to a large public his particular 'biographical' method of reading Pushkin. Although not a professional scholar, before emigration in 1922 Khodasevich had been associated with leading authorities on Pushkin. With his usual wit and unerring sense of proportion, Khodasevich traces masterfully – as only another accomplished poet could do – the intricate interplay of inspiration and technical skills in Pushkin's creative consciousness as a poetic text is produced. It is the specific impressions and experiences of the individual creative artist that are the raw material of a work of art, Khodasevich insists: '"Poet" and "Person" are the two hypostases of a single personality'; and he concludes that 'only by juxtaposing Pushkin's *Wahrheit* and *Dichtung* do we learn how he pondered the purpose of his own life [*kak filosofstvoval on nad svoeiu zhizn'iu*].' This appearance established Khodasevich as a specialist on Pushkin in the diaspora and, for the decade and a half following, arbiter in matters Pushkinian. Khodasevich's devotion to the 'wonder-working genius' (*chudotvornyi genii*) that was Pushkin lasted until his own death in 1939.

In this same anniversary year, Khodasevich's *Pushkin's Poetic Economy* (*Poeticheskoe khoziaistvo Pushkina*), compiled from a series of articles published in émigré periodicals, appeared anomalously in Leningrad in a notoriously corrupt edition. This study of 'autoreminiscences' (recurring words, phrases and autobiographical motifs) recreates the psychology of Pushkin's creative process. While aware of the role played by literary convention and technique in shaping a text, Khodasevich believed that life itself – as revealed to and processed by an accomplished and superior poet's creative intelligence – was the driving force of literary production.

Khodasevich's principal rival – and frequent adversary – in the ongoing engagement with Pushkin in the diaspora was Modest Gofman. Firmly established in Pushkin studies in pre-revolutionary St Petersburg as an associate of the newly established Institute for Russian Literature (located in Pushkin House, Leningrad), in 1922 Gofman had been dispatched to Paris by the Russian Academy of Sciences to negotiate the transfer to Russia of A. F. Onegin-Otto's famous hoard of Pushkiniana. In December 1923 at the Russian People's University, which had been established under the auspices of the Sorbonne, Gofman had begun a course of lectures on Pushkin and his era. He edited a volume of materials from this coveted 'Pushkin museum'[3] and drew on it for a number of other publications, but in 1924 made the decision not to return to Soviet Russia. Gofman became obsessed over a chimerical lost diary of Pushkin's allegedly in the possession of the poet's granddaughter, resident in Constantinople; but repeated promises of its discovery have yet to materialise despite continued hopes. A controversy erupted over Khodasevich's interpretation of *Rusalka* as related to an incident from Pushkin's biography (see Chapter 4). Gofman refused to admit the possibility (and probity) of Khodasevich's *psychological* reading, which remains valid even in the face of evidence soon produced that Pushkin's pregnant peasant mistress never actually drowned herself.

Gofman's contributions, often written in collaboration with the famed dancer Serge Lifar as the 1937 centenary drew near,[4] were numerous; and duly and critically reviewed by Khodasevich. Although he praised Gofman's French biography of Pushkin (Modeste Hofmann, *Pouchkine*, 1931) for its 'reliability' and new factual information, he faulted his approach for a lack of psychological acuity that gave a reliable but 'external' view of the subject.

The Lifar/Gofman enterprise went on to publish a collector's edition of 'Journey to Arzrum', a re-configured 'Egyptian Nights', and Gofman's popularising summary of Pushkin's amorous escapades.[5] The culmination of their endeavours was the appearance of a 'jubilee' edition of the original text (transcribed and in facsimile) of twelve of Pushkin's French letters to his future wife. This folio *de grand luxe*, in a limited printing, was initially available only by subscription.[6] The manuscripts had been obtained by Sergei Diaghilev after the death of Pushkin's granddaughter, and Lifar had managed to purchase them and other materials from the estate after his mentor's death. The texts were supplemented by Lifar's introduction, two translations, Gofman's commentary and his extended essay on Pushkin's wife, attesting her virtue and intelligence. The volume was illustrated by (misidentified) portraits of the two protagonists and by the imprint of Pushkin's supposed seal on the cover. Khodasevich's critical reaction to this 'pompous' publication of Pushkin's letters marked a resumption of hostilities and occasioned a furious public exchange of accusations and counter-accusations among the parties involved concerning the edition's cost and editorial philosophy.

The centenary celebration and its critical legacy

The centenary of Pushkin's death in 1937 evoked an extraordinary burst of energy in expatriate communities, centralised in Paris. On 21 November 1934, the Russian National Committee, under the chairmanship of theologian and civic leader A. V. Kartashev, adopted a resolution declaring that 'of course the general directorship for the affairs of the Pushkin jubilee should be assumed by a special "Pushkin Committee" (*Pushkinskii komitet*) of our outstanding writers, academicians, Pushkin scholars, journalists and other representative figures here in Paris. Local committees should everywhere be formed for collaboration with the centre.' The first major undertaking in advance of the jubilee was a successful fundraising concert of fragments from Pushkin-inspired operas and ballets on 17 February 1935 at the Salle Rameau, an event sponsored by the Union of Russian Writers and Journalists and a number of charitable organisations. This proved to be the model for a host of similar concerts, meetings and recitals leading up to the grandiose celebrations in February and March of 1937.

The first meeting of the Pushkin Committee was held on 26 February 1935: V. A. Maklakov (the Provisional Government's erstwhile ambassador to France) was elected chairman; Ivan Bunin (the 1933 Nobel laureate), Pavel Miliukov (editor of the largest émigré daily) and M. M. Fedorov were designated deputies. Khodasevich, Gofman, the critic Mark Aldanov, poet Konstantin Bal'mont, and distinguished writers Nadezhda Teffi, Boris Zaitsev, Ivan Shmelev as well as other luminaries from among the émigré literati attended the meeting; a resolution (by the Pushkin biographer Ariadna Tyrkova-Williams) to publish an affordable edition of Pushkin's collected works was adopted; fundraising committees were formed; announcements of the formation of local Pushkin committees in the US and Yugoslavia were made. At a grand concert on 17 March 1936, after the intermission, as a mark of solidarity on the part of the French cultural establishment, the audience was addressed by Paul Valéry (1871–1945), the Symbolist poet and

Professor of Poetry at the Collège de France. He and other prominent figures from French political, academic and literary spheres had been persuaded to participate in observances of the centenary of Pushkin's death (in partial exculpation of the crime of their countryman, d'Anthès, perhaps). André Gide (newly disillusioned with Soviet Russia) likewise made public statements lauding Pushkin. The committee held its own, exclusively French, convocation at the Sorbonne on 26 January 1937. Such events were conjoined, throughout France and in other centres of the diaspora, with observances of the Day of Russian Culture; and thus the educational effort to involve the youth of Russia Abroad was made a significant aspect of the whole impressive undertaking.

By January 1937, the Pushkin Committee could report that eighty-five local committees in thirty-seven countries on five continents had informed them of their plans and programmes for the jubilee observances: song recitals and dance performances; theatrical productions and readings of Pushkin's works; unveiling of monuments and renaming of streets; newly commissioned portraits and revelations of discoveries of Pushkiniana; and wider access to new editions of his writings, published to take advantage of interest in the poet fanned anew by the wide publicity. The Pushkin Committee's culminating assembly was held on 10 February. All this activity was naturally reported in the periodical press: supplements in the major newspapers, *Latest News* (*Poslednie novosti*) and *Renaissance* (*Vozrozhdenie*); a one-day newspaper entitled *Pushkin* issued by the Pushkin Committee; and special editions of the glossy weekly *Illustrated Russia* (*Illiustrirovannaia Rossiia*). These issues soon became collectors' items, replete as they were with articles, Pushkin materials, and statements from leading writers and public figures. On 28 February yet another important gathering in memory of Pushkin was held at the Orthodox Theological Institute, presided over by the metropolitan and with papers exploring the religious, philosophical and historical aspects of the writer's legacy.

A grand exhibition of Pushkiniana, *Pushkin et son époque*, organised by Lifar (who with Gofman's cooperation had begun preparations for it in mid-1934) was scheduled to open on 10 February at the Bibliothèque nationale, and it was eagerly awaited. But political considerations intervened: the Soviet ambassador Potemkin demanded that he be allowed to open the exhibition in the name of his government. Lifar refused, and at the eleventh hour it was moved to the large foyer of the Salle Pleyel and eventually opened on 16 March 1937. Jean Cocteau's poster advertising the exhibition was soon visible throughout Paris. Items dating from the 1820s and 1830s were drawn from museums, libraries and private collections, and they included manuscripts, portraits, paintings and drawings (mounted by artists

Alexandre Benois and Mstislav Dobuzhinskii), vintage porcelain, silver, fabrics, furniture and even the pistols used at the duel between d'Anthès and Pushkin. The exhibition was the site of numerous lectures, readings and other meetings and convocations, all of which were exhaustively chronicled in the newspapers. It was viewed by over 10,000 visitors before closing on 8 April.

Pushkin's image in émigré writing

The more ephemeral, visible bursts of public energy in émigré centres were the more immediate consciousness-raisers of community identity, but it might be said that the most important contributions were made aside from the official celebrations.[7] Factions were ranged across literary, political and theological spectra, and Pushkin was assimilated to them. From the dialogues there emerges a new set of identities for Pushkin as a philosophical and religious poet. A brief discussion of some of the more important written interventions follows.

Since the ill-fated publication of his book in Leningrad in 1924 and his address at the Sorbonne festivities in the same year, Khodasevich's reputation as the most erudite and discerning of Pushkinists had only increased, and he published a series of reviews, studies of the poet and his contemporaries, and comments on a wide range of matters Pushkinian. The total comes to over 100 items. His perceptive critiques were eagerly seized upon by the cultured younger generation in Paris and beyond, not least because they frequently generated controversy. His articles were a regular feature in *Renaissance* (*Vozrozhdenie*) from early in 1927 until his death in 1939; the most respected émigré quarterly *Contemporary Annals* (*Sovremennye zapiski*) was the other venue in which his work appeared sporadically. After the debacle over *Pushkin's Poetic Economy*, Khodasevich tempered somewhat his view of the intimate intersections of biographical fact and literary text, focusing with increasing refinement on factors that had specific bearing on the creative act. The salient feature of Khodasevich's work, often beginning with a strictly formal analysis, remained the concern to illuminate the mutual interpenetration of a text or set of texts and the author's life experience: 'life is organically and consciously merged with art'. In analyses of discrete texts and new editions; in reviews of books by key figures in the history of Pushkin studies in Russia and abroad; in articles about Pushkin's connections with contemporaries he demonstrated an encyclopedic knowledge of the period.

Writing pseudonymously as 'Gulliver', Khodasevich was publicly negative about the biographies undertaken in Soviet Russia by Iurii Tynianov and Georgii Chulkov. Notwithstanding old animosities (due to the critic's capricious readings of Khodasevich's poetry and acute political differences between the two), D. S. Mirsky's English-language writings on Pushkin and the fragments of biography, written for the 1937 jubilee after Mirsky's return to Russia, met with his approval. We are the poorer for not having Khodasevich's long-promised biography, which he had hoped to publish for the 1937 jubilee. A subscription appeal over the signatures of leading figures in the diaspora appeared in Paris newspapers at the beginning of 1935. However, because of ill health, the demands made by piecework required for mere subsistence, and the inaccessibility of archives and indispensable publications – coupled with his dim view of the hullabaloo around the jubilee observances – he eventually abandoned the project.[8] To meet his subscribers' demands, he revised his 1924 book and published it as *On Pushkine* (*O Pushkine*, Berlin, n.p., 1937). Khodasevich's final tribute was a scholarly edition of *Evgenii Onegin* (Brussels, Petropolis, 1937; illustrations by Dobuzhinskii). Basing his work on the final edition published in Pushkin's lifetime, he corrected misprints, restored the manuscript text and preserved the original orthography.

Gofman's major contribution – and a return to his expertise in textual criticism – was the collected works mandated by the Pushkin Committee, *Sochineniia Aleksandra Pushkina* (Berlin, Pushkin Committee, 1937). While less than complete, this edition became the standard text in the diaspora, surpassing in popularity and quality a hastily prepared one published by *Illustrated Russia* (*Illiustrirovannaia Rossiia*) (Paris, 1936). A more reliable edition from the publishing house Life and Culture (Riga, 1936) was based on current Soviet Russian scholarship. All of these efforts, of course, were hamstrung by lack of access to primary sources.

Although Pushkin studies from scholars and writers headquartered in Paris commanded the greatest attention, far from negligible contributions were made in other centres of Russia Abroad. A. L. Bem, the doyen of Russian studies in Prague was pre-eminent in establishing the Day of Russian Culture as an institution and wrote frequently about Pushkin. He headed the jubilee commemorations and published a collection of essays, *On Pushkine* (*O Pushkine*, Uzhgorod, Pis'mena, 1937).[9] Bem also collaborated with Roman Jakobson in editing a four-volume Czech *Selected Works* (*Vybrane spisy A. S. Puškina*, Prague, 1936–38). In this edition and elsewhere Jakobson published a series of brief articles on Pushkin; his most substantial contribution, again in Czech, was his seminal structuralist study 'Pushkin and his sculptural myth'.[10] Important discussions of Pushkin in Polish by Wacław Lednicki, who was reared and educated in Moscow (and then in Kraków and Wilno), had been appearing since the mid-1920s (and often reviewed by Khodasevich); he also lectured on Pushkin, in Russian, several times during the centennial observances in Paris and other west European capitals.

Demanding attention are such important publications as the series of articles by P. M. Bitsilli (based in Sofia) during this period, ranging from his chapter on Pushkin in *Studies on Russian Poetry* (*Etiudy o russkoi poezii*, Prague, Plamia, 1926), through his splendid centennial articles, and continuing into the post-war period.[11] Space permits here only a listing of S. Serapin's [S. A. Pinus], *Pushkin and Music* (*Pushkin i muzyka*, Sofia, Iugo-Vostok, 1926), and compilations such as the *Pushkin Collection* (*Pushkinskii sbornik*, Prague, Politika, 1929), the *Belgrade Pushkin Collection* (*Belgradskii Pushkinskii sbornik*, Belgrade, Pushkin Committee in Yugoslavia, 1937) and *Russia and Pushkin: a Collection of Articles 1837–1937* (*Rossiia i Pushkin. Sbornik statei. 1837–1937*, Kharbin, Manchuria, Akademicheskaia gruppa v Kharbine, 1937).

The year 1937 was also an *annus mirabilis* for assessments of Pushkin by leading philosophers, theologians, churchmen and religious and political thinkers. These synthetic statements by non-professional literary scholars are among the most lasting monuments of émigré thought on Russia's great poet.[12] They take their origin in principle in the Pushkin essays of the late nineteenth-century religious philosopher Vladimir Solov'ev, and in subsequent extensions and developments by men of letters including the philosophers Vasilii Rozanov (1856–1919) and Lev Shestov (1866–1938), the critic and historian Mikhail Gershenzon (1869–1925), the Symbolist novelist Dmitrii Merezhkovskii (1865–1941) and the poet Viacheslav Ivanov (1866–1949), all of whom flourished in the period often referred to as the Silver Age of Russian literature that began at the turn of the century and ended just before World War I. The last three continued to make important contributions to the philosophical discourse around the legacy of Pushkin in Russia Abroad. The hermeneutics developed by these thinkers is of lasting significance, and it has spurred some of the best interpretive criticism in Russia today.[13]

Typologically, these writings are akin in their view of Pushkin as prophet, teacher and spiritual ideal.[14] It is telling that his 1826 lyric 'The Prophet' was so frequently invoked and read as key to both his personal and aesthetic experience (see Chapter 2). This was in marked contrast to the use to which Pushkin was so often put by Soviet ideologues, that of ally in the fight against tsarism and serfdom, threats from abroad, latter-day capitalist exploitation and, in general, as predecessor of the communist utopia; a 'fellow-traveller,' in the jargon of the day.

The religious philosopher S. L. Frank's essays from the interwar period, 'Pushkin's religion' (1933), 'Pushkin as political thinker' (1937) and 'On the tasks of knowing Pushkin' (1937), were collected in the posthumous *Studies on Pushkin* (*Etiudy o Pushkine*, Munich, n.p., 1957). They contain profound explorations of Pushkin's personal convictions, his 'liberal conservative' political and social views, and his expressions of the 'ineffable originality of the Russian spirit'. The articles and notes on Pushkin by the political and social philosopher P. B. Struve are also worthy of attention, expressing as they do the émigrés' conviction that Pushkin was the embodiment of what was most profoundly Russian and could serve as an anchor of identity in their straitened circumstances.[15]

Vladimir Weidle's 'Pushkin and Europe' treated the relationships between Russia and Europe in Pushkin's work, his understanding of European culture and literature, the assimilation of the Western legacy in nineteenth-century Russia, and Pushkin's place in European literature and history. It is deserving of special notice because it puts to rights Dostoevsky's eccentric Slavophile views on Pushkin's significance in Russian culture, and remains the most sophisticated and knowledgeable treatment of the subject available.[16]

Of outstanding value was the essay by the medievalist and cultural historian Georgii Fedotov, 'Bard of empire and freedom' ('Pevets imperii i svobody'), published in the same centennial issue of *Contemporary Annals* (63) as the articles by Bitsilli, Weidle and Ivanov. Fedotov explores the seeming paradox between Pushkin's celebration of empire and his plea for a fundamental personal and creative freedom. With a nuanced reading of crucial texts, Fedotov evokes the evolution of Pushkin's political thought from his youthful radicalism and liberalism to his late 'free conservative' stance. His conceptualisation of Pushkin's final months is a convincing explanation of the poet's motives in pursuing the fatal encounter with d'Anthès. Fedotov traces these motives to Pushkin's deeply personal necessity for clarification, a desire to free himself from the pressures and demands of St Petersburg's social and imperial circles.

The papers read by Fedotov's and Weidle's colleagues, Fr Sergii Bulgakov, Vladimir Il'in, Mochul'skii and Kartashev, at the convocation at the Orthodox Theological Institute are of major interest.[17] In 'Pushkin's lot' ('Zhrebii Pushkina'), Bulgakov (theologian and dean of the institute) joined a discussion on a topic given prominence by Solov'ev during the 1899 jubilee. Reviewing the history of Pushkin's religious views and experiences, he posits a 'conversion' in the mid-1820s. 'Depending on how we comprehend "The Prophet" we understand the whole of Pushkin. If it is only an aesthetic invention . . . then there is *no* great Pushkin, and we have nothing to celebrate at this time. Or is Pushkin representing what actually happened to him, i.e. the vision of a divine universe beneath the pall of materiality?' queries Bulgakov, and answers in the affirmative. However, in the 1830s, with courtship and marriage, Pushkin fell victim to secular beauty and frivolous behaviour in St Petersburg. Thus did he lose his prophetic calling; and this was the proximate antecedent to his death. Only on his deathbed, Bulgakov declares, did Pushkin undergo catharsis and achieve a kind of Christian lucidity. It is hard not to agree with Khodasevich's sober-minded response to Bulgakov (and, by implication, to other religiously oriented critics). His is a less elevated view, a necessary corrective: Pushkin was not a prophet, teacher, leader of all things Russian; he was purely and simply a poet (*byl vsego lish' poetom*).[18]

The literary legacy of 1937: Tsvetaeva and Nabokov

Among the fruits gathered in the extraordinary harvest of the 1937 jubilee were some notable works of literature. Unlike Khodasevich's, the verse of another major poet among the older émigré writers, Marina Tsvetaeva, shared no direct relationship to Pushkinian poetics. Her prose writings on Pushkin were boldly idiosyncratic. She had marked the anniversary in 1924 with three poems, and she was an industrious participant in the celebrations of 1937, albeit not in émigré establishment circles. Four expressionistic poems (dated 1931), in her characteristically vigorous style, explored the relationship between the poet and political power; a fifth poem from the cycle appeared only in 1956. Tsvetaeva's extravagant prose experiments include 'Natal'ia Goncharova' (1929); although ostensibly devoted to the contemporary painter, the essay included discussion of her namesake and distant relative, Pushkin's wife, and Tsvetaeva's animosity toward the latter is patent.[19] Tsvetaeva's prose about Pushkin reached its culmination in two pieces for the jubilee year: 'My Pushkin' ('Moi Pushkin'), a charming psychological study of the author herself layered within peculiar memories of Pushkin from her earliest years and her adult reflections about him; and 'Pushkin and Pugachev', a juxtaposition of *The Captain's Daughter* with its historical sources.[20] A singular acknowledgement of Tsvetaeva's respect was her translations into French of several lyrics, eleven of which have been published.[21] She read them in a variety of settings: on 18 February 1937 to a literary festival organised by black Parisians (chaired by the minister of colonies and the Soviet ambassador!); on 21 February at a meeting of the Society for Return to the Homeland; on 2 March during a personal recital dedicated solely to Pushkin; and again, on 8 June, before a French audience to celebrate Pushkin's birthday. The texts chosen, 'The Prophet' ('Prorok'), 'Demons' ('Besy'), 'To the Sea' ('K moriu'), 'Poet', 'Solitary sower of freedom . . .' ('Svobody seiatel' pustynnyi . . .') and others, were fundamental to Tsvetaeva's own conception of a poet's mission; the translations were unmistakably in her own voice. They signify both her desire to honour the precursor she admired above all others and her determined effort to bridge the gap between Russian and French poetic practice. (At the same time, the venues and audiences before which she read these translations foreshadow Tsvetaeva's imminent decision to abandon Russia Abroad.)

Perhaps the most enduring tribute to Pushkin in the anniversary year was Vladimir Nabokov's novel *The Gift* (*Dar*, 1937–38). Little of his earlier prose was fixed so firmly in Pushkin, even though he is the subject of several lyrics from both the 'Russian' and 'American' years. The writing of *The Gift* began with what became the embedded biography (enclosed in an inverted sonnet) of the radical critic N. G. Chernyshevskii (1828–89), designed as a kind of Gogolian grotesque, an exposé of shoddy thought and muddled perception. (This 'politically incorrect' chapter was rejected for the serial publication; it eventually appeared only in the novel's first complete edition in 1952 in New York.) The 'biography' came to stand in implicit contrast to the loving representation of the protagonist's father, a virile explorer, entomologist and natural scientist, an individual who is through and through an embodiment of Pushkinian values, endowed with personal dignity and with clarity of thought and vision. As the conceptual framework of the narrative grew over three years of writing, it became a portrait of the artist as a young man, a novice writer in whose aesthetic education Pushkin assumes a defining role. Pushkin 'enters his bloodstream' as he imagines his father's biography, and that effort is specifically enabled by the study of exemplary texts drawn from Pushkin's prose. The novel concludes in a prose paragraph mimicking a perfect Onegin stanza, the protagonist's farewell to the novel he has just created, in imitation of Pushkin's envoi to his eponymous character. The novel's very title evokes a polemic with Pushkin's 1828 lyric, 'Futile gift, random gift' ('Dar naprasnyi, dar sluchainyi').

This grand homage to Pushkin and his legacy was among the major events of the opening of the jubilee year.[22] Following an introduction by his literary confrère Khodasevich, on 24 January 1937 Nabokov read the first two chapters to an émigré audience in Paris, and the serialisation of the novel began in the issue of *Contemporary Annals* (63) celebrating the Pushkin centenary. It was on this same reading tour that Nabokov delivered his 'Pouchkine ou le Vrai et le vraisemblance', an effort – including four verse translations – like Tsvetaeva's to introduce Pushkin to a French audience.[23] To round off his engagement with Pushkin during his émigré years, Nabokov wrote and published another novel in the same year. Produced during a brief hiatus in his work on *The Gift*, Nabokov's dystopian *Invitation to a Beheading* (*Priglashenie na kazn'*, 1938) is also full of allusions to Pushkin.[24] The novel's protagonist is figured as a unique consciousness; he is, once again, the creative artist in conflict with the mob (*chern'*), the masses which submit unthinkingly to totalitarian brainwashing. Examples from the life of Pushkin and his lyrics celebrating individual freedom provide a deep-seated, underlying model for the construction of the liberated self.

Such powerfully stated positions had been developed in the years between 1924 and 1937 and they had a particular, cumulative significance in the late 1930s, a time when writers and individuals in Stalin's Russia had fallen – and not always unwillingly – into the grip of state power. To a far greater extent than in the homeland, the diaspora could celebrate the Pushkinian ideals of personal freedom and devotion to the Russian tradition. As had been the case in Petrograd in 1921, individual engagements and communal ceremonies tapped the energy latent in Pushkin's image. The interpretations of the Pushkin phenomenon which were developed in Russia Abroad have proven durable, and their incorporation into the legacy is under way in today's Russia.

NOTES

1. The term 'Russia Abroad' (roughly equivalent to *russkoe zarubezh'e*) was given currency in Marc Raeff, *Russia Abroad: a Cultural History of the Russian Emigration, 1919–1939*, New York and Oxford, Oxford University Press, 1990.
2. On the celebrations in Soviet Russia in 1921, 1924, 1937 and 1999, see Stephanie Sandler, *Commemorating Pushkin: Russia's Myth of a National Poet*, Stanford University Press, 2004, pp. 85–135.
3. *Neizdannyi Pushkin. Sobranie A. F. Onegina*, Moscow and Petrograd, Gosudarstvennoe izdatel'stvo, 1923; first edn. 1922.
4. See Sergei Lifar', *Moia zarubezhnaia Pushkiniana. Pushkinskie vystavki i izdaniia*, Paris, n.p., 1966. Pushkin items figure prominently in the catalogue for the sale of his property: Sotheby Parke Bernet Monaco SA, *The Diaghilev-Lifar Library* (Monaco, 1975).
5. M. L. Gofman, *Pushkin – Don-Zhuan*, Paris, Izdanie Sergeia Lifaria, 1935; reviewed by Khodasevich in April 1935.
6. M. L. Gofman and Sergei Lifar', *Pis'ma Pushkina k N. N. Goncharovoi. Iubileinoe izdanie. 1837–1937*, Paris, n.p., 1936.
7. Recent anthologies of this material include *Tsentral'nyi Pushkinskii Komitet v Parizhe (1935–1937)*, ed. M. D. Filin, 2 vols., Moscow, Ellis Lak, 2000; *Pushkin v emigratsii. 1937*, ed. V. Perel'muter, Moscow, Progress–Traditsiia, 1999.
8. Khodasevich was silently dismissive of the amateur efforts at biography by A. Tyrkova-Williams (*Zhizn' Pushkina*, vol. i, Paris, YMCA Press, 1929) and P. Miliukov (*Zhivoi Pushkin [1837–1937]*, Paris, n.p., 1937). See Caryl Emerson, 'Our everything', *Slavic and East European Journal* (Spring 2004), 79–98.
9. Of surpassing interest are the informative letters from Khodasevich to Bem, 1934–37: Rashit Iangirov, 'Pushkin i Pushkinisty', *Novoe literaturnoe obozrenie* 37 (1999), 181–228. On Bem, see also: A. L. Bem, *Pis'ma o literature*, ed. M. Bubeníková and L. Vachalovská, Prague, Euroslavia, 1996; A. L. Bem, *Issledovaniia. Pis'ma o literature*, ed. S. G. Bocharov and I. Z. Surat, Moscow, Iazyki slavianskoi kul'tury, 2001.
10. R. Jakobson, 'Socha v symbolice Puškinove', *Slovo a slovenost* 3 (1937), 2–24. See also Hugh McLean, 'A linguist among the poets', *International Journal of*

Linguistics and Poetics 27, supplement: *Roman Jakobson: What He Taught Us*, ed. Morris Halle (1983), 7–19.

11. See P. M. Bitsilli, *Tragediia russkoi kul'tury. Issledovaniia. Stat'i. Retsenzii*, ed. M. Vasil'eva, Moscow, Russkii put', 2000.
12. Now collected in *Pushkin v russkoi filosofskoi kritike*, ed. R. A. Gal'tseva, Moscow, Kniga, 1990.
13. Among the best examples are the collected studies by I. Z. Surat in *Zhizn' i lira*, Moscow, Knizhnyi sad, 1995, and *Pushkin: biografiia i lirika*, Moscow, Nasledie, 1999; see also the excellent 'interior biography' by Surat and S. G. Bocharov, *Pushkin. Kratkii ocherk zhizni i tvorchestva*, Moscow, Iazyki slavianskoi kul'tury, 2002.
14. V. M. Markovich, '"Novoe" i "staroe" v suzhdeniiakh russkoi zarubezhnoi kritiki o Pushkine (1937)', in M. A. Vasil'eva (ed.), *Pushkin i kul'tura russkogo zarubezh'ia*, Moscow, Russkii put', 2000, pp. 9–32.
15. As collected in P. B. Struve, *Dukh i slovo*, Paris, YMCA Press, 1981.
16. First delivered at the meeting of the Religious-Philosophical Academy on 31 January, it appeared in print in *Sovremennye zapiski* 63 (1937), 220–31.
17. Omitting Mochul'skii's talk, they were collected in *Lik Pushkina*, Paris, Put' zhizni, 1938.
18. This respectful rejoinder is reprinted in an appendix to Gal'tseva (ed.), *Pushkin v russkoi filosofskoi kritike*, pp. 488–93.
19. See Liza Knapp's 'Tsvetaeva and the two Natal'ia Goncharovas: dual life', in B. Gasparov *et al.* (eds.), *Cultural Mythologies of Russian Modernism*, Berkeley, CA, University of California Press, 1992, pp. 88–108.
20. Published respectively in: *Volia Rossii* 5–9 (1929); *Sovremennye zapiski* 64 (1937), and *Russkie zapiski* 2 (1937). On Tsvetaeva's relationships with Pasternak as mediated through Pushkin, see Irina Shevelenko, *Literaturnyi put' Tsvetaevoi*, Moscow, NLO, 2002, *passim*. For a comprehensive discussion see Sandler, *Commemorating Pushkin*, pp. 214–65.
21. Iu. Kliukin, 'Pushkin po-frantsuzski v perevode Mariny Tsvetaevoi (k istorii sozdaniia)', in *Marina Tsvetaeva. Stat'i i teksty*, Vienna, Wiener slawistischer Almanach, 1992, pp. 63–84.
22. See Alexander Dolinin in his introduction and annotations in Vladimir Nabokov, *Sobranie sochinenii russkogo perioda*, vol. iv, St Petersburg, Simpozium, 2000. Compare Sergei Davydov's 'Weighing Nabokov's *Gift* on Pushkin's Scales', in *Cultural Mythologies of Russian Modernism*, pp. 415–28. Khodasevich had reworked his January 1937 introduction into a laudatory article, 'O Sirine' (*Vozrozhdenie*, 13 February 1937), and he consistently reviewed instalments of the novel as they appeared in 1937–38. For a sampling of critical studies in which Nabokov's inter-textual strategies involving Pushkin are explored, see *V. V. Nabokov: pro et contra*, St Petersburg, Izdatel'stvo Russkogo Khristianskogo gumanitarnogo instituta, 1997.
23. As published in the 1 March 1937 issue of the *Nouvelle Revue française*. For Dmitri Nabokov's English translation, 'Pushkin, or the Real and the Plausible', see *The New York Review of Books* 31 (March 1988), 38–42.
24. See Alexander Dolinin, 'Pushkinskie podteksty v romane Nabokova "Priglashenie na kazn'"', in Vasil'eva (ed.), *Pushkin i kul'tura russkogo zarubezh'ia*, pp. 64–85.

13

STEPHANIE SANDLER

Pushkin filmed: life stories, literary works and variations on the myth

Beginning with the earliest examples of Russian silent film, Alexander Pushkin and his work have remained popular subjects throughout the Soviet and post-Soviet period. Pushkin films, which number more than 100, vary in aesthetic quality, but they contain impressive achievements and telling experiments. As an art form, cinema has performed the pedagogical labour of transmitting Russian culture's fascination with Pushkin, and it has also contributed a large body of interpretive work about him. It is the latter that interests us here. How has cinema read Pushkin's life, his writings and the myths about him?

This chapter will treat three kinds of Pushkin films: life stories, literary adaptations and films alluding to Pushkin or his work. In their different ways, they extend and complicate the myth of Pushkin's foundational place in modern Russian culture. As a result, these films make new myths about poetic and cinematic inspiration. Confidence that an audience in Russia would know Pushkin's works well enough to catch both passing allusions and fully fledged allegory marks them all. Biographical films, many of them focused on Pushkin's fatal duel in 1837, have regularly retold the story of his life. The life stories make Pushkin's biography into an exemplary Russian life. They may also offer allegorical narratives about how Russia treats its poets and how poets should live their professional lives.

More varied when taken as a category are the quirky films in which Pushkinian motifs function as psychological or cultural turning points for modern-day characters. These films have ranged from melodramas that re-enact the triangle of Pushkin's last duel to coming-of-age stories that mix pathos, humour and occasional tragedy. All imply that his life and works are relevant to contemporary life, and the best of them use Pushkinian material as a springboard to new creative acts.

Finally, we will consider adaptations of his best-loved works, which have appeared as silent films, early black-and-white sound films and eventually colour extravaganzas in full historical costume. The adaptations of literary works reiterate Pushkin's centrality, while also asking whether the literary can function as a model for the cinematic. Tensions between the literary and the cinematic, in fact, are among their most interesting features. The best adaptations insist that cinema has the capacity to interpret literary material and to do so with insight; these films explore what Pushkin's fiction, poetry and drama mean at a given historical moment.

Biographical films

Although the vast majority of Pushkin films have been adaptations of the poems and stories, the first was a biographical film: *The Life and Death of A. S. Pushkin* (*Zhizn' i smert' A. S. Pushkina*, 1910, dir. Vasilii Goncharov). One review of this film put it simply: 'The poetry of Pushkin is his life.'[1] *The Life and Death of A. S. Pushkin* was extremely popular, despite its relatively primitive technique and poor acting.[2] Its mixed reception, splitting critical commentaries off from an enthusiastic public, begins an enduring pattern: the lessons of Pushkin films were often deemed insufficient, reflecting the high expectations for educating viewers who, in fact, already knew the poet's writings quite well. The Pushkin scholar Nikolai Lerner recounted his unfavourable impression of *The Life and Death of A. S. Pushkin*, dismissing the actors as poor likenesses and the details as historically inaccurate; the terms 'blasphemy', 'ignorance' and 'slander' are mentioned, which shows how high the stakes were for films about Pushkin.[3] Next to appear was *The Poet and the Tsar* (*Poet i tsar'*, 1927, dir. Vladimir Gardin). It focused exclusively on the romantic intrigues among Pushkin, Tsar Nicholas I, Pushkin's wife Natalia Nikolaevna and the Baron d'Anthès. While more a curiosity than a sophisticated account of the poet's last years, the film remained popular well into the late Soviet period when it was restored and re-released as a film for children in 1968.

In 1936, filmmakers turned to an earlier period in Pushkin's life. *The Poet's Youth* (*Iunost' poeta*, 1936, dir. Arkadii Naroditskii) tried to avoid criticisms of historical inaccuracy by enlisting several consulting specialists.[4] The lead-up to the jubilee celebrations in 1937, when the film was to be featured, was a highly charged moment in Stalinist consolidation of cultural control. *The Poet's Youth* complied with the ideological requirement that heroic figures be of appropriate working-class origins or, if from the nobility, that they display apparent class consciousness. Thus, the film shows Pushkin as something of a rebel at the Lycée in Tsarskoe Selo. His erotic adventures posed a problem for filmmakers, which they solved by referring, if only mutedly, to his relations with serf women.[5] Pushkin is shown reading aloud to his Lycée classmates a poem denouncing serfdom as slavery, an anachronism devised by the scriptwriters who moved forward by several years the compositional history of poems like 'Liberty. An Ode' ('Vol'nost'. Oda', 1817) and 'The Countryside' ('Derevnia', 1819). Still greater liberties were taken in *Journey to Erzerum* (*Puteshestvie v Arzrum*, 1936), made under precisely the same historical circumstances. Pressured to render Pushkin an appropriate hero for Soviet audiences, the filmmakers give undue emphasis to the ideology of the Decembrists. They endow Pushkin with beliefs much closer to those of the Decembrists than was the case.[6] *Journey to Erzerum* also implicitly raised the question of how much fiction one should permit in a biographical film, in this case seeking to recreate the atmosphere and circumstances of Pushkin's 1829 journey to the region.[7]

The next major film about the poet's life was made several decades later: *The Last Road* (*Posledniaia doroga*, 1986, dir. Leonid Menaker). Again, the era had its political tensions, for this film was made during Glasnost, the years when many previously closed subjects were opened for fresh debate. *The Last Road* was paradoxical – traditional in its turn to familiar cultural history and a confirmed hero, but also gently adventurous in its emphasis on unusual details in the story of Pushkin's last duel. Like *The Poet's Youth*, the film was to be part of an anniversary celebration, in this case the 150th anniversary of Pushkin's death. It has a distinctive backward glance at the Stalin period: as in Mikhail Bulgakov's play *The Last Days* (*Poslednie dni*, 1934–35), whose title it echoed, *The Last Road* virtually ignores Pushkin himself. Instead, the action revolves around his palpable absence, and the words of his friends and enemies make up all the dialogue. *The Last Road* uses much documented, verifiable language for characters' dialogue. Thus, for example, Vasilii Zhukovskii speaks words familiar from his poem on Pushkin's death and his letter to Pushkin's father. Other characters can also be heard incorporating phrases from known memoirs or epistolary material into their speeches. But the film invents some characters for heightened emotional effect, most memorably an unnamed officer who first carouses with friends of d'Anthès but later reacts strongly and as if with embarrassment to the news that Pushkin has been shot.

The film's interpretation of Pushkin's death is conveyed through this young man's consternation and horror. *The Last Road* demonises Pushkin's enemies far less than did Stalinist-era texts, including Bulgakov's play *The Last Days*; instead, it shows the weakness of his friends. Their failure to protect Pushkin is emphasised, and they lament their inadequate responses to what they knew to be a significant domestic and public crisis for the poet. The film spends far more time on Petr Viazemskii and Zhukovskii than the others, and van Heeckeren is impressively played by the great Innokentii Smoktunovskii; his scenes with d'Anthès are quietly unsavoury.

The Last Road screens as a solidly reliable movie, not venturing toward experimental cinematography. Music and whirling snow are used as transitional signals, for example, echoed by scenes of dancing couples swirling in a ballroom. The filmmakers are at great pains to keep to a fairly traditional look. As with their use of quoted speech, they include pictorial clues oriented toward the visual arts or material history, reminding viewers of historical and portrait paintings or photographs from the Pushkin Museum at Moika 12. Quasi-documentary fidelity to known artefacts and precedent becomes a strong principle of the film. *The Last Road* is perhaps the one film to create a kind of thematic pun on the formal principle of fidelity, since it argues that insufficient loyalty among Pushkin's friends was the hidden cause of his death.

Variations on Pushkinian themes

Whereas biographical films concentrate their full attention on Pushkin, films ostensibly made with unrelated plots and characters may nonetheless use Pushkinian motifs in telling and significant ways. In some of these films, the attention to Pushkin is ephemeral and nearly unfathomable. Quotations from poems and biographical references occur with deceptive casualness as though they were entirely incidental. This is the case with the repeated quotations from the poem 'Demons' ('Besy', 1830) in Vladimir Khotinenko's film *The Muslim* (*Musul'manin*, 1995). We might notice those quotations more because Khotinenko made a later movie, *Passion Boulevard* (*Strastnoi bul'var*, 2000), in which a man pastes on Pushkinian sidewhiskers and spouts Pushkin right and left. But that information will not change our response to *The Muslim*, a film that tells us a great deal more about the aftermath of the Soviet Union's disastrous invasion of Afghanistan than about Pushkin's presence in modern culture. Nor does it much matter, in Dinara Asanova's film about a strong teacher and the teenagers who admire her, *Key Without a Duplicate* (*Kliuch bez prava peredachi*, 1976), that the students take a field trip to Pushkin's apartment on the Moika. They hear poets recite in the courtyard, and some of the poets (Bella Akhmadulina, Bulat Okudzhava) appear in the same role in Marlen Khutsiev's film *I am Twenty* (*Mne dvadtsat' let*, 1964, a revised version of which appeared as *Zastava Il'icha* in 1988). This kind of oblique turn to Pushkin also occurs in the loosely structured post-Soviet film *Day of the Full Moon* (*Den' polnoluniia*, 1998, dir. Karen Shakhnazarov). In one of its many episodes, Pushkin makes an appearance, shown during his journey to Erzerum, and he seeks the kiss of a Kalmyk girl in a brief scene that parallels several of the film's unfulfilled moments of romance. That passage, one feels, might have been drawn from the work of any Russian writer, so uninflected is the turn to Pushkin.

For some films, however, the possibility of a parallel with Pushkin's life haunts a character seen on screen and gives that character's life its meaning if only for the moment. Sometimes this is very funny, as in *Wake up Mukhin!* (*Razbudite Mukhina!*, 1967, dir. Iakov Segel'), where a deeply bored university student dreams away his time in lectures by transporting himself backwards to the times under discussion. He tries to stop Pushkin's duel with d'Anthès, which the film makes interesting cinematically by shooting the duel scene as if it were a silent film, with appropriate piano music in the background. This film has to have been a model for Andrei Bitov's time-travel story 'Pushkin's Photograph (1799–2099)' ('Fotografiia Pushkina [1799–2099]', 1987), a fact which is important perhaps only because it shows an instance of film influencing the course of literary material about the Pushkin myth, rather than the other way around, as one might more readily expect.

In the pseudo-documentary film *Sidewhiskers* (*Bakenbardy*, 1990, dir. Iurii Mamin), a nationalist Pushkin club is formed to eradicate a free-spirited collective called Capella. Although *Sidewhiskers* has a very serious political agenda, it is also extremely funny as well as disturbing. The Pushkin club members grow sidewhiskers and strive to imitate Pushkin from the outside, but their fascist tendencies are more in keeping with the right-wing political group Pamiat', which was then on the rise. Whereas in *Wake up Mukhin!* one laughed at the physical humour and at the incongruous conversations based on time travel, in *Sidewhiskers* the humour comes from Capella's sexual and exaggeratedly theatrical antics. Words from Pushkin's fiery poem 'The Prophet' give an ominous beginning to *Sidewhiskers*, but a stanza from *Evgenii Onegin* gets roundly parodied when its iambic rhythms are used to motivate body-building youth in the Pushkin club.

In Soviet melodramas, we see the more serious side of evocations of the Pushkin myth. Domestic drama is featured in two films from the 1980s, *Direct Descendant* (*Naslednitsa po priamoi*, 1982, dir. Sergei Solov'ev) and *Keep Me Safe, My Talisman* (*Khrani menia, moi talisman*, 1986, dir. Roman Balaian). In these films, the public image of Pushkin is also felt, particularly in *Keep Me Safe, My Talisman*, which takes place in Boldino and includes comments from museum staff (all actors) and visiting poets and scholars, like Bulat Okudzhava, who play themselves. In one scene, these visitors argue about Pushkin's image, but what matters more in the argument scene is the evolving erotic triangle among the three lead actors. A reporter and his young wife seek the same refuge from urban problems that took Pushkin to Boldino or Mikhailovskoe, but they have their idyll disrupted by a sinister, intrusive young man. He behaves as if he were d'Anthès pursuing Natalia Nikolaevna, and even rehearses a few pet theories about d'Anthès.[8] This melodrama makes modern Soviet life seem trivial and immoral when compared with Pushkin's era.

Direct Descendant features a barely pre-teenage girl, Zhenia, who believes that one of her forebears was the unknown addressee of a love letter Pushkin wrote in Odessa in 1823. Zhenia lives in an unnamed seaside town in the south, where she is able to imagine that a deserted building on the beach was the backdrop when Pushkin wrote the letter. Composed in French, the letter turns up in the film in Russian translation, principally in a key line about love, pride and gentility: 'I love you with so much tenderness, so much modesty, that my love cannot wound your pride.'[9] The film tells a love story, though, in which there is neither tenderness nor nobility, at least not on the part of the young man in whom Zhenia places her trust. Splendidly unmoved by his betrayal, she comes to his rescue in the end, emerging as the sole exemplar of genuine moral and emotional strength in the film. Her reward is a nod of approval from a spectre of Pushkin himself, and the two of them sit gazing out at the sea in silent satisfaction as the film ends. *Direct Descendant* is a film that reminds one of nothing so much as Rolan Bykov's *Scarecrow* (*Chuchelo*, 1985), which it must surely have influenced: there, an equally idiosyncratic young heroine also shaves her head in mockery of her peers, and dances a similarly defiant dance for them. *Scarecrow* does without the Pushkinian motifs, telling instead the story of a forebear who was a serf painter. The point of both films, though, is to create a zone of creative authenticity around a daring heroine on the cusp of sexual maturity. *Direct Descendant* proves that Pushkin retains the capacity to create that zone of safety, one which can provide safe passage toward maturity for even the quirkiest young woman. Rather than fantasising about various women as Pushkin's muse, *Direct Descendant* offers us a glimpse of Pushkin himself as the muse to a young girl seeking to create her own destiny.

One cannot leave a discussion of films with Pushkinian motifs without considering a last and very unlikely genre, the cartoon. There is an extraordinary animated film that began as three short films with titles taken from Pushkin's poetry, which were then assembled as a sixty-five-minute film shown on Soviet television, *My Favourite Time* (*Liubimoe moe vremia*, 1987, dir. Andrei Khrzhanovskii).[10] One hears Pushkin writings throughout this film, as performed by two men, Innokentii Smoktunovskii and the excellent comic actor Sergei Iurskii. *My Favourite Time* presents Pushkin's works as sound text against a visual background based on his drawings and manuscripts. The camera moves across still objects as if it were alive. At times, the lens zooms in to examine a pained self-portrait, or pulls us back from a seductive line drawing; a manuscript page turns, rocks and shakes (as in the recitation of the poem 'Arion' [1827]). There is always a lot happening on the screen: we might see drawn figures or horses or demons in motion, an overlay of diagonal lines to suggest rain, lighting changes from black to white background, all as we hear the falling rain, some bit of Pushkin's writings, and orchestral music to intensify the sequence's mood. The celebrated avant-garde composer Alfred Schnittke wrote piano and other music for the film, which contributes powerfully to its success.

The fascination of *My Favourite Time* with Pushkin's inner world makes the film a pleasurable antidote to the melodrama and tragedy that pervade Pushkin films (despite the fact that *My Favourite Time* still moves inexorably toward Pushkin's death). The film attempts to show the act of poetic creation by focusing on Pushkin as he writes, draws, doodles and improvises witticisms in conversation with his friends. Some segments strive to replicate Pushkin's creative process, as when the first line of *The Gypsies* (*Tsygany*, 1824) is heard to change from its first to its final versions. At times, we hear the scratching pen as it transfers words from mind to page. These sequences animate Pushkin's handwriting. The opening sequence shows a foot's inscription of an arabesque as if onto ice (we hear skates cutting across the ice), setting up this moment when a drawing is produced as prologue to many sequences in which poetry will be produced. The best scholar of Pushkin's drawings, Abram Efros, noted in 1945 that the drawings appear in the manuscripts as a kind of pause in the writing process, but the film suggests that these activities were simultaneous.[11] Every kind of mark that Pushkin made when he put pen to page is in fact used: the numbers found on some pages, for example, are given as his mental calculations of his debts; ink blots and cancellations across a face are reproduced in order to show Pushkin's dissatisfaction with the self-images he drew. Thus the film explains the pun of its title: although late autumn was Pushkin's favourite time of year, and references to autumn come at spaced intervals in the film, Pushkin loved autumn because he associated it with his own capacity for work, as in the Boldino autumn of 1830. The film suggests that Pushkin's most cherished periods of time were when he sat, pen in hand, wrote, and drew pictures.

My Favourite Time is anchored by its visual focus on Pushkin's drawings, as indicated by its subtitle ('According to Pushkin's sketches', 'Po risunkam Pushkina'). The director, Andrei Khrzhanovskii, has said that the drawings show Pushkin's ability to reconstruct and to reincarnate an object when he drew it.[12] He suggests that the object has mystical properties in Pushkin's drawings, and his film exudes an almost pagan belief in Pushkin's magical powers. The poet who wrote of statues that come to life (in *The Bronze Horseman* most notably, a poem of which *My Favourite Time* makes good use) is a fitting subject for a film based on the technology of animation.[13] Russians call animated films *mul'tiplikatsionnye fil'my*, using a mathematical metaphor to indicate the medium's capacity, in increasing the number of images before a viewer, to create the illusion of movement, but when we think of this film, the inherent pun in *animated films* remains: in Russian, to animate is to give an object a soul (*odushevit'*), and just as Pushkin is said by Khrzhanovskii to have breathed life into the objects he drew (and, of course, others would say that he does the same thing with words), so this film takes on the task of bringing Pushkin's world to life. In that sense, it achieves the highest task of any of the films that use Pushkinian motifs: *My Favourite Time* establishes Pushkin as an exemplary creator of art, a creator who can yet teach poets and writers and one whose work stands as a model for the filmmakers who use him as their subject.

Adaptations

Pushkin's fiction and drama have long been a vital part of Russian cinema, with dozens of film adaptations having been made since the first, *The Queen of Spades* (*Pikovaia dama*, dir. Petr Chardynin) in 1910. Some of his writings have generated better movies than others, and it is intriguing to see the far greater cinematic success with the story 'The Queen of Spades' as compared with, for example, *Evgenii Onegin*. When a British film production company filmed *Onegin* in 1999 (dir. Martha Fiennes), the poetry was simply dropped in favour of prose, although bits and pieces of Pushkin's writing were dispersed through the characters' lines to peculiarly stilted effect.[14] Poetry has seemed to work well on film principally in the *Little Tragedies* (*Malen'kie tragedii*, of which the best version was Mikhail Shveitser's 1979 film) or occasionally in films based on the fairytales, such as *Ruslan and Liudmila* (1971–72, dir. Alexander Ptushko).

Costume pageantry and lavish settings became the principal attraction of filmed versions of *The Captain's Daughter* (*Kapitanskaia dochka*, most recently recreated as *The Russian Uprising* [*Russkii bunt*, 1999, dir. Alexander Proshkin]). We cannot know much about the first version of the film (*Kapitanskaia dochka [Emel'ka Pugachev]*, 1914, dir. Grigorii Libken and Sigismund Veselovskii), made in Yaroslavl, since the film has not been preserved; it surely was overshadowed that year by the lavish version of *Anna Karenina* directed by Vladimir Gardin. Its negative attitude towards the rebel hero Pugachev was evident.[15] A 1928 version with a screenplay by the noted Formalist critic Viktor Shklovskii was also made ideologically charged by details added to emphasise the economic complexities of life in the late eighteenth century and to give a salacious tinge to some scenes involving the hero Grinev, his beloved Masha and Catherine II. Grinev's rival Shvabrin little resembles the malevolent traitor created by Pushkin, instead becoming a rebel hero in his own right. He tries to save Masha Mironova in one scene, which is about as far as one can get from Pushkin's novel. The film has been called the most scandalous adaptation of any of Pushkin's writings.[16] Surely it now has strong competition from *The Russian Uprising*, with its air of depredation befitting Russia's post-Soviet audiences far more than the admittedly critical view Pushkin took of Catherinian Russia. Shklovskii's 1928 version was not a unique departure from Pushkin's text. A 1958 version, *The Captain's Daughter* (dir. Roman Kaplunovskii), also took liberties with Pushkin's text, emphasising the battle between Pugachev's Cossacks and the Imperial soldiers more than the family drama so important to Pushkin.

The Russian Uprising presents a good test case for the relevance of Pushkinian themes in a time of national transition. The film was made for the 1999 jubilee, although not released until shortly thereafter. It appeared with great fanfare, and received prizes at the Sochi Film Festival as well as being shown in the Berlin Festival in 2000. That quick release to a western audience tells us much about the film's strategy for drawing attention to itself: *The Russian Uprising* targets an audience both within and outside Russia, showing the 'new Russians' lots of lavish decor and scenes of wealthy consumption with which they can identify all the while that foreigners are treated to a spectacle of the imagined 'Russian soul'. Passionate excess branded as peculiarly Russian marks one lengthy sequence of celebrating Cossacks, led by Pugachev who cuts his own hand and waves it as he dances, dripping blood. The insane *khorovod* of men holds up to the West a vivid blood-red image of abasement before power and simulated pleasure in a dance before death. The film seems to know that its audiences, East and West, will prefer eroticism to sheer force, although many scenes are gratuitously violent. In the ending, a lascivious Catherine II has a young lover at her side when she offers her pardon to Masha Mironova. Perhaps more shocking to readers of Pushkin is an earlier scene of sexual groping between Masha and Grinev, which poses a much deeper challenge to the ethos of Pushkin's tale about honour.

Fidelity to Pushkin's text is only one measure of a film's success, of course, and in the case of *The Russian Uprising*, the strong performances of a few of the actors, especially Sergei Makovetskii as Pugachev, almost compensates for the near incoherence in aesthetic or historical terms. Judging from the extant versions, *The Captain's Daughter* may have posed a greater challenge to filmmakers than they imagined. To reduce Pushkin's ironies and quick characterisation to simple visual drama, no matter how extravagant the costumes, is essentially to transform his short tale into something more like the historical fiction of Pushkin's contemporaries, the popular novelists Faddei Bulgarin and Mikhail Zagoskin.

Paradoxically, the deft short story 'The Queen of Spades' has made a better subject for film than the historical novel, probably because its essential qualities of mystery and incomplete explanation work remarkably well in visual terms.[17] The success of Tchaikovsky's well-known adaptation of Pushkin's story for his opera *The Queen of Spades* facilitated further creative interpretations on the part of filmmakers. The first film of the story, in fact, was based on the opera: *The Queen of Spades* (1910, dir. Petr Chardynin). More interesting, though, is the 1916 silent version directed by Iakov Protazanov, which reproduces the fascination with scientific illusion found in Pushkin's story. Pushkin refers to mesmerism, galvanism and alchemy to mark this innovation, while Protazanov foregrounds the illusion that is film itself. James Card, writing about early films, found them to be 'a mixture of science, physiology and illusion'.[18] His observation helps us to see another reason why adaptations of 'The Queen of Spades' occurred quickly and often in cinema, and why they have often been so successful. Even in Pushkin's written tale, Germann attends to the story of the Countess's magic three cards as if he were watching a performance, and so inserted material can occur as if naturally in Protazanov's screen recreation of the tale. He also transposes the central interpretive work of Pushkin's verbal narrative. Protazanov shows Germann as an observer of others. By making him a spectator to nearly all of the film's major events, Protazanov exposes to our view the process by which Germann tries to make sense of what occurs before his eyes.[19] We spend a remarkable amount of the film watching Germann watch others. Some of these moments flow naturally from the plot of 'The Queen of Spades', where we know, for example, that Germann is a careful observer at the opening gambling scenes. While others exclaim or react to Tomskii's story about his grandmother, Germann is stiff with attention. His body often faces the camera, turned slightly away from the others, as if he were closing off all other distraction in order to concentrate entirely on what he hears – and as if the director wanted to make sure that an audience could similarly view Germann without distraction. The film consistently offers Germann as a focal point for understanding how acts of observation and interpretation occur in the story; the viewer is invited to copy Germann's intensity of attention although not perhaps his increasingly wild imagination. In this respect, Germann's mixed record as an interpreter of people and events gives him a function uncannily similar to that of the film's earliest audiences. It is a truism of film criticism to claim that early viewers were easily overwhelmed by the new thrills of the cinema. The Lumières' film *The Arrival of a Train at La Ciotat Station* (1895), with its onrushing train headed straight out into the cinema audience, is said to have caused panic. But audiences may have been entirely capable of seeing events from the viewpoint of the screen protagonist. Yuri Tsivian helpfully disputes the claim that early viewers were incapable of distinguishing between mimesis and real events. As he points out, viewers had long been educated in a variety of cultural codes, from the theatre and opera to literature itself. These codes prepared them well for the new art form of cinema: they would have understood as well as felt how the multiple viewpoints of the montage created a relativism in contrast to Germann's obsessive point of view.[20]

In Igor Maslennikov's 1982 film *The Queen of Spades* (*Pikovaia dama*), the assurance of an audience's aesthetic sensibilities leads to a different set of cinematic decisions. Certainly by the 1980s, all anxiety about cinema and its viewers was long gone, and the aesthetic concern had shifted toward the potential contrast between literature and film. Maslennikov assumes that his viewers want their Pushkin pure, and he offers a film that tries to revert to almost entirely verbal art. Epigraphs are printed on screen (not unlike the inter-titles that were used in silent cinema, in fact). Interpolated dramatic scenes are nearly always told rather than shown (no sight of the young Countess learning the secret of the three cards, for example). Any number of scenes in the story, in fact, are only described (the 'repulsive secrets' of the old Countess's toilette, for example). Maslennikov gives Pushkin's words to a narrator, the acclaimed stage and film actress Alla Demidova, who appears in modern dress. She walks from one scene to another, as if motivating the transition from Narumov's dining room where gambling opens the film to the Countess's bedroom, or she stands outside buildings to tell viewers what is happening inside (the old Countess's funeral). Her presence is commanding: she often speaks at length, and subtly, barely copies the actors' body language as if nearly performing their parts herself. Demidova plays her part extremely well, looking stern when she describes Germann's stiff demeanour, gently sad when she elaborates on the difficulties of Liza's life as a companion to the old Countess, and truly disturbed when she recounts the scene of Germann's final misplayed card. It is she who becomes the focal point for acts of interpretation in the film, rather than Germann, as was the case in Protazanov's version: we watch the narrator as she watches the actors, and we see her extremely expressive face register their surprise or disappointment, or her own ironic amusement.

Maslennikov draws his viewers back into a world of literary narration. He leaves many scenes (the young Countess losing then regaining money, Germann in the insane asylum) safely in the viewer's imagination. His film is directed toward an audience that comes to the movies in search of literary pleasures, where words conjure up images; *The Queen of Spades* in this version is meant to create the illusion not that viewers have been to the movies, but that they have read a book. One can read along in the story as the film proceeds (which would have been all the easier at home – and this movie was made for television), noting how rarely the spoken words stray from Pushkin's text. Even the music is taken from Pushkin's era with all melodies taken from the work of Dmitrii Bortnianskii. Maslennikov pushes to an extreme the principle of fidelity to Pushkin found in other Pushkin films.

Alexander Orlov made a new version of 'The Queen of Spades' in the last years of Soviet power, changing the title to mark his strong departure from an extremely literary model: *These . . . Three Faithful Cards* (*Eti . . . tri vernye karty*, 1988). The new title also indicates his interpretation of Pushkin's tale: Maslennikov had suggested with Demidova's narration that the story's magic was in Pushkin's narrative prose, but Orlov implicitly argues that this is a tale about cards. His film thus opens with the card-playing scene at Narumov's, here much extended and used as background for the opening credits; when the final credits roll, the card playing resumes, creating a frame for the film. Germann, expertly played by Alexander Feklistov, is obsessed with cards, not merely keenly interested in them. He is driven to near-insanity as soon as he hears Tomskii's story about the Countess, and so in the very first card-playing scene he answers the question 'What time is it?' with the mangled reply 'A quarter to the ace' ('bez chetverti tuz'). Orlov plays freely with Pushkin's details, in this instance by changing and bringing forward a sentence found later in the original story.

The film, however, does more than show us the power of cards to make someone obsessed. *These . . . Three Faithful Cards* also presents an idea of what cards can mean in a gambler's life. More even than a liberated freedom to 'sacrifice what is necessary for the superfluous' pleasure of life, cards represent the possibility of a life lived for high stakes, a life of passionate intensity and recklessness.[21] Germann incarnates that willingness in the film, but so does Liza, especially as played by Vera Glagoleva. Orlov emphasises the emotional intensity of Pushkin's tale, making it a Gothic horror tale at the expense of Pushkin's irony. The film's emphasis on passion affects the exchange between Germann and the old Countess in her bedroom: he imagines that he speaks to her as a young beauty. Their conversation is oddly affectionate, and the old Countess caresses his face when he begins to speak. Germann is nearly a positive hero, one who feels instantly that he has committed a grave wrong. Once he loses at cards, Germann becomes insane. The film concludes with an extended scene of deranged behaviour in a madhouse where Germann ends his days.

Conclusion

One could argue that the madhouse scenes that conclude *These . . . Three Faithful Cards* are so extended because the filmmaker saw his own culture descending into a chaos that reminded him of this madness. Such glances around at the present are common in Pushkin films, but their strength lies perhaps more significantly in what they venture to say about Pushkin and his world. These films often portray themselves as faithful to some deeper vision of Pushkin's world, and they value characters who display that capacity for fidelity. They also, however, value the moments of creative departure, showing us the achievements of bold individuals who dare to strike out on their own. The contemporary world of Soviet Russia and now its post-Soviet variant does not always reward such appreciation for risk, which may be another reason for the long scene of madness at the end of *These . . . Three Faithful Cards*, but film as an aesthetic object works best when it takes some risks of its own. Memorable movies have now been made that retell the life of Pushkin, that recreate some of his writings, and that use Pushkinian motifs toward new ends. Taken together, this body of work constitutes a key piece of twentieth-century culture's response to Pushkin, and there is every reason to think that this response will endure as the new century continues.

NOTES

1. *Velikii kinemo: katalog sokhranivshikhsia igrovykh fil'mov Rossii 1908–1919*, Moscow, NLO, 2002, p. 47. All translations in this chapter are the author's own.
2. E. Barykin and V. N. Antropov (eds.), *Pushkinskii kinoslovar'*, Moscow, Sovremennye tetradi, 1999, pp. 16–18.
3. *Velikii kinemo*, p. 49.
4. See Barykin and Antropov (eds.), *Pushkinskii kinoslovar'*, p. 39, for the list of scholars.
5. As discussed in Karen Petrone, *Life Has Become More Joyous, Comrades: Celebrations in the Time of Stalin*, Bloomington, IN, Indiana University Press, 2000, pp. 133–35.
6. As noted in Barykin and Antropov (eds.), *Pushkinskii kinoslovar'*, p. 38.
7. N. N. Efimov praises the film's invention of characters or conversations to fill out the historical picture. See his 'Biograficheskie fil'my o Pushkine', *Pushkin. Issledovaniia i materialy* 5 (1967), 311.
8. On *Keep Me Safe, My Talisman*, see Stephanie Sandler, *Commemorating Pushkin: Russia's Myth of a National Poet*, Stanford University Press, 2004, chap. 4, where longer analyses of *Sidewhiskers*, *The Last Road* and *Little Tragedies* also appear.
9. See A. S. Pushkin, *Sobranie sochinenii*, 10 vols., Leningrad, Nauka, 1977–79, vol. x, pp. 52, 595. I have made my English closer to the Russian as heard in the film.

10. For a description of each short film (the titles are 'Ia k vam lechu vospominan'em . . .', 'I s vami snova ia . . .' and 'Osen''), see Barykin and Antropov (eds.), *Pushkinskii kinoslovar'*, pp. 105–07.
11. See Abram Efros, *Avtoportrety Pushkina*, Moscow, Goslitmuzei, 1945, p. 14.
12. Quoted in E. O. Vysochina, *Obraz, berezhno khranimyi*, Moscow, Prosveshchenie, 1989, p. 212.
13. On the aesthetic thrill that cartoons give by making the inanimate improbably animate, see Iurii Lotman, 'O iazyke mul'tiplikatsionnykh fil'mov', in Iurii Lotman, *Izbrannye stat'i*, 3 vols., Tallinn, Aleksandra, 1993, vol. iii, pp. 323–24.
14. One can read choice bits of the dialogue on the website of the Internet Movie Database at http://www.imdb.com/title/tt0119079/quotes
15. Barykin and Antropov (eds.), *Pushkinskii kinoslovar'*, p. 28.
16. Ibid., p. 36.
17. For a discussion of all versions, see Anatoly Vishevsky, '"The Queen of Spades" revisited, revisited, and revisited: how time changed accents', *Russian Studies in Literature* 40:2 (Spring 2004), 20–44.
18. James Card, *Seductive Cinema: the Art of Silent Film*, New York, Alfred A. Knopf, 1994, p. 26.
19. See the discussion of unique forms of 'spectatorial address' in still earlier film (before 1908) in Tom Gunning, '"Now you see it, now you don't": the temporality of the Cinema of Attractions', in *Silent Film*, ed. Richard Abel, New Brunswick, NJ, Rutgers University Press, 1996, pp. 71–84; see esp. p. 74.
20. Yuri Tsivian, *Early Cinema in Russia and its Cultural Reception*, translated by Alan Bodger, University of Chicago Press, 1998, p. 136.
21. On the symbolic and cultural significance of gambling, see Ian Helfant, *The High Stakes of Identity: Gambling in the Life and Literature of Nineteenth-Century Russia*, Evanston, IL, Northwestern University Press, 2002.

14

EVGENY DOBRENKO

Pushkin in Soviet and post-Soviet culture

Pushkin's unique place in the Russian national consciousness owes less to his greatness as a poet than to the fact that a myth of Pushkin lies at the heart of the Russian national identity which is defined by a conflict between a lofty image of Russia's majesty, and the bleakness of her past and uncertainty of the present. It can be described as a cross between an inferiority complex and a superiority complex. Russianness is realised in a dichotomy that was engendered by Pushkin. It was he who created that Russia which, in the words of the nineteenth-century poet Fedor Tiutchev, 'the mind cannot grasp' by creating an enchanting fairytale about this huge, cold, bleak and cruel land. Pushkin made possible Turgenev's young noblewomen, Tolstoy's noble heroes, Chekhov's good-natured protagonists, Bunin's dark alleys and Blok's beautiful stranger, the captivating music of Tchaikovsky and Rachmaninov, the painter Isaac Levitan's melancholy canvases and Diaghilev's exquisite ballets. That is why Pushkin is of such vital importance to Russians, and why his status in Russia is so hard for foreigners to fathom.

The one writer who falls out of this magical list is Dostoevsky. It is no coincidence that he was the first to articulate the idea of Russia's messianic role using the image of Pushkin, for he found himself at the heart of the Pushkin myth. Dostoevsky was the first to reveal the depth of the national trauma. Dostoevsky is Pushkin in reverse. He is the inner side of Russian national identity, whilst Pushkin is its radiant exterior. Maxim Gorky (1868–1936), the founding father of Soviet literature, understood this only too well. He wanted the world to see Russia through the eyes of Pushkin, not Dostoevsky, because Dostoevsky's talent was 'sick', whilst Pushkin's was 'psychologically healthy'. In the 1860s, Apollon Grigoriev had declared that for Russians Pushkin was 'our everything'. That is true insofar as Pushkin incorporates everything that Russia wants to be and everything that it fails to be. For the more clearly Pushkin was seen as a European and 'a free individual', the less concrete the lofty image of Russia that he embodied became.

The Soviet myth of Pushkin was shared by everyone from the leader down to the collective farmer (a truly national cult!), because it has less to do with politics than with the trauma of Russian national identity. On 6 June 1949, at the opening of a meeting in the Bolshoi Theatre held to commemorate the 150th anniversary of Pushkin's birth, the leading Soviet writer Alexander Fadeev said:

> We understand and value Pushkin's love of freedom because we are the freest nation, a genuinely free nation, the only free nation in the world . . . We alone can truly appreciate the Russianness of Pushkin's poetry because we are the free descendants of that great nation which gave birth to Pushkin. We find inspiration in the exuberance of his poetry because we are the most exuberant and happy nation in the world, confident of our strength and of our future.[1]

This talk of freedom, exuberance, greatness and self-confidence bespeaks a profound trauma. It goes without saying that the Soviet people, tormented by hunger and an ongoing state of terror, possessed nothing of the sort. Pushkin is on a completely different plane of existence from the qualities here ascribed to 'the nation'. Pushkin is cheerful and free, talented and high-spirited. Russia is morose and enslaved ('unwashed Russia – a country of slaves, a country of masters', in Lermontov's words; 'from the highest to the lowest, all are slaves', in Chernyshevskii's), cold and harsh. The unique paradox of the Pushkin myth as a patriotic myth of a national poet is that it is impossible to love both Pushkin and the real Russia – as opposed to the one he invented – at the same time.

Pushkin is a barometer of freedom (which he referred to as 'secret freedom') lacking in a Russia that is undoubtedly the least free of those European countries with whom it identifies. This uniqueness is the source of Russia's national complexes. Pushkin is both the medium through which the trauma is expressed and the means by which it is overcome. Russia finds its voice in Pushkin, and thereby prevails over the gravitational pull of reality. This is the perspective from which we will consider changes in the Pushkin myth after the Russian Revolution.

Pushkin in early Soviet culture

> 'Don't forget, I won't let you talk disrespectfully about the work of the authorities, I mean, that Pushkin and so forth!'[2]

These are the words with which a provincial official addressed Vladimir Mayakovsky during the tour of Russian cities he and his fellow Futurists had undertaken. Unsurprisingly, after the Revolution, left-wing artists, whose entire creative enterprise was based upon rebellion against the artistic canon and 'the authorities', continued to see Pushkin as the embodiment of the hateful tyranny of beauty. They were less exercised by the social content of the classics than by their status, a status to which left-wing art itself laid claim. The historical and social conditions offered the Futurists (members of the modernist movement called Futurism dedicated to dynamic change) the chance to set about systematically destroying the official national canon, and the Pushkin myth with it. The Russian Empire had fallen apart; its past was seen as shameful; its foundations, be they national ('the prison of nations'), international ('the policeman of Europe'), moral, religious or aesthetic, were crumbling in plain view, as the 'nests of gentlefolk' and the churches went up in flames. Pushkin had not simply stopped being a figure of 'authority': he had become a target for attack. 'Why hasn't Pushkin been attacked? And the other generals of the classics?', asked the Revolutionary poet Vladimir Mayakovsky indignantly in 1918;[3] as early as 1912 he had called for Pushkin to be 'thrown over the side of the steamship of modernity'.

In the years immediately after the Revolution, the Futurists drew their support from proletarian culture. But in the mid-1920s when the era of War Communism came to an end, the New Economic Policy was introduced, and the 'workaday building of socialism' began. The Futurists and the Proletarian Culture Organisation (*Proletkult*), founded in 1917 to produce a truly proletarian art created by proletarians for proletarians, fell out of favour with the Party elite. The ideals of the Proletkult started to fade from view, and left-wing art experienced a profound crisis. As early as 1924 (the 125th anniversary of Pushkin's birth), Mayakovsky's tone changes completely. While he still refuses to regard Pushkin as a figure of 'authority', Russia's foremost Revolutionary poet talks with Pushkin as with a 'comrade', enlists him in his 'company', and claims that their earlier misunderstandings had been nothing to do with Pushkin, but the canon in which he was included: 'I love you, but living, not mummified.'[4] At that very moment a cry rang out, unthinkable in the first years after the Revolution, but now sanctioned by the Party: 'Back to Pushkin!'

The very nature of the Russian Revolution prompted these changes. The 1920s were an age in which Russian literature was downgraded, declared imperialistic, 'politically unengaged'; and downplayed as the critical school known as Formalism deprived it of the magic means by which it fulfilled its main function: that of a cosmetic to be applied to the otherwise gloomy and unattractive face of Russian reality. The Revolution did not need literature for this purpose. On the contrary, it presented literature as an 'accomplice' which had conspired with the hateful regime to conceal the 'ulcers of tsarism'. There was simply no room for the Pushkin myth in Revolutionary culture.

Formalist literary criticism regarded Pushkin's writing merely as a set of literary devices, treating its development purely as a matter of style, and accounting for its distinctiveness in comparative terms. Sociological criticism in the 1920s and early 1930s (as practised by Pavel Sakulin, Vladimir Friche and especially by their students from the Communist Academy, the supporters of Valerian Pereverzev) was focused upon 'class analysis'. It claimed that Pushkin's entire output showed him to be nothing more than a 'nobleman in disguise', an adherent of the ideology of the 'minor landed gentry'; it claimed that he had capitulated before the tsar, becoming a servile poet, and that at best he was a representative of 'the enlightened aristocracy'.

This last view was held by one of the most influential of the semi-official Pushkinists, Dmitrii Blagoi, for whom 'class analysis of creativity' meant totalling up Pushkin's income: 'his professional life as a "scribbler", as a writer who lived on his own "earnings", to a large extent set Pushkin apart not only from the "nobility of old", but from the nobility in general, placing him instead in the intermediate layers of the working urban intelligentsia'.[5]

Nevertheless, sociological critics, in contrast to the radicals of the Left Front of Art and Proletkult movements, did try to understand Pushkin positively, claiming that he had turned his back on the aristocracy and become 'an adherent of the ideology of the self-capitalising landowners' (a view which can be traced back to the Bolshevik theorists Georgii Plekhanov and Anatoly Lunacharskii). Some of the ideas put forward were downright peculiar in their attempt to invent for Pushkin a class content stemming from the 'nobility-peasantry'.[6] Pushkin was transformed into a Romanticised outcast from his social milieu, who 'left his own class and entered another without any idea about the theory of social classes and class struggle . . . His fate is the fate of an outcast in the midst of his own class, who began to make the break at a time when there was no class for him to move into.'[7] That is the fundamental conflict reflected in Pushkin's writing, and the culmination of Marxist sociological criticism before its return to the embraces of the messianic nationalist myth.

Until the mid-1930s, an air of remarkable political redundancy clung to Pushkin studies. Pushkin was made just *one* of the Russian classics. Deprived of his pivotal role in Russian national identity, he ceased to be an all-time great, in whose presence all the other greats were but fashions. But this hiatus was significant in itself: another reason why the Revolution did not need Pushkin was that for a short time it cured the Russian nation of its chronic inferiority complex. The Revolution opened the gates to Europe. Thanks to its truly universal European project – socialism – Russia could proudly take its place in world history. The Russian socialist experiment banished the complexes of the new political elites. A national myth would just have restricted the new Russia's messianic drive. And so it remained until the early 1930s, when the doctrine of 'socialism in one country' replaced the messianic internationalist project of 'world revolution'.

Popular taste had no patience for avant-garde gimmicks. The reality was popular demand for the classics (conventional, comprehensible art), a huge popular desire to take control of one's 'cultural heritage' and to reap its benefits. Cultural organisations such as RAPP (the Russian Association of Proletarian Writers), AKhRR (the Association of Artists of Revolutionary Russia) and RAPM (the Russian Association of Proletarian Musicians) came into being. Their programmes amounted to nothing more than aesthetic traditionalism and 'learning from the classics'. These organisations more or less gained a monopoly on culture under Stalin in the early 1930s, thanks to active encouragement from the leadership. The classics occupied a key position in their aesthetic programmes, but they were robbed of any national content whatsoever, seen as nothing more than a repertoire of 'virtuoso techniques' to be acquired by proletarian writers, artists and composers so that they could create an art which was 'accessible to the people' and 'comprehensible to the masses'. That is why Pushkin first returned to the forefront of culture not in his capacity as a national poet, but as the leading 'craftsman', a kind of 'bourgeois professional' (*spets*).

Pushkin as canonical Soviet figure

> It was a Pushkin winter. His verses permeated everything: the snow, the sky, the frozen river, the garden in front of the school . . . Some extract or another from Pushkin could be heard over the loudspeaker every day, morning and evening. In the newspapers, alongside cartoons of Franco and Hitler, photographs of award-winning writers and Georgian dancers who had travelled to Moscow for a festival of Georgian art, alongside angry headlines which read, 'No mercy for the traitors!' and 'Wipe the traitors and murderers off the face of the earth!', were printed portraits of a tender, curly-haired youth and a gentleman in a top hat, who was sitting on a bench or strolling along the banks of the Moika.[8]
>
> (Trifonov, *Ischeznovenie*)

Here, Gorik, the protagonist of Iurii Trifonov's autobiographical final novel, published after the writer's death, recalls his childhood, when, as a schoolboy, he participated in the celebrations marking the centenary of Pushkin's death, which took place against the background of Stalin's Terror. The album which he and his family lovingly put together receives no mention in a competition for the best piece of work done for the occasion. First prize goes to an older boy who has made a plasticine model called 'The young Stalin reads Pushkin'.

Trifonov's novel was called *Disappearance* (*Ischeznovenie*), and it told of how entire generations and strata of the intelligentsia disintegrated, disappeared and were refashioned in the crucible of the Terror. This intelligentsia was extremely diverse: veterans of the Revolution who had fallen out of favour in the Stalinist system; the children and grandchildren of the pre-Revolutionary cultural elites who had melted away into the never-ending corridors of communal flats; the daughters of Moscow professors who had married 'commissars in dusty helmets'; the writers who in the past had been implacable champions of the avant-garde, and who were now winners of Stalin Prizes and members of the state's 'creative unions'.

If anything held this fractured society together, it was 'Great Russian Literature', in which Pushkin was the leading figure. The writer Lidiia Libedinskaia, then a schoolgirl, later recalled these times: 'To Pushkin we dedicated poetry, essays and dreams. We dreamed about Pushkin. We talked to him as though he were alive . . . Pushkin, Pushkin, Pushkin.'[9] Pushkin became a veritable fetish whilst remaining at the heart of the literary canon, and literature once again assumed its central position on the Russian Parnassus. With the ascendancy of 'Russocentric populism'[10] in the mid-1930s, the revolutionary project receded into the past. The Soviet nation, born in the paroxysms of the Terror, yet the sole heir to the glory of 'great Russia', needed Pushkin first and foremost in the capacity of 'Russian national poet' and a projection of its own greatness. The myth of Pushkin had reached its finest hour.

It carefully dismantled the Silver Age myth of Pushkin, which had denied Pushkin any ideological significance, perceiving his real value to lie not in 'civic' and national themes, but in the themes of the poetic vocation and the freedom of creativity. It was not enough just to cite the ode 'Liberty' ('Vol'nost''), the poems 'To Chaadaev' ('K Chaadaevu'), 'To the Slanderers of Russia' ('Klevetnikam Rossii'). Something had to be done about the Pushkin who, as the author of 'The Poet and the Crowd' ('Poet i tolpa'), had written contemptuously about 'the rabble'. The theory of 'art for art's sake' was no longer invoked; rather, his contempt was interpreted as merely an idiosyncratic means of self-defence against 'the rabble' to be seen in the context of the post-Napoleonic restoration of Europe and the reaction of the reign of Nicholas I. This 'rabble', it transpired, was 'not the people as a whole, whom great art always serves, and who always revere their poets, hanging on their every word'; on the contrary, the faults of the mob were redefined in Soviet criticism to mean what Pushkin disliked in 'high society' or equated with the 'repulsive egotism' of western democracy.

The re-evaluation of the Silver Age myth of Pushkin entailed reversing a central idea of Russian modernism, namely, the idea of return according to which 'the start of the twentieth century and the start of the nineteenth century were similar, parallel epochs in culture . . . [and] the linear progression of time should be rejected'.[11] It was now claimed that 'the new Russian literature which originated with Pushkin has become Soviet literature'.[12] The idea of progress and linearity reached truly ludicrous heights when projected onto the Pushkin myth in particular. Assertions abounded that Soviet Russia had outstripped the West not only in its industrialisation, but in the spiritual arena, too. What had taken Europe centuries to achieve was knocked off by Pushkin, that hero of national construction, in a record time which would have impressed even Stakhanov: 'What took Europe four hundred years took us a few decades and Pushkin just twenty years.'[13]

In contrast to this complete reworking of the Silver Age myth, the myth of Pushkin articulated by Dostoevsky merely had some finishing touches added to it, and its fundamental feature – messianism – was preserved: 'Dostoevsky said that "our impoverished and disorderly land" might ultimately deliver a new message to the world', might reveal 'the solution to Europe's misery in its Russian soul'. Apparently this was already present in the artistic genius of Pushkin's wise humility.[14] Without the Pushkin myth, the 'Soviet people' could not realise their potential, without it they were deprived of their crucial positive aspects (a 'free', 'great' people, 'rooted in history'). Pushkin became a screen onto which a new identity and a new legitimacy were projected.

In accordance with the Romantic ideology in whose service his image was employed, Pushkin himself was turned into a heroic Romantic rebel – a Decembrist, an enemy of autocracy and the tsar, a persecuted genius, a lover of the people cast out by his class and by society, an internationalist and a patriot.[15] As Paul Debreczeny has noted, the Soviet myth of Pushkin was modelled on hagiography, which was why it functioned not only as a myth of the national poet,[16] but also as a quintessentially Soviet heroic myth.[17]

That is why Pushkin continued to be 'collectivised'. Headlines in the newspapers published in his anniversary year read: 'Pushkin is among us', 'Pushkin and us'; a book by the Stalinist literary critic V. Kirpotin had the title *Communism and the Legacy of Pushkin*; Andrei Platonov wrote an article entitled 'Pushkin is our comrade'. Pushkin was 'among us' in the trenches of the civil war ('I took vengeance for Pushkin at Perekop', wrote the poet Eduard Bagritskii), he was with the crew of the Cheliuskin as they got stuck in the ice floe, he was in Red Square during public celebrations – amid the workers, the collective farmers and the heroes of industry:

> Look, it's him! There he stands on the platforms,
> As the marches resound in Red Square,
> He is affable, friendly and ardent,
> And his head, just like ours, is left bare.
> Where the spurs of the blue-coloured mountains
> Gather snow, which looks sure to descend,
> Down the Military Highway to Georgia,
> There we walked by his side, just like friends.

He was toughened in campaigns and battles,
And today he's both reader and tome.
He has learned that a life never-ending
Is not rest, but our anxious hearts' moan.[18]

He was with the Komsomol and with Party members as they sat in the smoke-filled offices of the Party committees:

At local Party meetings
They all discuss his verse.[19]

Pushkin was a participant in the construction of socialism who saw his dream realised in contemporary Soviet society. Everything that had once cast a shadow over the poet's life had now disappeared forever:

Past is an age of fear and repression,
Alexander Sergeich, just look –
The late emperor,
His Third Section,
Now that's all gone for good.[20]

Pushkin remained omnipresent even in wartime:

For Stalin, our guide and our light: to the line of attack!
Do battle for Pushkin,
For Lenin's invincible flag![21]

All this took place against a publishing boom. From 1918 to 1936, 335 editions of Pushkin were produced, with 18.6 million copies printed in total;[22] the editions published for the 1937 anniversary alone ran to 13.4 million copies.[23] The Russian national poet attained a quite fantastic readership in the multi-ethnic Soviet state. In the entire century which had elapsed between the publication of his first poems and the Revolution, only a few of his works had been translated into thirteen of the languages of the peoples who made up pre-Revolutionary Russia, and just 35,000 copies had been printed. All told, in the period from 1918 to 1954 Pushkin was indisputably the most widely published writer in the country (in all its languages, including Russian): more than 84.5 million copies of his works appeared in 1,932 editions in eighty-two languages.[24] For the 150th anniversary of his birth in 1949, 252 editions and 10 million copies of his works appeared in Russian, as well as an additional 1.5 million copies in translation into seventy-six minority languages (twenty-five of which had had no written form prior to the Revolution).

Figure 1. Mass meeting, 1937, near the Pushkin Monument on Tverskoi Boulevard, Moscow. The verse at the bottom of the billboard of Pushkin is from his 'Epistle to Siberia'. Reproduced from Iu. Molok, *Pushkin v 1937 godu: materialy i issledovaniia po ikonografii*, Moscow, NLO, 2000, p. 27

Figure 2. Boris Knoblok, poster, 1936. The verses are the same as those quoted on the billboard (figure 1) and describe the day when freedom will come 'and on the ruins of autocracy / will our names be written'. Here, the names of Stalin, Pushkin, Molotov, Gorky, Kaganovich and Mayakovsky are written on the red volumes carried by the masses. Reproduced from Molok, *Pushkin v 1937 godu*, p. 55

The interval which separated this anniversary from the 1937 celebrations had seen Pushkin definitively Russified and transformed into a tool at the disposal of the authorities. For instance, he was actively deployed in the battle against 'servility before all things foreign' and cosmopolitanism: 'As an ardent fighter for the national dignity of the Russian people in the face of "the slanderers of Russia", both foreign and domestic, Pushkin is our ally in the battle with all manifestations of cosmopolitanism and servility before the West. Bourgeois "democracy" was no less repellent to Pushkin than were the feudalism and serfdom which he so hated.'[25]

Pushkin's pronouncements even proved useful in battle with the concrete manifestation of universal evil – America. On the date of Pushkin's birthday the editorial in *Pravda* wrote that 'Pushkin's irascible words which reveal the celebrated American "democracy" to be specious and hypocritical, masking the almighty power of the omnipotent money-bag . . . are extremely acute and exceptionally relevant today', that they were 'a blistering and ruinous indictment of contemporary American reactionaries'.[26]

The Stalinist Pushkin was a bridge between what ought to be and what actually was. In this capacity he embodied the basic principle of the Soviet aesthetic vision: his lofty Russia was akin to the Socialist Realist 'life in its Revolutionary development'. Thus, in the end, Pushkin was a form of compensation for the disparity between Russia's real past and the glorious new image of that past. There was no danger that anyone would remark the disparity during the festivities marking the centenary of the poet's death. But the unmistakable conversion of Russia's hateful and shameful past (the past that it had had literally just five years previously) into a pageant of outstanding victories and accomplishments (the new patriotic national myth) was conclusive proof of the transforming power of Stalinist mythology, which had equal success in distilling the no less shameful present, with its communal apartments, shortages, queues, poverty and Terror, into the celebratory heroic myth of the 1930s and 1940s. Pushkin stood at the very centre of this myth.

The Pushkin myth of the intelligentsia and poets from Akhmatova to Brodsky

'We were music in ice' (Boris Pasternak)

Pushkin's personality was too free, his genius too lightly borne, his creations too vital, to become completely petrified in this myth. In the writings of Akhmatova, Tsvetaeva and Mandelstam,[27] whose works were forced out of public culture almost entirely and remained the property of just a small circle of admirers, the Pushkin myth reaches maturity. It loses its political thrust, ceases to be an article of faith, and, by becoming a medium through which 'secret freedom' is realised, it finds its full artistic expression. It becomes a myth in the true sense of the word. The fullness of expression which it finds in Akhmatova is of unprecedented scope. In her poetry, myth permeates the very air of Tsarskoe Selo, 'where the poets lived', becoming its *genius loci*. It flourishes in the complex inter-textual web woven by Akhmatova's long poems, in their subtexts, motifs and themes. And, ultimately, it becomes the subject of Akhmatova's literary criticism. The vapid, one-dimensional political remake found in Soviet schoolbooks and editorials pales by comparison.

Sergei Gandlevskii, a representative of the post-Akhmatova generation in Russian poetry, observed that 'Akhmatova, who had fortuitously survived the terror, was seen by her immediate circle as the guardian of the homestead of classic culture. The impetuous Pasternak, caught in "some sort of perpetual childhood", was not suitable for this solemn and noble responsibility. But the regal Akhmatova was a different proposition . . . Akhmatova was, amongst many other things, the high priestess of culture.'[28] According to Gandlevskii, the deity in this temple was still Pushkin: 'The leading poet is Pushkin; that holds for the twentieth century, too. All the rest trail in second and third place.'[29]

Transformed in the work of the greatest Russian poets of the twentieth century, over time the Pushkinian legacy becomes a sort of 'music in ice'. Pushkin's accessibility notwithstanding, he remains a pocket of 'secret freedom' for the dissident intelligentsia. Analysing the classics makes it possible to dissect 'eternal' themes and conflicts such as the people and power, power and freedom, political violence, etc. The classics become the sites of secret ideological battles.

Tynianov tried to demythologise the Pushkin era in his historical novels, most notably in *Pushkin* (1935–43). He stripped it of its customary 'poetry' and pathos, showing Russia to be a country with no freedom whatsoever, into which a genius doomed to solitude and ruin was born. In Mikhail Bulgakov's play *Last Days* (*Poslednie dni*, 1934–35) Pushkin himself does not appear at all, but his death is presented as the result of a court conspiracy (an explanation which enjoyed great popularity at the time of the 1937 anniversary, when there were conspiracies and conspirators at every turn). Indeed, at the climax of the play Bulgakov makes explicit the real political motive for his murder. The burial scene is reminiscent of the demonstrations of 1905 and 1917: a student climbs a lamppost to declaim to the crowd Lermontov's forbidden poem 'On the Death of a Poet'; a noble officer addresses those assembled with the words, 'Fellow citizens! Pushkin was the victim of premeditated murder. And this despicable crime is an offence against our people . . . A great citizen has died because unlimited power has been placed in the hands of unworthy men who treat the people like slaves.'[30] Even if they related to events a century old, such speeches were much too dangerous for 1937. Performance of the play was banned.

The Pushkin myth preserved the positive aspect of the Russian national character in such a concentrated form that it retained a huge utopian potential. Platonov's series of articles on Pushkin published in the journal *The Literary Critic* in 1937 was a declaration of the faith of a 'Pushkin man'. Platonov spoke of the realisation of the Pushkinian ideal in the triumph of socialism in the poet's native land. He immersed Pushkin in the ideal world of a dream come true, apparently overlooking the realities of 1937. The Pushkin myth acquired a humane and therapeutic dimension. It was a form of escapism from the real tragedy of an unrealisable ideal. Such a declaration of faith apotheosises the spirit of Pushkin as the realisation of creative and humane principles.

A highly mythologised perception of Pushkin informed virtually everything Platonov said about the poet: 'Pushkin is nature operating in its rarest form: poetry. That is why truth, veracity, beauty, depth and anxiety automatically coincide in him.'[31] Seen in this radiant light, the 'Pushkin' about whom Platonov writes is in no way equivalent to Pushkin himself; rather, he stands for the entire Russian nation:

> In Pushkin the nation found inspiration and learned the true value of a life comprised not just of ideal things, but also of ordinary ones, a life lived not just in the future, but also in the present. This in itself eased the lot of the ordinary worker, the one real man, to whom nothing had ever been promised on this earth, save the Kingdom of Heaven.[32]

But history was fraying the edges of this pretty picture.

If Platonov picked out the 'serious' side of the myth formulated by Blok (the part about the purpose of the poet), the critic and writer Andrei Sinyavsky took up another aspect, which Blok had summed up in the phrase: 'Pushkin is a jolly name'. He made one of the first determined efforts to peel Pushkin the myth away from Pushkin the poet. In *Strolls with Pushkin* (*Progulki s Pushkinym*), which he wrote when he was in a prison camp in the mid-1960s, he tried to see Pushkin from outside the myth. The casual manner in which he talked with the poet, the lack of reverence in the conversation, revealed an unexpected new Pushkin. The tone of his discussion with a classic author and about classic literature was so unusual that the publication of the book in London in 1975 prompted a wave of attacks on Sinyavsky in the émigré press, and its publication in the USSR during

Perestroika caused an even greater scandal than the publication of Solzhenitsyn's *The Gulag Archipelago* had done.

Pushkin's freedom, his conversational style, 'Pushkinian lightness and elegance'[33] were inherited by the foremost Russian poet of the post-Akhmatova generation, Joseph Brodsky. But it was not only his use of language which made Brodsky Pushkin's direct heir; the way in which he shaped his own image to escape the bounds of the 'national tradition', narrowly understood, and his literary independence were also part of Pushkin's legacy. Sometimes the relationship between them is one of contrast: the drama of Pushkin's enforced service at court stands as a curious counterpoint to Brodsky's conflict with the Soviet authorities, who accused him of being a 'sponger'; another contrast is to be found in their exiles, in the fact that Pushkin, effectively imprisoned within Russia, strove to travel abroad, whilst Brodsky was kicked out of the country. It is no coincidence that Brodsky made most use of those poems in which Pushkin actively creates his own image, such as 'The Prophet' ('Prorok'), and 'Autumn' ('Osen'').[34] Brodsky was the first of the great poets to begin playing with the Pushkin myth.

He effected a change which was to be the starting-point for Andrei Bitov (born 1937) in *Pushkin House*, in which the Pushkin myth is brought down to earth. The novel's protagonist, the talented young philologist Lev Odoevtsev – 'a namesake rather than a descendant' of the St Petersburg aristocrats – has an ordinary background: his grandfather was a victim of state persecution whose son renounced him for the sake of his career. The atmosphere of treachery within the family shapes Odoevtsev's character in large measure. But Bitov is interested in finding an existential reason for the protagonist's conformity. In his opinion, people like Odoevtsev have survived into the twentieth century thanks only to 'the single technique of not asking oneself any questions', of ignoring reality: 'Unreality is a requirement for life.'[35] The Pushkin myth was just such a means of ignoring reality, replacing it by poetry, and thus it becomes clear that the myth operated on the micro level of individual psychology as well as on the macro level of political culture.

Bitov describes how this mindset works. At the very end of the novel the reader is introduced to a text Lev's grandfather wrote in the 1920s:

> The bonds have been broken, the secret has been lost forever . . . A mystery has been born! Culture is left only in the form of statues whose contours are destroyed. In this sense I can rest easy about our culture – it has already *been*. It is no more. It will live on without any meaning for a long time after I am gone . . . When everything had perished – that is when classic Russian culture was born, for all time . . . Russian culture will be a sphinx in the eyes of our descendants, just as Pushkin was a sphinx in Russian culture.[36]

Thus a connection is established between the 'unreal time' of the protagonist's life and the unreal – unending – cultural lifespan of the Russian literary classics. There can be no more accurate way of describing the fundamental conflict embodied in the Pushkin myth in modern Russia.

The culture of Perestroika and post-Soviet Pushkin

> Pushkin is an extreme, perhaps even the only, manifestation of the Russian spirit: he is Russian man in his final form, as he might appear in two hundred years' time. (Nikolai Gogol[37])

Soviet critics bridled at Gogol's words, since officially 'Russian man in his final form' had already appeared in the image of the new Soviet man (*homo Sovieticus*). But when the 200th anniversary of Pushkin's birth coincided with the collapse of the Soviet state, Russian man, now further than ever from the Pushkinian ideal, once again found himself alone with Pushkin. As a recent commentator has noted, this anniversary was notable because it saw the cult of Pushkin rapidly lose its official status.[38] The process had begun long before the anniversary itself.

The official Soviet myth of Pushkin had always invited parody, but the first writer to gain renown for parodying it consciously was Daniil Kharms. He undermined it in anecdotes and absurdity. Kharms's *Anecdotes from the Life of Pushkin* (*Anekdoty iz zhizni Pushkina*, 1937) were a parody of the innumerable memoirs which had been especially popular at the time of the 1937 anniversary celebrations. They were also a challenge to the semi-official image which robbed Pushkin of even the smallest hint of vitality. Kharms's Pushkin broke his legs, brawled in the street and threw stones at passers-by. It was a 'broken' myth, one that had got out of control.

During Perestroika of the 1980s and 1990s, Conceptualist poetry and art (a post-modern, ironic and self-referential style) released a torrent of texts directly connected with Pushkin in the semi-official literature. (Important examples can be found in Dmitrii Prigov's obituaries and his *Enchanting Star of Russian Poetry* [*Zvezda plenitel'naia russkoi poezii*]), in the rhythms of the underworld song (*blatnaia pesnia*) and the cruel romance (in much of Timur Kibirov's poetry, in Vladimir Druk's poem *Iosif Vissarionovich Pushkin*), in the style of everyday speech (in Lev Rubinshtein), in the quasi-realist novel (Mikhail Berg's *An Unhappy Duel* [*Neschastnaia duel'*]), and in quasi-poetic Romanticism (Prigov's *Pushkin's Evgenii Onegin*).[39] In order to debunk the Pushkin myth, Prigov first acknowledged it, and then dissociated the poet's image from his work:

Figure 3. Boris Orlov, *All-Russian totem*, 1982. The representation likens Pushkin to the general secretary of the Communist Party, Leonid Brezhnev. Reproduced from *Shinel' Pushkina*, Moscow and St Petersburg, Pentagraphic Ltd, cover

Consider the matter with care, should you want to:
You'll notice that Pushkin, once famed for his words,
Is nowadays more like a god of good harvests,
A nation's dear father and watcher of herds.

If only I could, in every last village
I'd place a fair image which carries his name.
And then – you know what? – well, I'd tear up his poems:
They spoil the impression, don't add to his fame.[40]

In the Perestroika period when the former historical mythology was beginning to collapse there was a popular joke which went: 'Russia is a country with an unpredictable past.' Prigov, Kibirov, Druk and Mamin argue that so-called 'historical consciousness' is in essence nothing more than a collection of stereotypes, a sort of mosaic in which the tiles can be moved around to form any pattern whatsoever. Rather than eroding the Pushkin myth, these games exposed how deeply it was embedded in popular consciousness.[41]

It goes without saying that the Conceptualist storm passed the average reader by. In post-Soviet society Pushkin was virtually the only point of cultural consensus. National identity remained just as tightly bound to his name as before. As the poet Vladimir Smirnov remarked, 'we have a writer of an "earthly" gospel – Pushkin. He is a supra-literary phenomenon. Pushkin is Russia's greatest statesman.'[42] And although Pushkin is studied today by people with a remarkably diverse range of opinions – from those who talk in earnest about a transcendental divine principle in Pushkin and about Pushkin as first and foremost a poet of Russian Orthodoxy, to those who say that Pushkin is not a poet, but a 'refined debauchee', and that his poetry is 'blasphemy' and 'abuse'[43] – his status remains unchanged. And that means that his tremendous susceptibility to manipulation for ideological purposes remains unchanged, too. He has been transformed from a Soviet non-believer, a militant atheist almost, into a holier-than-thou believer; from 'an ardent Revolutionary' who in his grave welcomed the Great October which had given the people their long-awaited 'liberty' and which had shattered the accursed 'despotism' into 'fragments' on which 'were written' the names of Pushkin, the Decembrists, the Revolutionary democrats, and so on, into a respectable monarchist and a staunch conservative.

And yet, as Andrei Zorin commented, 'the anniversary celebrations of 1999 showed us the Pushkin of the end of the second millennium. He turned out to be fun, homely, vivid, well-dressed, prosperous, importunate, a little banal: an idealised portrait of contemporary Russian democracy, perhaps. Of all the Pushkins that Russia has known, this one is far from the worst.'[44] Reaction to Pushkin as always is a barometer of ongoing changes. At the end of the 1920s, Tynianov made an acute observation: 'Every generation in literature battles against Pushkin, enrols him in their ranks . . . or, having started out doing the former, ends up doing the latter.'[45] And only, one might add, in order to start the whole process all over again.

In the crucible of the Revolution and the Stalinist Terror of the 'Pushkin winter' of the 1930s a new – Soviet – nation was born. This nation desperately needed a cultural heritage as a pedigree. And it also needed Pushkin because it was still the same eternal Russia. When the old Marxist guise of national Bolshevism disappeared at the end of the 1920s, when the bright hopes for change and 'socialism with a human face' faded away in the 1960s, and now at the beginning of the twenty-first century when the young Russian democracy has sunk into oblivion, it is hard not to wonder whether the world sees standing before it the same old Russia – a cold and austere empire in Europe's backyard which believes in its messianic destiny and which dreams of unparalleled eminence to come. In *The Bronze Horseman*, Pushkin famously acclaimed Peter for opening a geo-political 'window onto Europe'. The window onto European culture was opened by Pushkin himself. From him Russia received its first intoxicating taste of freedom. Without this ideal inspired by Pushkin Russia would cease to be itself – torn between the West (Pushkinian 'fun' and 'freedom') and the East (a gloomy imperial police state, embittered with the whole world, and a beggar, despite its countless riches). Without the Pushkin myth this romantic vision which forms the very essence of Russian national consciousness could not exist. Pushkin will remain at the very core of it as long as Russia is neither West nor East. In other words, for as long as there is a Russia.

NOTES

1. Alexander Fadeev, *Za tridtsat' let*, Moscow, Sovetskii pisatel', 1957, p. 490.
2. Vladimir Mayakovsky, 'Dva Chekhova', in *Polnoe sobranie sochinenii v trinadtsati tomakh*, Moscow, Khudozhestvennaia literatura, 1955, vol. i, p. 296.
3. Mayakovsky, *Polnoe sobranie sochinenii*, vol. xii, p. 45.
4. Ibid., vol. ii, p. 215.
5. Dmitrii Blagoi, *Sotsiologiia tvorchestva Pushkina*, Moscow, Mir, 1931, p. 50.
6. Valerii Kirpotin, *Nasledie Pushkina i kommunizm*, Moscow, Khudozhestvennaia literatura, 1936, p. 240.
7. Ibid., pp. 260–1.
8. Iurii Trifonov, *Vremia i mesto*: *Povest', romany*, Moscow: Izvestiia, 1988, pp. 172–73.
9. Lidiia Libedinskaia, *Zelenaia lampa*, Moscow, Sovetskii pisatel', 1966, p. 70.
10. David Brandenberger, *National Bolshevism: Stalinist Mass Culture and Formation of Modern Russian Nation Identity 1931–1956*, Cambridge, MA, Harvard University Press, 2002, p. 215.
11. Irina Paperno, 'Pushkin v zhizni cheloveka Serebrianogo veka', in Boris Gasparov, Robert P. Hughes and Irina Paperno (eds.), *Cultural Mythologies of Russian Modernism: from the Golden Age to the Silver Age*, Berkeley, CA, University of California Press, 1992, pp. 19–20.
12. I. K. Luppol, *Literaturnye etiudy*, Moscow, Khudozhestvennaia literatura, 1940, p. 38.
13. Ibid., p. 43.
14. Ibid., p. 71.
15. For criticism of the mythology of Soviet Pushkin scholars, see works by M. N. Virolainen and Iurii Druzhnikov in the Guide to Further Reading.
16. See Stephanie Sandler, *Commemorating Pushkin: Russia's Myth of a National Poet*, Stanford University Press, 2004, pp. 107–19; Karen Petrone, *Life Has Become More Joyous, Comrades: Celebrations in the Time of Stalin*, Bloomington, IN, Indiana University Press, 2000, pp. 113–48; Iu. Molok, *Pushkin v 1937 g.*, Moscow, NLO, 2001.

17. See Paul Debreczeny, "'Zhitie Aleksandra Boldinskogo': Pushkin's Elevation to Sainthood in Soviet Culture" in *Late Soviet Culture*, ed. Thomas Lahusen, Durham, NC, Duke University Press, 1993, pp. 47–68.
18. Pavel Antokol'skii, *Stikhotvoreniia i poemy*, Leningrad, Biblioteka poeta, 1982, p. 143.
19. Alexander Zharov, *Novyi mir* 1 (1937), 13.
20. Boris Kornilov, *Novyi mir* 1 (1937), 12.
21. The Uzbek poet Sheikh-Zade in *O rodine*, Moscow, 1934, p. 179.
22. G. Novogruskii, '18,6 milliona eksempliarov proizvedenii Pushkina', in *Pravda* 43 (1937).
23. 'Pered pushkinskimi dniami', in *Pravda* 5 (1937), 1–4.
24. Maurice Friedberg, *Russian Classics in Soviet Jackets*, New York, Columbia University Press, 1962, p. 190.
25. S. N. Durylin, *Pushkin na stsene*, Moscow, Akademiia nauk, 1951, p. 189.
26. 'Slava i gordost' russkogo naroda', in *Pravda* 157 (1949), 1.
27. See Sandler, *Commemorating Pushkin*, pp. 175–265.
28. Sergei Gandlevskii, 'Olimpiiskaia igra', in *Russkii zhurnal* (13 February 1998).
29. Sergei Gandlevskii, 'Iskusstvo nad spravedlivost'iu smeetsia', in *Ural* 1 (2001), 198.
30. Mikhail Bulgakov, *P'esy*, Moscow, Sovetskii pisatel', 1986, pp. 284–85.
31. Andrei Platonov, 'Pushkin – nash tovarishch', in *Literaturny kritik* 1 (1937), 37.
32. Ibid.
33. Valentina Polukhina, *Joseph Brodsky: a Poet for our Time*, Cambridge University Press, 1989, pp. 61, 194.
34. See Andrei Ranchin, *Na piru Mnemozimy: Interteksty Iosifa Brodskogo*, Moscow, NLO, 2001, pp. 200–85.
35. Andrei Bitov, *Pushkinskii dom*, Moscow, Sovremennik, 1989, p. 353.
36. Ibid., p. 353.
37. N. V. Gogol', *Polnoe sobranie sochinenii*, 14 vols., Moscow, Akademiia nauk SSSR, 1937–52, vol. viii, p. 50
38. Andrei Zorin, 'Den' rozhdeniia Aleksandra Sergeicha', in Andrei Zorin, *Gde sidit fazan . . . Ocherki poslednikh let*, Moscow, Sovremennik, 2003, p. 122.
39. See Mikhail Berg (ed.), *Shinel' Pushkina*, Moscow, Pentagraphic, 2000.
40. Ibid., p. 140.
41. For a similar experiment see Timur Kibirov's poem 'In the framework of *glasnost'*. 2' ('V ramkakh glasnosti. 2'), where he describes how a statue of Stalin is changed into one of Pushkin.
42. Vladimir Smirnov, 'Ischeznet poeziia – ischeznet Rossiia', in *Literaturnaia gazeta* (26 September 2001), 10.
43. Archpriest M. Ardov, *Vozvrashchenie na Ordynku*, St Petersburg, Inapress, 1998, p. 278.
44. Zorin, 'Den' rozhdeniia', p. 124.
45. Iurii Tynianov, *Arkhaisty i novatory*, Leningrad, Priboi, 1929, p. 228.

APPENDIX

Verse-forms

The standard metrical unit in Russian versification is the foot. A foot is composed of two (binary metres) or three syllables (ternary metres). The alternation of stressed or unstressed syllables determines the type of foot. Russian words have a single stress and the placement of that stress is inherent. The most common foot in Russian poetry is the iamb, consisting of an unstressed syllable followed by a stressed syllable. The second most common foot is the trochee, consisting of a stressed syllable followed by an unstressed syllable. The number of feet, normally between two and six, determines the length of the line. Hence the iambic tetrameter consists of four iambic feet (composed of eight or nine syllables), and the iambic pentameter consists of five iambic feet (composed of ten or eleven syllables). Iambic tetrameter was the metre of choice for narrative verse and lyric poetry in the early nineteenth century. Many of Pushkin's narrative poems, including *Ruslan and Liudmila, The Fountain of Bakhchisarai, The Gypsies* and *The Bronze Horseman* are written in this metre, using an irregular rhyme scheme that mixes couplets and alternating rhyme.

Further features that add expression and variety to poetic speech are rhythm, intonation and enjambment. Rhythm is the result of the actual rather than theoretical stress pattern. In the standard iambic line the words, ordered according to rules of syntax, fall into a pattern of alternating unstressed and stressed syllables. In an iambic line of eight or nine syllables the metre calls for up to four metrical stresses. But the rules also allow the poet to vary the frequency of stresses and create lines that have fewer stressed syllables than the maximum, with the effect of creating a more understated pattern. In theory, therefore, an iambic pentameter (a line made up of five iambs) will have five stressed syllables, which are separated at regular intervals by one unstressed syllable. But in practice the verse-line is much more flexible because the rules permit the poet to substitute an unstressed syllable for a stressed syllable. The omission of stress to create a rhythmic effect most often happens in the second, third and fourth feet. It is this variation from the theoretical norm that creates the rhythm of the line and gives individual poets their poetic profile, and rhythm often adds to the expressive effect of individual lines and poems. Like most other poets of the first decades of the nineteenth century, Pushkin wrote lines in which stress tended to occur in the the first, second and fourth feet, while stress was increasingly omitted on the third foot. In the poem 'Lines Written at Night during Insomnia', discussed in Chapter 2, Pushkin takes advantage of this rhythmic flexibility. The omission of the usual trochaic stress in lines 1, 2, 4, 7, 8, 11, 12 and 14 slackens the rhythm, de-poeticising the speech. By contrast, the unusual stressing of two consecutive syllables in iambic or trochaic verse results in a foot called the spondee: spondaic stresses are uncommon and highly emphatic (see Chapter 5 for an example).

Intonation relates to tone and melody. The rhetorical nature of the sentence (interrogative, declarative, conversational) affects intonation. Caesura, a word-break that occurs in longer lines like the iambic pentameter (as in *Boris Godunov*), can be used to create a pause in the line in imitation of a speech rhythm. Enjambment is a syntactic event that occurs when the ending of the poetic line and the sentence do not coincide, and the sense overflows to the next line. This effect, which can alter intonation, is common in narrative poetry and in soliloquies.

Although iambic tetrameter is also common in lyric poetry, Pushkin's corpus does contain significant variety. Different verse-lines and stanzaic patterns often carried connotations about genre and meaning. Russian iambic hexameter was derived from the French Alexandrine, the twelve-syllable line with a caesura after the sixth syllable. For instance, in 'To the Grandee' (1830), Pushkin's epistolary poem about the European Grand Tour and life of an Enlightenment aristocrat, Pushkin uses a form of the Alexandrine, that is, a line of six iambic feet with regular caesura. Pushkin chose a form associated with neoclassical verse writing and didactic genres that suited the poem's presentation of an earlier age. Similarly, in keeping with this, the poem uses a more elevated diction full of archaic-sounding words. In drama such as *Boris Godunov* and *Mozart and Salieri* Pushkin employed blank verse or iambic pentameter, thereby associating himself with Shakespeare's use of the metre in dramatic soliloquies (see Chapter 4).

Evgenii Onegin is also written in iambic tetrameters organised in a fourteen-line stanza form devised by Pushkin expressly for his novel-in-verse. The Onegin stanza contains three quatrains bearing three different schemes of regular feminine and masculine rhyme (alternating, couplets and enclosed) followed by a couplet ending in masculine rhymes. The stanza is ingeniously structured and lets Pushkin carefully pace the speed at which information is released to the reader. He tends to concentrate the narrator's chatty interjections in the first quatrain, reserving much of the content, including meditations and advancement of the plot, for the next eight lines; the final couplet normally allows him to point a moral wittily, to underscore a transition. Despite its fixed metrical shape, the stability of the versification and flexibility of the syntax made it a brilliant vehicle for Pushkin's narrative and poetic aims. The Onegin stanza proved a durable invention and was used and sometimes parodied by other Russian poets and enjoys an English afterlife in 'The Nutcracker' by the English poet Jon Stallworthy (1987) and in Vikram Seth's Pushkinian novel-in-verse, *The Golden Gate* (1986). Pushkin's formal accomplishment in handling complex stanza forms is also on display in other narrative works, like *The Little House in Kolomna* and *Count Null*. In one of his greatest lyric poems, 'Autumn' (1831), a capacious and syntactically flexible stanza form of eight lines of iambic hexameter allows Pushkin to unfurl majestically the details of the season and the poet's changes of mood and inspiration.

GUIDE TO FURTHER READING

STUDIES IN ENGLISH

Bakhtin, Mikhail, *The Dialogic Imagination: Four Essays*, Michael Holquist (ed.), trans. C. Emerson, Austin, TX, University of Texas Press, 1981

Bayley, John, *Pushkin: a Comparative Commentary*, Cambridge University Press, 1971

Bethea, David, *Realizing Metaphors: Alexander Pushkin and the Life of the Poet*, Madison, WI, University of Wisconsin Press, 1998

Binyon, T. J., *Pushkin: a Biography*, London, HarperCollins, 2002

Bocharov, Sergei, 'The stylistic world of the novel', in S. Hoisington (ed. and trans.), *Russian Views of Pushkin's Eugene Onegin*, Bloomington, IN, Indiana University Press, 1988, pp. 122–68

Briggs, A. D. P., *Alexander Pushkin: Eugene Onegin*, Landmarks of World Literature, Cambridge University Press, 1992

Clayton, J. Douglas, *Ice and Flame: Aleksandr Pushkin's 'Eugene Onegin'*, University of Toronto Press, 1985

Dalton-Brown, Sally, *Pushkin's 'Eugene Onegin'*, Critical Studies in Russian Literature, London, Duckworth, 1997

Davydov, Sergei, 'Nabokov and Pushkin', in V. E. Alexandrov (ed.), *The Garland Companion to Vladimir Nabokov*, New York and London, Garland Publishing, 1995, pp. 482–96

Debreczeny, Paul, *The Other Pushkin: a Study of Alexander Pushkin's Prose Fiction*, Stanford University Press, 1976

Social Functions of Literature: Alexander Pushkin and Russian Culture, Stanford University Press, 1997

Dixon, Simon, *The Modernisation of Russia 1676–1825*, Cambridge University Press, 1999

Driver, S., *Puškin: Literature and Social Ideas*, New York, Columbia University Press, 1989

Emerson, Caryl, *Boris Godunov: Transpositions of a Russian Theme*, Bloomington, IN, Indiana University Press, 1986

'Tatiana', in S. Hoisington (ed.), *A Plot of Her Own: the Female Protagonist in Russian Literature*, Evanston, IL, Northwestern University Press, 1995, pp. 6–20

Evdokimova, Svetlana, *Pushkin's Historical Imagination*, New Haven, CT, and London, Yale University Press, 1999

Freeborn, Richard, *The Rise of the Russian Novel from Eugene Onegin to War and Peace*, Cambridge University Press, 1973

Gasparov, Boris, *Five Operas and a Symphony: Word and Music in Russian Culture*, New Haven, CT, Yale University Press, 2005, chap. 3

Ginzburg, Lidia, *On Psychological Prose*, trans. J. Rosengrant, Princeton University Press, 1991

Gofman, M. L., 'Pushkin i ego epokha. Iubileinaia vystavka v Parizhe', *Illiustrirovannaia Rossiia*, special issue: 'A. S. Pushkin i ego epokha' (Paris, 1937), 114–31

Greenleaf, Monika, *Pushkin and Romantic Fashion: Fragment, Elegy, Orient, Irony*, Stanford University Press, 1994

Gregg, Richard, 'Rhetoric in Tat'jana's last speech: the camouflage that reveals', *Slavic and East European Journal* 25 (1981), 1–12

Gustafson, Richard, 'The metaphor of the seasons in *Evgenij Onegin*', *Slavic and East European Journal* 6 (1962), 6–20

Hoisington, Sonia, '*Eugene Onegin*: an inverted Byronic poem', *Comparative Literature* 27 (1975), 36–152

Hughes, Lindsey, *Peter the Great. A Biography*, New Haven, CT, and London, Yale University Press, 2002

Hughes, Robert P., 'Pushkin in Petrograd, February 1921', in B. Gasparov *et al.* (eds.), *Cultural Mythologies of Russian Modernism: from the Golden Age to the Silver Age*, Berkeley, CA, University of California Press, 1992, pp. 204–13

Kahn, Andrew, *Pushkin's Bronze Horseman*, Critical Studies in Russian Literature, London, Duckworth, 1998

Leighton, L. G., 'A bibliography of Alexander Pushkin in English: studies and translations', *Studies in Slavic Language and Literature* 12 (1999), 102–16 and 258–64

Levitt, Marcus C., *Russian Literary Politics and the Pushkin Celebration of 1880*, Ithaca, NY, Cornell University Press, 1989

Lezhnev, Abram, *Pushkin's Prose*, Ann Arbor, MI, Ardis, 1983, 190–206

MacCarthy, Fiona, *Byron. Life and Legend*, London, John Murray, 2002

O'Bell, Leslie, 'Through the magic crystal to *Eugene Onegin*', in D. Bethea (ed.), *Puškin Today*, Bloomington, IN, Indiana University Press, 1993, pp. 152–70

Reyfman, Irina, *Ritualized Violence Russian Style: the Duel in Russian Culture and Literature*, Stanford University Press, 1999

Sandler, Stephanie, *Commemorating Pushkin: Russia's Myth of a National Poet*, Stanford University Press, 2004

Distant Pleasures: Alexander Pushkin and the Writing of Exile, Stanford University Press, 1989

Scherr, Barry, *Russian Poetry: Meter, Rhythm, and Rhyme*, Berkeley, CA, University of California Press, 1986

Semenko, I. M., 'The "Author" in Eugene Onegin: image and function', *Canadian-American Slavic Studies* 29:3–4 (1996), 233–55

Taruskin, Richard, *Musorgsky: Eight Essays and an Epilogue*, Princeton University Press, 1993

Tertz, Abram, *Strolls with Pushkin*, trans. Catharine Theimer Nepomnyashchy and Slava I. Yastremsky, New Haven, CT, Yale University Press, 1993

Todd, William Mills, III, *The Familiar Letter as a Literary Genre in the Age of Pushkin*, Princeton University Press, 1976
Fiction and Society in the Age of Pushkin: Ideology, Institutions, and Narrative, Cambridge, MA, Harvard University Press, 1986
Vickery, Walter, 'Byron's *Don Juan* and Pushkin's *Evgenij Onegin*: the question of parallelism', *Indiana Slavic Studies* 4 (1968), 181–91
Vitale, Serena, *Pushkin's Button*, New York, Farrar, Straus and Giroux, 1999
Wachtel, Michael, *The Development of Russian Verse: Meter and its Meanings*, Cambridge University Press, 1998
Wolff, Tatiana (ed.), *Pushkin on Literature*, London, Athlone Press, 1986; rev. edn., Stanford University Press, 1986
Woodward, J. B., *Form and Meaning: Essays on Russian Literature*, Columbus, OH, Slavica, 1993

STUDIES IN RUSSIAN AND OTHER LANGUAGES

Abramovich, Stella, *Pushkin: Poslednii god*, Moscow, Sovetskii pisatel', 1991
Akhmatova, Anna, *O Pushkine*, St Petersburg, Sovetskii pisatel', 1977
Annenkov, P. V., *Materialy dlia biografii Pushkina*, 2 vols, St Petersburg, Voennaia tipografiia, 1855; new edn., Moscow, Kniga, 1985
Druzhnikov, Iurii, *Duel' s pushkinistami. Polemicheskie esse*, Moscow, Khroniker, 2001
Gillel'son, Maksim, *Molodoi Pushkin i Arzamaskoe bratstvo*, Leningrad, Nauka, 1974
Gofman, M. L. 'Pushkin i ego epokha. Iubileinaia vystavka v Parizhe', *Illiustrirovannaia Rossiia* (1937), 114–31
Grekhnev, Vsevolod, *Mir pushkinskoi liriki*, Novgorod, Volgo-Viatskoe knizhnoe izdatel'stvo, 1994
Iezuitova, R. V., and Ia. L. Levkovich (eds.), *Utaennaia liubov' Pushkina*, St Petersburg, Akademicheskii proekt, 1997
Ivanov, Viacheslav, 'O Pushkine', *Sovremennye zapiski*, 63 (1937), 177–95
Izmailov, N. V. (ed.), *Ocherki tvorchestva Pushkina*, Leningrad, Nauka, 1975
(ed.), *Stikhotvoreniia Pushkina 1820–1830-kh godov. Istoriia sozdaniia i ideino-kudozhestvennaia problematika*, Leningrad, Nauka, 1974
Khodasevich, Vladislav, *Pushkin i poety ego vremeni*, ed. Robert Hughes, 2 vols., Berkeley Slavic Specialties, 1999–2001
Kikta, V., *Pushkinskaia muzykal'naia panorama XIX–XX vekov: kratkii informatsionnyi spravochnik*, Moscow, Muzyka, 1999
Koshelev, V. A., *'Onegina' vozdushnaia gromada*, St Petersburg, Akademicheskii proekt, 1999
Lotman, Iurii, *Aleksandr Sergeevich Pushkin. Biografiia pisatelia*, Leningrad, Prosveshchenie, 1981
Pushkin, St Petersburg, Iskusstvo, 1995
Roman A. S. Pushkina 'Evgenii Onegin': Komentarii, Leningrad, Prosveshchenie, 1980
Meynieux, André, *Pouchkine homme de lettres et la littérature professionelle en Russie*, Paris, Librairie des cinq continents, 1966

Modzalevskii, B. L., *Biblioteka A. S. Pushkina: Bibliograficheskoe opisanie*, St Petersburg, Imperatorskaia Akademiia nauk, 1910; reprinted Moscow, Kniga, 1998

Pushkin i ego sovremenniki: Izbrannye trudy (1898–1928), ed. A. Iu. Balakina, St Petersburg, Iskusstvo, 1999

Ospovat, A. L., and R. D. Timenchik, *'Pechal'nu povest' sokhranit": ob avtore i chitateliakh 'Mednogo vsadnika'*, Moscow, Kniga, 1985

Proskurin, Oleg, *Poeziia Pushkina, ili podvizhnyi palimpsest*, Moscow, Novoe literaturnoe obozrenie, 1999

Literaturnye skandaly pushkinskoi epokhi, Moscow, OGI, 2000

Reitblat, A. I., *Kak Pushkin vyshel v genii: istoriko-sotsiologicheskie ocherki o knizhnoi kul'ture pushkinskoi epokhi*, Moscow, Novoe literaturnoe obozrenie, 2001

Shanskii, N. M., *Po sledam 'Evgeniia Onegina': kratkii lingvisticheskii kommentarii*, Moscow, Russkoe slovo, 1999

Shchegolev, Pavel, *Duel' i smert' Pushkina*, Moscow, Zhurnal'no-Gazetnoe Ob"edinenie, 1936

Iz zhizni i tvorchestva Pushkina, Leningrad, Khudozhestvennaia literatura, 1981

Skvoznikov, V. D., *Pushkin: istoricheskaia mysl' poeta*, Moscow, Nasledie, 1999

Slonimskii, A., *Masterstvo Pushkina*, Moscow, Gosudarstvennoe izdatel'stvo khudozhestvennoi literatury, 1959

Smirnov-Sokolskii, Nikolai, *Rasskazy o prizhiznennykh izdaniiakh Pushkina*, Moscow, Izdatel'stvo vsesoiuznoi knizhnoi palaty, 1962

Surat, Irina, *Pushkin: biografiia i lirika*, Moscow, Nasledie, 1999

and S. G. Bocharov, *Pushkin: kratkii ocherk zhizni i tvorchestva*, Moscow, Iazyki slavianskoi kul'tury, 2002

Tomashevskii, Boris, *Pushkin. Kniga pervaia (1813–1824)*, Moscow, Akademiia nauk, 1956.

Pushkin: Kniga vtoraia, materialy k monografii (1824–1837), Moscow, Leningrad, Izdatel'stvo AN SSSR, 1961

Tsiavlovskii, M. A., *Stat'i o Pushkine*, Moscow, Akademiia nauk, 1962

Tynianov, Iurii, *Pushkin i ego sovremenniki*, Moscow, Nauka, 1968

Vatsuro, Vadim *et al.* (eds.), *A. S. Pushkin v vospominaniiakh sovremennikov*, 2 vols., Moscow, Khudozhestvennaia literatura, 1974

and S. A. Fomichev (eds.), *Pushkin v prizhiznennoi kritike 1820–1827*, St Petersburg, Gosudarstvennyi Pushkinskii teatral'nyi tsentr, 1996

Vinogradov, V. V., *Iazyk Pushkina: Pushkin i istoriia russkogo literaturnogo iazyka*, Leningrad, Academia, 1935

Virolainen, M. N. (ed.), *Legendy i mify o Pushkine*, St Petersburg, Akademicheskii proekt, 1994

Zhuikova, R. G., *Portretnye risunki Pushkina. Katalog attributsii*, St Petersburg, Dmitrii Bulanin, 1996

INDEX

CAMBRIDGE COMPANIONS TO LITERATURE

The Cambridge Companion to Greek Tragedy
edited by P. E. Easterling

The Cambridge Companion to Roman Satire
edited by Kirk Freudenburg

The Cambridge Companion to Old English Literature
edited by Malcolm Godden and Michael Lapidge

The Cambridge Companion to Medieval Women's Writing
edited by Carolyn Dinshaw and David Wallace

The Cambridge Companion to Medieval Romance
edited by Roberta L. Krueger

The Cambridge Companion to Medieval English Theatre
edited by Richard Beadle

The Cambridge Companion to English Renaissance Drama
2nd edition
edited by A. R. Braunmuller and Michael Hattaway

The Cambridge Companion to Renaissance Humanism
edited by Jill Kraye

The Cambridge Companion to English Poetry, Donne to Marvell
edited by Thomas N. Corns

The Cambridge Companion to English Literature, 1500–1600
edited by Arthur F. Kinney

The Cambridge Companion to English Literature, 1650–1740
edited by Steven N. Zwicker

The Cambridge Companion to English Literature, 1740–1830
edited by Thomas Keymer and Jon Mee

The Cambridge Companion to Writing of the English Revolution
edited by N. H. Keeble

The Cambridge Companion to English Restoration Theatre
edited by Deborah C. Payne Fisk

The Cambridge Companion to British Romanticism
edited by Stuart Curran

The Cambridge Companion to Eighteenth-Century Poetry
edited by John Sitter

The Cambridge Companion to the Eighteenth-Century Novel
edited by John Richetti

The Cambridge Companion to Gothic Fiction
edited by Jerrold E. Hogle

The Cambridge Companion to Victorian Poetry
edited by Joseph Bristow

The Cambridge Companion to the Victorian Novel
edited by Deirdre David

The Cambridge Companion to Crime Fiction
edited by Martin Priestman

The Cambridge Companion to Science Fiction
edited by Edward James and Farah Mendlesohn

The Cambridge Companion to Travel Writing
edited by Peter Hulme and Tim Youngs

The Cambridge Companion to American Realism and Naturalism
edited by Donald Pizer

The Cambridge Companion to Nineteenth-Century American Women's Writing
edited by Dale M. Bauer and Philip Gould

The Cambridge Companion to Victorian and Edwardian Theatre
edited by Kerry Powell

The Cambridge Companion to the Literature of the First World War
edited by Vincent Sherry

The Cambridge Companion to the Classic Russian Novel
edited by Malcolm V. Jones and Robin Feuer Miller

The Cambridge Companion to the French Novel: from 1800 to the Present
edited by Timothy Unwin

The Cambridge Companion to the Spanish Novel: from 1600 to the Present
edited by Harriet Turner and Adelaida López de Martínez

The Cambridge Companion to the Italian Novel
edited by Peter Bondanella and Andrea Ciccarelli

The Cambridge Companion to the Irish Novel
edited by John Wilson Foster

The Cambridge Companion to the Modern German Novel
edited by Graham Bartram

The Cambridge Companion to the Latin American Novel
edited by Efraín Kristal

The Cambridge Companion to Jewish American Literature
edited by Hana Wirth-Nesher and Michael P. Kramer

The Cambridge Companion to Native American Literature
edited by Joy Porter and Kenneth M. Roemer

The Cambridge Companion to the African American Novel
edited by Maryemma Graham

The Cambridge Companion to Canadian Literature
edited by Eva-Marie Kröller

The Cambridge Companion to Contemporary Irish Poetry
edited by Matthew Campbell

The Cambridge Companion to Modernism
edited by Michael Levenson

The Cambridge Companion to American Modernism
edited by Walter Kalaidjian

The Cambridge Companion to Postmodernism
edited by Steven Connor

The Cambridge Companion to Postcolonial Literary Studies
edited by Neil Lazarus

The Cambridge Companion to Feminist Literary Theory
edited by Ellen Rooney

The Cambridge Companion to Australian Literature
edited by Elizabeth Webby

The Cambridge Companion to American Women Playwrights
edited by Brenda Murphy

The Cambridge Companion to Modern British Women Playwrights
edited by Elaine Aston and Janelle Reinelt

The Cambridge Companion to Twentieth-Century Irish Drama
edited by Shaun Richards

The Cambridge Companion to Homer
edited by Robert Fowler

The Cambridge Companion to Virgil
edited by Charles Martindale

The Cambridge Companion to Ovid
edited by Philip Hardie

The Cambridge Companion to Dante
edited by Rachel Jacoff

The Cambridge Companion to Cervantes
edited by Anthony J. Cascardi

The Cambridge Companion to Goethe
edited by Lesley Sharpe

The Cambridge Companion to Dostoevskii
edited by W. J. Leatherbarrow

The Cambridge Companion to Tolstoy
edited by Donna Tussing Orwin

The Cambridge Companion to Chekhov
edited by Vera Gottlieb and Paul Allain

The Cambridge Companion to Ibsen
edited by James McFarlane

The Cambridge Companion to Flaubert
edited by Timothy Unwin

The Cambridge Companion to Pushkin
edited by Andrew Kahn

The Cambridge Companion to Proust
edited by Richard Bales

The Cambridge Companion to Thomas Mann
edited by Ritchie Robertson

The Cambridge Companion to Kafka
edited by Julian Preece

The Cambridge Companion to Brecht
edited by Peter Thomson and Glendyr Sacks

The Cambridge Companion to Walter Benjamin
edited by David S. Ferris

The Cambridge Companion to Lacan
edited by Jean-Michel Rabaté

The Cambridge Companion to Nabokov
edited by Julian W. Connolly

The Cambridge Companion to Chaucer, second edition
edited by Piero Boitani and Jill Mann

The Cambridge Companion to Shakespeare
edited by Margareta de Grazia and Stanley Wells

The Cambridge Companion to Shakespeare on Film
edited by Russell Jackson

The Cambridge Companion to Shakespearean Comedy
edited by Alexander Leggatt

The Cambridge Companion to Shakespeare on Stage
edited by Stanley Wells and Sarah Stanton

The Cambridge Companion to Shakespeare's History Plays
edited by Michael Hattaway

The Cambridge Companion to Shakespearean Tragedy
edited by Claire McEachern

The Cambridge Companion to Christopher Marlowe
edited by Patrick Cheney

The Cambridge Companion to Ben Jonson
edited by Richard Harp and Stanley Stewart

The Cambridge Companion to John Donne
edited by Achsah Guibbory

The Cambridge Companion to Spenser
edited by Andrew Hadfield

The Cambridge Companion to Milton, 2nd edition
edited by Dennis Danielson

The Cambridge Companion to John Dryden
edited by Steven N. Zwicker

The Cambridge Companion to Molière
edited by David Bradby and Andrew Calder

The Cambridge Companion to Aphra Behn
edited by Derek Hughes and Janet Todd

The Cambridge Companion to Samuel Johnson
edited by Greg Clingham

The Cambridge Companion to Jonathan Swift
edited by Christopher Fox

The Cambridge Companion to Mary Wollstonecraft
edited by Claudia L. Johnson

The Cambridge Companion to William Blake
edited by Morris Eaves

The Cambridge Companion to Wordsworth
edited by Stephen Gill

The Cambridge Companion to Coleridge
edited by Lucy Newlyn

The Cambridge Companion to Byron
edited by Drummond Bone

The Cambridge Companion to Keats
edited by Susan J. Wolfson

The Cambridge Companion to Shelley
edited by Timothy Morton

The Cambridge Companion to Mary Shelley
edited by Esther Schor

The Cambridge Companion to Jane Austen
edited by Edward Copeland and Juliet McMaster

The Cambridge Companion to the Brontës
edited by Heather Glen

The Cambridge Companion to Charles Dickens
edited by John O. Jordan

The Cambridge Companion to Wilkie Collins
edited by Jenny Bourne Taylor

The Cambridge Companion to George Eliot
edited by George Levine

The Cambridge Companion to Thomas Hardy
edited by Dale Kramer

The Cambridge Companion to Oscar Wilde
edited by Peter Raby

The Cambridge Companion to George Bernard Shaw
edited by Christopher Innes

The Cambridge Companion to W. B. Yeats
edited by Marjorie Howes and John Kelly

The Cambridge Companion to Joseph Conrad
edited by J. H. Stape

The Cambridge Companion to D. H. Lawrence
edited by Anne Fernihough

The Cambridge Companion to Virginia Woolf
edited by Sue Roe and Susan Sellers

The Cambridge Companion to James Joyce, 2nd edition
edited by Derek Attridge

The Cambridge Companion to T. S. Eliot
edited by A. David Moody

The Cambridge Companion to Ezra Pound
edited by Ira B. Nadel

The Cambridge Companion to W. H. Auden
edited by Stan Smith

The Cambridge Companion to Beckett
edited by John Pilling

The Cambridge Companion to Harold Pinter
edited by Peter Raby

The Cambridge Companion to Tom Stoppard
edited by Katherine E. Kelly

The Cambridge Companion to Brian Friel
edited by Anthony Roche

The Cambridge Companion to Herman Melville
edited by Robert S. Levine

The Cambridge Companion to Nathaniel Hawthorne
edited by Richard Millington

The Cambridge Companion to Harriet Beecher Stowe
edited by Cindy Weinstein

The Cambridge Companion to Theodore Dreiser
edited by Leonard Cassuto and Claire Virginia Eby

The Cambridge Companion to Willa Cather
edited by Marilee Lindermann

The Cambridge Companion to Edith Wharton
edited by Millicent Bell

The Cambridge Companion to Henry James
edited by Jonathan Freedman

The Cambridge Companion to Walt Whitman
edited by Ezra Greenspan

The Cambridge Companion to Ralph Waldo Emerson
edited by Joel Porte and Saundra Morris

The Cambridge Companion to Henry David Thoreau
edited by Joel Myerson

The Cambridge Companion to Mark Twain
edited by Forrest G. Robinson

The Cambridge Companion to Edgar Allan Poe
edited by Kevin J. Hayes

The Cambridge Companion to Emily Dickinson
edited by Wendy Martin

The Cambridge Companion to William Faulkner
edited by Philip M. Weinstein

The Cambridge Companion to Ernest Hemingway
edited by Scott Donaldson

The Cambridge Companion to F. Scott Fitzgerald
edited by Ruth Prigozy

The Cambridge Companion to Wallace Stevens
edited by John N. Serio

The Cambridge Companion to Robert Frost
edited by Robert Faggen

The Cambridge Companion to Sylvia Plath
edited by Jo Gill

The Cambridge Companion to Ralph Ellison
edited by Ross Posnock

The Cambridge Companion to Eugene O'Neill
edited by Michael Manheim

The Cambridge Companion to Tennessee Williams
edited by Matthew C. Roudané

The Cambridge Companion to Arthur Miller
edited by Christopher Bigsby

The Cambridge Companion to David Mamet
edited by Christopher Bigsby

The Cambridge Companion to Sam Shepard
edited by Matthew C. Roudané

The Cambridge Companion to Edward Albee
edited by Stephen J. Bottoms

CAMBRIDGE COMPANIONS TO CULTURE

The Cambridge Companion to Modern German Culture
edited by Eva Kolinsky and Wilfried van der Will

The Cambridge Companion to Modern Russian Culture
edited by Nicholas Rzhevsky

The Cambridge Companion to Modern Spanish Culture
edited by David T. Gies

The Cambridge Companion to Modern Italian Culture
edited by Zygmunt G. Baránski and Rebecca J. West

The Cambridge Companion to Modern French Culture
edited by Nicholas Hewitt

The Cambridge Companion to Modern Latin American Culture
edited by John King

The Cambridge Companion to Modern Irish Culture
edited by Joe Cleary and Claire Connolly

The Cambridge Companion to Modern American Culture
edited by Christopher Bigsby